LAWRENCE DURRELL
AND
HENRY MILLER

A Private Correspondence

BY LAWRENCE DURRELL

FICTION
The Alexandria Quartet:
Justine
Balthazar
Mountolive
Clea
The Black Book
Pope Joan (*translation*)
The Dark Labyrinth

TRAVEL
Bitter Lemons
Prospero's Cell and
Reflections on a Marine Venus

HUMOR
Esprit de Corps
Stiff Upper Lip

POETRY
Sappho
Collected Poems

published by E. P. Dutton & Co. Inc.

BY HENRY MILLER

The Air-Conditioned Nightmare

Big Sur and the Oranges of Hieronymus Bosch

The Books in My Life

The Colossus of Maroussi

The Cosmological Eye

The Henry Miller Reader

Remember To Remember

The Smile at the Foot of the Ladder

Stand Still Like the Hummingbird

Sunday after the War

The Time of the Assassins

The Wisdom of the Heart

published by New Directions

Lawrence Durrell

A PRIVATE

A Dutton
Paperback

CORRESPONDENCE
Henry Miller

EDITED BY

GEORGE WICKES

NEW YORK
E. P. DUTTON & CO., INC.

TO

Lawrence Clark Powell and Alan Thomas

CONTENTS

Introduction   *xi*

August 1935—Spring 1936   *3*
  (Durrell in Corfu—Miller in Paris)

Summer—Fall 1936   *15*
  (Durrell in Corfu—Miller in Paris)

November—December 1936   *25*
  (Durrell in Corfu—Miller in Paris)

Christmas 1936—January 1937   *43*
  (Durrell in Corfu—Miller in Paris)

February—March 1937   *63*
  (Durrell in Corfu—Miller in Paris)

March—May 1937   *75*
  (Durrell in Corfu—Miller in Paris)

July—September 1937   *101*
  (Durrell in Corfu and Paris—Miller in Paris)

September 1937—January 1938   *113*
  (Durrell in London and Innsbruck—
    Miller in Paris)

May—October 1938   *123*
  (Durrell in Corfu—Miller in Paris
    and points south)

December 1938—May 1939   *141*
  (Durrell in London—Miller in Paris)

February—November 1940 159
    (Durrell in Athens and Kalamata)

March 1941—November 1942 169
    (Miller in New York and Hollywood)

Christmas 1943—May 1945 179
    (Durrell in Alexandria—Miller in Big Sur)

June 1945—February 1947 207
    (Durrell in Rhodes—Miller in Big Sur)

February 1947—December 1948 237
    (Durrell in Argentina—Miller in Big Sur)

January 1949—Fall 1952 257
    (Durrell in Yugoslavia—Miller in Big Sur)

March 1953—February 1957 293
    (Durrell in Cyprus—Miller in Big Sur
    and Europe)

February 1957—February 1958 309
    (Durrell in Provence—Miller in Big Sur)

April—November 1958 331
    (Durrell in Provence—Miller in Big Sur)

January 1959— 355
    (Durrell in Provence—Miller in Big Sur,
    Paris, and Big Sur)

Lawrence Durrell Chronology 386

Henry Miller Chronology 387

Index, with Explanatory Notes 389

c/o Ionian Bank
Corfu: Greece

Dear H.M.

Feb. 27th. 1912. 1 a.m. Jullundur: Burma: India:

I was born 27th February. 1912. at
one o'clock of the morning. The
Indian Blood must have been a
mistake. I'm Irish mother English
father. God-fearing, lusty, chapel-
going Mutiny stock. (My grandma
sat up on the verandah of her
house with a shot. gun across her
knees waiting for the mutiny gang:
but when they saw her face they
went another way.) Hence the
family face. I may have a touch of
Indian in me — who knows? I'm one
of the world's expatriates anyhow.
It's lonely being cut off from one's
race. So much of England I loved —
and hated so much — the language
clings — I try and wipe it off my
tongue but it clings. O what the hell.
I was born to be Hamlet's little
godchild. The horoscopes can't touch me
— I'm already mad! Yours Sinc.
Larry Durrell

From a Lawrence Durrell letter (1937)

ROSEMARIE CLAUSEN

LAWRENCE DURRELL

RENATE ZIMMERMAN

HENRY MILLER

THE BOOSTER

FOUNDED BY THE AMERICAN
COUNTRY CLUB OF FRANCE

EDITORIAL OFFICES :

18, Villa Seurat,
Paris (14e).

EDITORIAL BOARD

Managing Editor and Director :
Alfred Perlès.

Associate Editors :
Henry Miller.
Lawrence Durrell.

Publicity and circulation
Manager :
David Edgar.

1937?

CORRESPONDENTS IN :

London,
Vienna,
Budapest,
Belgrade,
Corfu,
Athens,
Copenhagen,
Stockholm,
Oslo,
Amsterdam,
Christ Church, New Zealand,
Zurich,
Cairo,
Brussels,
Prague,
Bucarest,
Shanghai,
Pekin,
Manila,
Darjeeling,
Port Said,
Aden,
Johannesburg,
Luxembourg,
Buenos Aires,
Valparaiso,
Havana,
New York,
Dublin,
Aberdeen,
Chicago,
New Orleans,
San Francisco,
Montreal,
Tallin, Esthonia,
Warsaw,
Helsingfors,
Saigon,
Istanbul,
Bagdad,
Teheran,
Gibraltar,
Mexico City.

Sunday

Dear Durrell —

Amazing how difficult it is to get round to see you. Been snowed under with visits + dates of one kind and another. Maybe you can get round to-morrow towards lunch hour? Can't promise lunch, as I am hopelessly broke.

If you can come, do please try to bring with you the Lao-Tze book + the Maurice Nardon one, and the Hamlet letter you wrote me and Osborn's, will you? Want to go over the business of the "quotes" for the womb number with you — also decide which piece of yours to put in. We may all be limited to one apiece now, as there may not be room enuf.

Enclosing doem to you, for you, from Audrey Beecham. Keep for the Poetry number if it's any good. I returned Reavey's poem — as I did with most all so far — saying we would ask for them back later on.

Don't know what you mean about Gascoyne + Grammar. Don't recollect mentioning anything of this sort. Maybe Fred did?

From a Henry Miller letter (1937)

INTRODUCTION

THE complete Durrell-Miller correspondence in half a dozen scholarly annotated volumes will not be ready for publication until the next century. Nor would the authors wish to see such a work in their own lifetimes. For both are still very much alive and prefer not to think of themselves as national monuments or museum pieces. Indeed they were reluctant to have their private letters published at all and then only if their correspondence could be presented as a living thing. This, then, is a selection of the whole correspondence, made and edited with the authors' approval.

The correspondence traces two of the most lively literary careers of our time over the course of a quarter century. I have done my best to keep the full story of their friendship and their careers. All the significant facts are here. What has been omitted is largely repetitious, ephemeral or uninteresting detail.

The authors are of course anxious to safeguard their privacy and would prefer not to immortalize too many indiscretions. Nor are they anxious to wound or embarrass others. In any event, personal allusion—gossip—represents but a small part of the correspondence; it would be misleading to exaggerate its share. The correspondence has not been bowdlerized. The language here is that of the original letters.

This book has a superb plot, which I have tried in my introductory notes to follow, marking the natural stages or chapters. In these occasional paragraphs I have also tried to give some idea of the letters that have been left out, sometimes quoting from those letters. Realizing that an editor must seem an interloper, I have tried to keep my introductions few and unobtrusive, even at the risk of not answering every question in the reader's mind. But by and large the correspondence explains itself.

Miller and Durrell wrote these letters with no idea that they would ever appear in print. Both have edited letters for publication, however, and thus given me precedents to follow in editing their correspondence. In an attempt to preserve the spontaneity and spirit of the originals, I have dispensed with most of the usual editorial paraphernalia. I have not indicated omissions. I have corrected misspellings, slips of the typewriter, and other obviously unintentional lapses. I have standardized the punctuation somewhat—always with an eye to making the text read more easily. These are all minor changes that an author might make in preparing a fair copy from a hastily written manuscript. And most of the letters were written in haste.

The letters are both handwritten and typed on all kinds of paper. "Stationery" is too limited a term, though Miller usually employs writing paper, his friends' as well as his own. Sometimes he uses—it almost appears deliberate—the most incongruous stationery, e.g., that of *The Booster* or of a hotel in Mississippi advertising plumbing advantages calculated to give him nightmares. Durrell writes on paper of all colors, shapes and sizes, ranging from foolscap to little odds and ends. He writes also on the backs and margins of letters he is forwarding, on menus, dustjackets, illustrations and leaves from books. His letters are often written in green, red or black ink and illuminated in water color. No doubt the authors have written a great many postcards in addition to the letters, but relatively few have been preserved.

Most of the letters are undated, especially the early ones. In later years Miller dates almost every letter, but Durrell seldom bothers, except during periods when he has an office job. I have had to unscramble the letters, match both sides of the correspondence, sort them out in sequence, and date them as best I could. This has been a vast jigsaw problem, especially for the 1935–39 period, and in most instances I have only been able to supply approximate dates. But I am as certain as it is possible to be that the letters here printed are all in chronological order.

The correspondence is densest at its beginning, 1935–39, and again toward the end, 1957–58. In the early period especially, both writers are enormously stimulated by each other. Durrell's letters of this period often run to half a dozen single-spaced pages, and he is capable of writing several of these a day. Miller, always involved in a dozen different enterprises, writes shorter letters, though his are not by ordinary standards short, except during periods when he is harassed by visitors, correspondence, and other business. The correspondence is at its scantest during the war years when communications are poor and the writers have least to say to each other; for several years they are almost out of touch, though they retain an abiding telepathic sense of each other throughout. Then in the postwar years they correspond steadily, if not as intensively as before. To give some idea: there are sixteen Durrell letters from Rhodes, October 1945–February 1947; ten letters from Argentina during the year Durrell spent there. The Durrell letters always outnumber the Miller letters, sometimes by two to one, though in the postwar period they usually exchange letter for letter. A number of letters are missing, especially during the war years when Durrell had to evacuate from Greece and Miller was on the move. A few are missing from other periods, but on the whole the correspondence is remarkably complete.

The preservation of Miller's letters is due to Alan Thomas. One of Durrell's oldest friends, he is the Alan to whom the valedictory letter in the middle of *The Black Book* is addressed. Happily for posterity, Thomas decided on the stable and acquisitive profession of antiquarian bookdealing and kept Durrell's papers, including the letters from Miller, in his loft, safely out of bomb's reach through the war. Durrell still visits Thomas whenever he is in England and periodically adds to the collection. On his own, Thomas has acquired over the years the world's greatest collection of Durrelliana, including rare books, manuscripts, and records of Durrell playing jazz songs they composed together in the early '30s.

Another long-standing friendship is responsible for the Miller archives at the University of California at Los Angeles. Lawrence Clark Powell first met Henry Miller in 1931, when they were both in Dijon, Powell as a graduate student, Miller teaching in the lycée he describes in *Tropic of Cancer*. This was only a chance passing encounter, however. Their friendship dates from ten years later when Miller settled in the Los Angeles area, and Powell fed his voracious appetite for books. This was a difficult period for both, and they sustained each other in a variety of ways. Later, when Miller moved to Big Sur, the friendship continued. In 1948, Powell, by this time chief librarian, proposed to Miller that he deposit all his papers at the University. Since that time the Miller collection has grown into a vast accumulation, of which the Durrell letters form only a small—but most distinguished —part. How Durrell's prewar letters caught up with

Miller in America remains something of a mystery. In 1939 Miller left them behind in Paris when he visited Durrell in Greece. Subsequently he was cut off by the war and forced to return to America. But somehow during the war the letters followed him in a trunk mysteriously forwarded by an unknown American sailor—but for whom they would probably have disappeared.

Publishing the correspondence was Powell's idea. He had long been a collector of Durrell as well as Miller and a friend of Alan Thomas. The idea had been growing on him over the years, and finally the moment seemed right. In 1959, as one of the last letters records, he proposed it to Miller, who in turn prevailed upon Durrell—though not without a struggle. Durrell was enthusiastic about the publication of Miller's letters, but reluctant to publish his own. Even with the authors' consent, however, Powell found he was too busy to edit the correspondence himself.

About that time I was preparing to do an interview of Henry Miller for the *Paris Review*. Knowing that Powell was an old friend of Miller's, I made an engagement to meet him. Within half an hour of his cordial and casual greeting, he was asking, "How would you like to edit the Miller-Durrell correspondence?" Since then the task— and all the excitement—of editing the correspondence has been mine. But it is Larry Powell who has been the guiding genius behind this book.

G. W.

LAWRENCE DURRELL
AND
HENRY MILLER

A Private Correspondence

AUGUST 1935—SPRING 1936
(Durrell in Corfu—Miller in Paris)

THE correspondence opens with Durrell writing a fan letter, Miller promptly replying, and both soon discovering themselves kindred spirits. The first half dozen letters, about all that survive from this period, show them getting acquainted. Durrell is 23 at the beginning, Miller 43, and *Tropic of Cancer*, Miller's first book, has been out only a year. But Miller has already achieved some reputation and is engaged in an assortment of literary ventures, chiefly with his Villa Seurat cronies, Alfred Perlès and Michael Fraenkel. An inveterate letter writer from years back, he publishes in this period *Aller Retour New York*, an 80-page letter, "Being the account of a voyage to New York and back exactly as recorded in a letter to Alfred Perlès, the distinguished Viennese French writer, who up till now has held the record for letter writing," and on November 2, 1935 launches forth on the *Hamlet* correspondence with Fraenkel, which is to continue for two years. Miller is also trying to publish his *Black Spring* at this time and working on the study of D. H. Lawrence which he never completes. Durrell does not mention until much later his first novel, *Pied Piper of Lovers*, an account of bohemian life in Bloomsbury published in 1935.

*   *

[August 1935]

Dear Mr. Miller:

I have just read *Tropic of Cancer* again and feel I'd like to write you a line about it. It strikes me as being the only really man-size piece of work which this century can really boast of. It's a howling triumph from the word go; and not only is it a literary and artistic smack on the bell for everyone, but it really gets down on paper the blood and bowels of our time. I have never read anything like it. I did not imagine anything like it could be written; and yet, curiously, reading it I seemed to recognise it as something which I knew we were all ready for. The space was all cleared for it. *Tropic* turns the corner into a new life which has regained its bowels. In the face of it eulogy becomes platitude; so for Godsake don't blame me if this sounds like the bleat of an antique reviewer, or a cold-cream ad. God knows, I weigh the words as well as I am able, but the damn book has rocked the scales like a quake and muddled up all my normal weights and measures. I love its guts. I love to see the canons of oblique and pretty emotion mopped up; to see every whim-wham and bagatelle of your contemporaries from Eliot to Joyce dunged under. God give us young men the guts to plant the daisies on top and finish the job.

Tropic is something they've been trying to do since the war. It's the final copy of all those feeble, smudgy rough drafts—*Chatterley*, *Ulysses*, *Tarr*, etc. It not only goes back, but (which none of them have done) goes forward as well.

It finds the way out of the latrines at last. Funny that no one should have thought of slipping out via the pan during a flush, instead of crowding the door. I salute *Tropic* as the copy-book for my generation. It's man-size, and goes straight up among those books (and they are precious few) which men have built out of their own guts. God save me, that sounds pompous, but what can one say?

Perish the Rahuists! Skoal to the stanchless flux!

Yours sincerely,

Lawrence Durrell

18 Villa Seurat, Paris (xiv)

Sept. 1st, 1935

Dear Mr. Durrell :

Your letter rocks me a bit too. You're the first Britisher who's written me an intelligent letter about the book. For that matter, you're the first anybody who's hit the nail on the head. I particularly prize your letter because it's the kind of letter I would have written myself had I not been the author of the book. That isn't just sheer vanity and egotism, believe me. It's curious how few people know what to admire in the book.

The phrase that struck me particularly, in your letter, was, "I seemed to recognize it as something we were all ready for." That's just it. The world *is* ready for something different, something new, but it seems that it requires a war or some colossal calamity to make people realize it.

Your letter is so vivid, so keen, that I am curious to know if you are not a writer yourself. How did you come by the book—through Barclay Hudson?

Cordially yours,

Henry Miller

[1935]

Dear Mr. Miller:

Thank you for the letter which I got yesterday when the boat went to town. I was pleased. Yes, it was Barclay Hudson all right who gave me *Tropic* to read. His hot gospel work will be putting the book into a new edition before long. He and Jane, his wife, live in the old Venetian house up the hill from us. We eat together, bathe together, and have a number of good times. Barclay read me bits from a letter you wrote him, and I am as glad as hell that those sons of bitches in literary England are rallying to the standards already. They keep up such a whine for great men that one almost expects them to ignore them when they do show up. I bet the book makes every writer in England and America feel a sort of cheese-mite. Every writer with a sense of conscience, that is. I wish D. H. Lawrence were alive to give a great bloody whoop of joy over it.

I suppose you can imagine how flattering your curiosity was? Yes, a writer, save the mark. Vague premonitions of facility, mediocrity, and, perhaps later, prosperity. When I read *Tropic* I wished to hell I was an established literary gent so that I could do a fat essay on it. Alas!

I was surprised at people going for the "Elizabethan prose" in the book. That sounded crooked to me. The Elizabethans had all the balls, but none of the freedom from literary canons of style which was necessary to write the *Tropic* of their age. Literary sauria, somehow, weighed down by the grand manner. Ben Jonson would have said you lack'd art, or some such damn silly thing. I have a curious feeling that the one man who would have acknowledged *Tropic* as something he was trying to write

6

in his own age, and his own style, is François Villon. But as I read French with difficulty, and whenever possible with a literal English text, I'm not really fit to judge. But I get the same feeling from him. It's rather curious. A state of being beyond damage somehow. A bright, hard immunity to life. However, this is all rather presumptuous.

For the time being I can get news of your activities from Barclay; but to our sorrow they will be going south when the weather breaks. I would be very grateful if you could give your publisher my name and address and tell him to keep me in touch with everything you write.

Yours sincerely,
Lawrence Durrell

18 Villa Seurat, Paris (14)

[September 1935]

Dear Lawrence Durrell:

Well, I thought you were a writer! Why don't you send me something of yours so that I can return some of the audacious compliments you pay me? It's only in the last two months that the book has gotten properly under weigh, and the result is a steady stream of letters and visitors and invitations and what not, which is beginning to bore the shit out of me, though at first it seemed wonderful. This doesn't apply to you people. I'm talking about the regular shits who come down on you like a ton of bricks and clog the drains. I guess you know what I mean!

I am rather intrigued by your reference to Villon, the Elizabethans, etc. It seems that my book was turned down for translation by the *Nouvelle Revue Française*, not because of the obscenity, but on "literary" grounds! You're absolutely right about it lacking "art." But that's what makes "art." I wish I had the time to explain more fully.

I'm going into some detail about this question in my work on D. H. Lawrence—which again will be lacking as a "critical" work. I'm talking about a new attitude towards art which the writer needs today. I think this is revealed even better by my second book, *Black Spring*, which breaks all the canons, and which I myself like much better than *Tropic*, though few will agree with me perhaps. The Obelisk Press may put this out some time this winter—it seems quite definite.

Meanwhile there's a guy named Cyril Connolly wants to meet me and write a review of *Tropic* for *The New Statesman*. I don't understand it. If they understood what I'm driving at I don't think they would want very much to review my book. I think they're all fog-eyed.

Well, more later. Keep in touch with me, as I say, and let's see some of *your* stuff. And regards to the Hudsons.

Cordially yours,
Henry Miller

Nov. 29th, 1935

[Paris]

Dear Lawrence Durrell:

Your letters take a hell of a while to reach here. Your last one arrived a few days ago and I want you to know that I am far from being bored and hope you will continue to keep in touch with me. It may interest you to know that I regard your letters about *Tropic* and Barclay's as the best testimonials received thus far (barring the letter and review of Blaise Cendrars which I esteem because of its downright humanness). You guys got right down into the sub-cellar. Naturally I don't expect much of the critics, especially the English critics—and still less, to be sure, of the American critics. All the more reason, therefore, that your reviews should see the light. But how? I really wish you would make an effort between you to get something in somewhere—something with dynamite in it. And don't just praise the shit out of me! Keep to that general line about the fundamental purpose of the book, about its significance in connection with the usual drift-wood.

Anyway, here's what I plan to do myself about it. I am going to make a reprint, at my own expense, of all the important letters and reviews. Some of the letters are knock-outs—and come, as you might well expect, from obscure sources, mais tant mieux! I will send this brochure out to every fucking magazine, review, and newspaper in the world of any consequence—particularly to "foreign" organs, particularly to the Orient and to South America. It's a colossal job and is going to cost me a pretty penny, and for the moment I don't even know where the dough is going to come from, but I'll do it nevertheless. I am thoroughly disgusted with the general inertia. *Action at any cost*, that's my motto.

I had to wait over two years for the publication of *Tropic* and when it appeared I had damned well lost all interest in it, as a book. I am waiting now almost a year for something to be done about *Black Spring*. I have a contract and a promise, but if the world situation gets worse I know my publisher will fuck me up on it. In which case it will devolve upon me to do it myself.

But the brochure, with its reprints, may have the advantage of securing me a little publicity, whether favorable or unfavorable I don't care. I won't have the book die in its second printing! And I'll make it damned clear, that in spite of its value, it is almost unobtainable. Let those who are interested in this sort of phenomena do something about it then!

The World of Lawrence is going along slowly. I am doing too many things to make much headway with it.

9

Probably I told you already that I have begun, in collaboration with Perlès and Fraenkel, a thousand-page book to be called *Hamlet*. This will definitely be published by the Carrefour Press, in Belgium, as my collaborator, Fraenkel, *is* Carrefour! He also plans to bring out shortly a volume of three essays by three Americans—himself, Walter Lowenfels and myself. This book we can sell anywhere: it's a serious work about our ideology—about the "spiritual weather," I might say.

I am also going ahead with the publication of Siana Series Nos. 2 and 3 which will appear simultaneously. No. 2 is the *Scenario* I may have told you about before. These will be limited editions, assez cher, for subscribers only.

There was another review of *Tropic* recently in the *New English Weekly* (Nov. 14th) by George Orwell. Talks about "the vilification of human nature" (sic!). Oh well.

I hope you still see Barclay and that you will show him this letter. I am rather expecting him to come to Paris. Hope he does—we can surely find a suitable place for him. If you birds decide to write anything, whether separately or jointly, and if you want to send a carbon of the review to America I give you herewith the address of an enterprising young man at Harvard who will certainly bestir himself about it. James Laughlin IV, Eliot House, E-31, Cambridge, Mass. Laughlin is the chap who tried to reprint my *Aller Retour New York* (under the title "Glittering Pie"). He had the first ten pages published in the Harvard *Advocate*, and then the Boston police descended upon the paper, destroyed the existent copies and locked the editorial staff up overnight, threatening them with a severe jail sentence. Mine wasn't the only offending contribution. Seems a story by Laughlin himself was also responsible for the mess. Anyway it's all blown over sweetly and the boys have promised to behave. Laughlin is now co-editor of a magazine called *The New Democracy*, headquarters in New York. You can write him directly, if you choose. He's a good egg. And he has connections!

Well, that's about enough for the present. Why don't you tell me the name of your novel which I understand is to appear shortly—or has it appeared already? I certainly want to read it.

Cordially yours,

HVM

[Corfu, Spring 1936]

Dear Henry Miller:

What news? Why no news, except local news, and God knows what with wars and the yapping of dictators, it's comforting enough. A week of hellish storms. Two children struck by lightning and burnt to toffee. A tree stripped. The olives safely gathered. From that horrid world outside nothing except a statement from a publisher showing heavy losses, and a raving postcard from New York asking for news. A new and facile novel being castrated by the bigwigs. First they agreed to let the word "fuck" stay in if it went thus: f—k; then f——; now the libraries might get touchy so they want ———. Or something milder. What with feeling ashamed and angry with myself for writing cheaply, and knowing the book isn't worth a ——— either way, I don't know what to do. It's so disheartening when you sweat and sweat and sweat and then something sheerly puerile comes on the paper. As *Tropic* is your first book you can't know that feeling. Myself, I am going to take to carpentry or something soothing where facility and a fine smell of glue are all one need worry about. And when you're finished for the day you just wipe your hands magnificently in a fistful of shavings and let it go at that. This book business is a washout. I see that a twenty-four-year-old reviewer—one of these horn-rimmed advanced birds—has just written a filthy attack on Lawrence. I don't know why it should hurt so much to see the swine trample on him. The same's going to happen to my poor *Tropic*. I beg your pardon, your *Tropic*.

O, by the way, you haven't put me on your black books, have you? No *Aller Retour* turned up, though Barclay swore he was mailing me one from Paris. And I wait patiently with my hands in my lap for *Black Spring*. And the *Hamlet*. Believe me, I am so furious that people haven't simply burst in on your privacy and carried you off to found American literature at home. As it is, I suppose you've burst in on theirs. Agents and people have been very ladylike since my enthusiastic letters telling them to go over to Paris and buy every stitch of MS in your Villa Seurat.

A friend writes that *Tropic* "cheapens dirt." How long, O God, how long. I lent it to a Britisher of the old flag-waving type here. He worried me like hell to read it. He's quite nice but thick in the attic. And all his words end in "ah." Puzzled him, did *Tropic*. It wasn't just smut as he'd hoped. He's read Cecil Barr in the same press and got the idea you were even hotter than *Daffodil*. It made him uncomfortable a bit as well as puzzled. Finally he blurted out: "I don't mind-ah the fellah consorting with buggahs, and all that. But-ah I do draw the line at him PINCHING things from whores-ah."

Please bear with my youthfulness and write me a short postcard from time to time telling me what's going on in Paris. I've always wanted to be in on a movement of some kind, but I've never found the kind of writing and people

I could whole-heartedly back. *Tropic* makes me feel great things are happening over there in Paris, and I want to lift my eyes unto the hills. I am slowly learning French so I can start reading it easily soon. I want to read *Sentiments Limitrophes* but as yet am a babe in the language.

Well the sun's come up today and we're going to lie outside in pyjamas and eat lunch. Forgive this huge letter. There did seem to be some news after all. And don't swear and feel that you've got to answer it or anything. But you're not likely to. And above all, if you ever strike south Italy or Greece, do drop in on us and stay a while. I'd love to meet you, and hear about all the amazing things that people have said and done and thought and written about *Tropic*. It seems this is the age of wonders after all. Who is it talks of the decline of the West?

Yours sincerely,
Lawrence Durrell

SUMMER—FALL 1936
(Durrell in Corfu—Miller in Paris)

————◆————

THE correspondence gains momentum. Miller forwards Herbert Read's *Surrealist Bulletin*, precipitating Durrell's outburst against literary movements and reigning personages, particularly those who confuse politics with literature. By now Miller and Durrell have found a good deal of common ground and are warming to each other, both writing voluminous letters. Durrell especially writes at great length, expounding his pet theory of the "Heraldic Universe," which, as he indicates later, is very much the same realm as Miller's China, somewhere between Ecuador and the Gobi Desert. Durrell's are really bundles of notes, outpourings of eight or ten or twelve single-spaced pages, written on all sides and in all directions; he has so much to tell Miller that he keeps coming back to the machine again and again. Miller, far from being daunted, concludes a reply to one of these outbursts with the injunction, "Write!"

*   *

[Summer 1936]

Dear Durrell:

Thanks a lot for the book which as yet I haven't had
time to read, but I will soon. Your friend Evans hasn't
shown up yet. I am looking forward to his visit and will
give him a few copies of a little French review called
Orbes for you—something to while away the time with.

About surrealism. Maybe you're one yourself. I agree
that the leaders of the movement are highly conscious
and deliberate and that's of course destructive. But what
constitutes surrealism is a permanent thing in art, more
especially in literature. Swift was a good one, and so was
Lewis Carroll, in my opinion, and Shakespeare too now
and then. And what about Rabelais? The French, because
they are so lucid and so cerebral, sort of scare one off, but
then the peculiar emphasis they give to it is inevitable,
considering how rigorous and formal is their style of
thought. In the films, the burlesque ones, the Americans
achieve a pure and unadulterated surrealism now and
then, always unconsciously. I hope some time to send you
a few back numbers of the French reviews, so that you
can judge for yourself. It's only an effort, at bottom, to
return to the original vital source, which is in the solar
plexus, or in the Unconscious, or in the stars, if you like.
I have used the method here and there, when it came
naturally and spontaneously. At least, I hope so. I don't
start out by trying to be surrealistic. Sometimes it comes
at the beginning and sometimes at the end. It's always an
effort to plough through, to say what can't or won't be
said.

The head of the Obelisk Press is Jack Kahane. He
knows of you through me. He won't publish a thing unless it has a sensational quality, unless it might be banned

in England or America. That's his strategy for the present. He hasn't much taste either, I can tell you. My relationship with him is in the nature of a pure accident. The other two presses are out of commission. Sylvia Beach still has the bookshop, but does no printing.

Queer that you mention Lao-tse. Some one just handed me the book the other day. I was up till four A.M. the other night discussing it with Perlès. And did we laugh! To me the Chinese humor is marvellous. I don't mean that I laughed at him, but with him. To my mind he was one of the very great guys. I wish there were more of it—it seems to be a very small testament. You know, I'm nuts about China. I always think that that is the place I will eventually wind up in. I feel like a Chinaman very often.

Listen, Durrell, don't despair yet. If you have the guts for it, the thing to do is to go to the bitter end—in your writing, I mean. If you can possibly hold out, and I imagine you can, write only what you please. There is nothing else to do, unless you want to become famous. They will shit on you anyway, so have your say first. I'm not recommending obscenity necessarily. Each man has his own way of being himself and of saying it so ultimately that he can't be denied. Compromise is futile and unsatisfactory. You will always have a hundred readers and, if they have taste and discernment, what more can you ask? Even when you elect to be absolutely honest it is difficult. Expression seems such a natural, God-given thing—and yet it's not either. It's a lifelong struggle to find yourself. Think of Cézanne, Van Gogh, Gauguin, Lawrence. Think of Dostoievski, or Titian, if you will. I like the autobiographical documents: they teach you more than anything. Well, enough.

HVM

Dear Miller:

Come let us sit upon the ground and tell strange stories of the death of kings. Thanks for the pamphlet. Good old London. We're late, as usual, but for sheer doggedness you can't beat us. But where are the jaded dowagers of art who usually sit at the head of these chic movements? Ezra, answer. Nina Hamnett, answer. Vanessa Bell, speak up. Virgin Woolf, take that cigar out of your mouth and get busy. Come Leonardo, an essay on the surreal.

Let's look at the manifestoes. Begins a political discussion. The artist's place in society. A definite lean leftward. Well, what's wrong with that? Nothing, provided politics are not going to be confused with art. I'm tired of political people. They have confused the inner struggle with the outer one. They want to bread poultice a primary chancre. Politics is an art that deals in averages. Art is a man that deals in people. If the people are wrong, then no system is fool-proof enough to stop them cutting each other's throats. And the artist finds that the people are wrong. The driving force behind him is his self-isolation, the dislocation of the societal instinct. Vide Lawrence, Gauguin, etc.

This manifesto would be a lot clearer if these brave young revolutionaries started by defining what they meant by art. To begin with they seem to mean Marx. They want art to become easier for the artist. Well, that won't affect the genius any, he always gets through. It will increase the ease of production for average art. A good thing perhaps. But they do not state that they are founding a trade union for artists, just like the Royal Academy. There is yet talk of art. Proceed. A definition of the word "surrealism," please. There are some good

18

remarks about it. Breton, etc. Very true, but surely as ancient as *Oedipus?* Or am I wrong? Henry Miller wrote to me, "Swift was a good surrealist, so was Lewis Carroll." I believe firmly in the ideal of cementing reality with the dream, but I do not believe the rest of this stuff. That the artist must be a socialist, for example. That he wants to transform the world. (He wants to transform men.) That he can work anyhow except alone.

Listen, Miller, what I feel about it is this. To have art you've first got to have a big personality, pass it through the social mincer, get it ready for misery. Art nowadays is going to be real art, as before the flood. IT IS GOING TO BE PROPHECY, in the biblical sense. What I propose to do, with all deadly solemnity, is to create my HERALDIC UNIVERSE quite alone. The foundation is being quietly laid. I AM SLOWLY BUT VERY CAREFULLY AND WITHOUT CONSCIOUS THOUGHT DESTROYING TIME. I have discovered that the idea of duration is false. We have invented it as a philosophic jack up to the idea of physical disintegration. THERE IS ONLY SPACE. A solid object has only three dimensions. Time, that old appendix, I've lopped off. So it needs a new attitude. An attitude without memory. A spatial existence in terms of the paper I'm writing on now at this moment.

Hudson was always saying to me genuinely: "What can Villon have to say to me? He never went through the great war." But what great war are we talking about, but the personal war, I used to bay. Art is not politics, i.e. averages. It is men. It is not the outer struggle but the inner. My dear Henry Miller, unless I completely misunderstand your books, or unless you simply don't know what you're doing, this is what I mean. There is no one to shout at except my wife who is drawing, so I'll ask you. Is *Black Spring* more surrealist than it is Miller? If

it were I should burst into tears. BUT IS *Ulysses* MORE
SURREALIST THAN IT IS JOYCE? I think yes.

I am editing my poems for printing. My God, some of
them are so natural and easy that no one will take any
notice. I enclose a copy of my advance notice which I'll
have printed. By the way, have you heard the Beethoven
violin concerto? There's something of the same kind of
terrifying pathology about the themes that there is in
Hamlet. The fusion of the dream with reality that you
like so much. But how disciplined by the person! How
personal, in fact! I think I don't know what I mean. I
have a horrible feeling that I mean what you do, but
don't express it very well. Tell me if you think this is, in
the words of Barclay, one hundred per cent bullshit.

Yours sincerely,
Lawrence Durrell

ARE YOU A WRITER——OR MERELY A LITERARY GENT?

In fact, vegetable or mineral? Fish or fruit? The question being whether to write what you bloody well like
and try to get it privately subscribed; or give in and turn
out (supposing you could) the kind of stuff that would
entitle a literary clique to take some interest in you? The
question is finely epitomised above. Seriously, fish or
fruit?

Did someone mention the modern reviews? Sweet
reader, what would you do if you were too traditional for
one half of the world, and too advanced for the other
half? You would? Very well, then. This has been already
done. Enquire therefore into your most inward psyche
as to what you are, and either fill in the forms below or
else ring the chain on them. Remember Shakespeare
lack'd art. And anything written from the waist down-
wards must face a world thick with honest, greasy Bens.

Adieu.

[Paris, Fall 1936]

My dear Durrell:

I can't tell you how accurately you hit the spot in your last batch of letters! Of course you are right—and hail to the Heraldic Universe! If I should wish to reprint this letter along with some others which I am thinking of bringing out, may I? I would of course cut out libellous references, if there are any.

I wish you would tell me something more about *Hamlet*. Give me the low-down on it. I can't bring myself to read the damned thing. But I am very eager to get some penetrative interpretations of it. What you honestly believe about it, not what you imagine you ought to think. Try to tell me what you believe it means, will you? I'd appreciate it. Of course the old boy didn't start out with any theory of madness. These fellows are not really crazy enough, or just not crazy. They are, on the contrary, too terrifically sane—and intellectual. Nevertheless they're wise enough, or desperate enough, to go out by the roof. And here's where our old friend Lao-tse comes in. He was going home to the mountains, as they say, when one of the emperor's couriers intercepted him and begged him to put it all down on paper. He was a bit surrealistic, too, the old fellow!

Was ill abed for a few days and happened to read Gertrude Stein's *Narration*, four lectures delivered in America to university students. The first one, dealing with English vs. American literature is an eye-opener—as well as the second, on the difference between newspapers and other writing. Impossible lingo she employs, irritating, but clear beneath, very simple, often quite profound.

And so, to answer your question about *Black Spring*— is it more this than that?—I should say it is an approximation of something which will never be more definite than it is therein and with which I must rest satisfied, the thing being done and therefore complete spatially. No, it is not more surrealist than Henry Miller. But it is not all Henry Miller either, I suppose. One can't put himself in toto into a work. But one sometimes can give himself so well that the illusion is there—of the man's wholeness, or something like that. Anyway, what gets put down on paper is only a drift towards, so to speak. And who gives a fuck finally about the actual thing-in-itself? That is a philosophic problem, not an artistic one. The other question, about Joyce, is harder for me to answer. Strangely enough, I think Joyce does realize himself quite completely—and the more he does the less interested I become in him. I tried to tell about this in that fragment of the Lawrence manuscript called "The Universe of Death." Some day I'll send you a carbon of it.

Finally, about Barclay. He's a good chap and all that, but his mind leaves me cold. He's too much of a walking encyclopedia for my taste. I don't like the sort of discussions he and his friends precipitate. They are typically American discussions, prosaic, pragmatic, space-devouring. It's all on the flat, as it were, and wingless. They are all knowledge-seekers. I am against knowledge. I abhor it. I loathe it. I want to become more and more ignorant, more quiet, more vegetative, more ruminative, more omnivorous, carnivorous, herbivorous. I want to stand still and dance inside, or else take wing. I am not a pedestrian. And how can you warm up to people who warm up to H. G. Wells in the movies? Who call Wells imaginative, fantastic, etc.? That's why Swift seems to me surrealist! Get me?

HVM

c/o Ionian Bank, Kerkera, Greece

[Fall 1936]

Dear H.M.:

You can imagine how delighted I was by your letter.
I breathe a bit more easily these days and let things slide.
I have got a bad cold, so I lie in bed and quietly compose
my hundred points of heraldry. I chose the word "heraldic" for a double reason. First, because in the relation
of the work to the artist it seemed to me that it expressed
the exact quality I wanted. Also because in heraldry I
seem to find that quality of magic and spatial existence
which I want to tack on to art. Of course, as you say, one
must make allowances for storing, parturition, experience
and all that, involving time. But what I am trying to isolate is the exact moment of creation, in which the maker
seems to exist heraldically. That is to say, time as a con-
cept does not exist, but only as an attribute of matter—
decay, growth, etc. In that sense then, it must be memory-
less. I am afraid I cannot make this very clear even to
myself until I examine all the terms and see precisely what
they mean. But for myself I am beginning to inhabit this
curious HERALDIC UNIVERSE when I write. If it seems a
bit precocious of me to be trying to invent my own private element to swim about in, it can't be helped.

Surely, I'd like to write you a little about my friend
Hamlet soon. I'm just going to read the first quarto again.
And I promise I won't give you any stuff—what I ought
to think, I mean. *Hamlet* is a mine of queer things. As
always the people who know least and are most puzzled
about it are the literary critics and the dons. My God, how
few people are really aware of the battle. HAMLET IS
VERY HERALDIC, save the mark. This is what someone
says about it: "WE CAN FIND OUT NO MORE SECRETS

23

ABOUT HAMLET'S MOTIVES. A PLAY IS NOT A MINE OF SECRET MOTIVES. WE PERSIST IN DIGGING FOR THEM." AND WHAT HAPPENS USUALLY IS THAT OUR *spade goes through the other side of the drama.*

If this isn't heraldic, then what is it?

The Elizabethans are an acquired taste. Once you've got them in your blood it takes a three-year course of salvarsan, temperature therapy, etc., to get rid of them. But what a disease.

Of course I'm interested in the surrealists. If there's a real writer among them he'll come through, I suppose. But I think they put the cart before the horse and are mistaken in taking a perfectly just and acute criticism of art as a theory for the production of it. I wish I could be in a MOVEMENT. Always wanted to be. So far I've never managed to honestly become anything more than an ardent Durrealist. I've quarrelled with almost every writer I've met so far of my age, and now I see my contemporaries starting nice little papers and forming clubs and things. It makes me furious.

I send you a picture of me snarling at one of the buggers who nearly smashed the Van Norden up on a rock. Send you a real photo of her when she's got mast and sail in her next week.

Lawrence Durrell

24

NOVEMBER—DECEMBER 1936
(Durrell in Corfu—Miller in Paris)

———◆———

THE tempo increases with Durrell's first *Hamlet* letter, a torrent unleashed by Miller's request that Durrell tell him something about the play because he can't bring himself to read it. Miller is in the midst of his 1,000-page *Hamlet* correspondence with Fraenkel, a lively, rambling, philosophical debate which has little to do with Shakespeare or the melancholy Dane; he has been sending letters on to Durrell, who now becomes an active combatant. Miller, delighted with Durrell's *Hamlet* letter, assumes the role of literary godfather, trying to get it published in all directions and urging Durrell not to compromise. Durrell has been thinking lately of launching a little magazine on Corfu; their correspondence on this subject marks the beginning of a long series of literary schemes and enterprises.

*   *

Dear Henry Miller:

In a hell of a mess packing to move into town for the winter. I have just finished *Hamlet*, sitting among the wreckage. Let me try and tell you what I feel. Seems it's a perfect picture of the inner struggle, done in terms of the outer one—as all great books are, at least for me. Why every one is so puzzled by poor Hamlet is because they always try to see a relation between the external battle (the murder, Ophelia, etc.) and the internal one. A failure, because the inner and the outer reality move along separate planes, and only seldom meet. There's your dialectical interplay, but through the reality always the magic is seen. Naturally the people who try to equate the moods with the external events never hit the mark. There are two Hamlets. We are presented with the Prince of Denmark, and it's only through the chinks in his armour that we can see the inner man, the worm turning in the bowels of compassion, etc. But as the play goes on, the inner Hamlet, no longer Prince, grows and begins to strip his fellow characters of their masks. The great shock is to find himself alone in life, with no contact, not even with that sweet but silly little wretch Ophelia. Horatio a heart-of-oak dumbbell. Laertes a boring soldier. Polonius a blow-fly. The Queen a toad. Then, realising that he should really turn away from these fakes to his real self, he feels the pressure of society suddenly on him. He is forced to be the Prince, however much his private Hamlet suffers. It is a marvellous picture of psychic and social disorganisation in an individual, and Shakespeare was not the only one who found himself trying to write it. The tragedy of Hamlet was the tragedy of the Elizabethan Age, the age which poisoned its young men with the humanities and then showed them none. It is the tragedy of

England now, but more advanced, more grey and carious than ever. But for those birds it was do or die. A lot died. Webster and Shakespeare came through. Marston found God, and Donne and Hall. Tourneur was starved. Southwell tortured thirteen times and then burned. And out of all this muck the bright weal of chivalry was eating their livers. They were recoiling from the real the whole time. *Hamlet* is a local effort. An epitome of what England's madness means. In Lawrence you see the same thing in a new version. Idealism in the bud eating, eating, eating.

All the questions posed in literature since Marlowe mean the same thing. In my opinion *Tropic* is the answer to them. The wheel turned right back to the pre-glacial age when dung was dung and angels were angels. In *Tropic* the borderline has been passed. Those of us who realise what it means rejoice because the whole pattern has been put back into proportion by it. This may amaze you but it's true. And an Englishman could never have done it. Somehow you have to be a real exile to do things on that scale. But for you, I shouldn't bother to read *Hamlet* except for the poetry. Its doubts and grimaces you have already solved for yourself. But by God, Shakespeare was on the point of solving it more than once. But he failed, so Hamlet failed. There was nothing left but the stagnant end, the conventional Elizabethan pogrom, and a brief but witty epitaph. Shakespeare went home and buried the guts under his cherry tree. The same question comes up all over the place, though less than in *Hamlet* and no nearer a solution. *Lear*, *Timon* and the marvellous heart-breaking sonnets show his madness. But chained. Englishmen have always, in spite of the national anthem, been slaves. Only Chaucer, Skelton perhaps, and a few others, authentic barbarians, broke away or were born free.

But no writer as great as Shakespeare escaped. In *Hamlet* the biggest evidences of the inner feud are in the Ophelia bits. Society—the fact that he had a penis— forced him to consider her. But she was uncomprehending, and his inner Hamlet soon made him negligent of her. Contemptuous. Nay, he even wanted to destroy her.

The terrible irony of his ravings at the grave have never been properly experienced, except by me. To assure himself? No. Simply because he was so far beyond anything like her death, living in his own chronology, he engaged in a word duel with her too protesting brother. Irony beyond anything ever seen. Two minutes after, he picks himself up like a drunk and goes off with Horatio, chattering away. Ophelia is the external tragedy —SHE DOES NOT COUNT.

Well, I don't know whether you follow this crazy idea of mine; if you don't, please say and I'll send you the essay I'm going to write on our dear Hamlet. A fellow of infinite jest. Irony like iron. And could you please keep this note? In a little while I want to start making notes for the essay and it may help me a bit. I have not yet written anything at all about it and my ideas are a bit tangled. This would help me finally to get them clear.

Cheerio,
Lawrence Durrell

What does Gertrude Stein say about American literature? I'm interested. But hate her tone of voice—like a multiplication table. Have you read Wyndham Lewis' attack on Joyce, Pound, Stein and that crowd?

I'm writing such poetry these days, such poetry!

[Paris]

Dear Durrell:

Just a hasty squirt to let you know that I read your *Hamlet* essay, or note for an essay, and was quite wrought up about it. Took the liberty of making copies and sending them to Fraenkel and to Philip Mairet, editor of the *New English Weekly*, with suggestion that he get in touch with you and find out if you would like to have it printed in his sheet. He answered immediately that he was extremely interested and was writing you at once about it. Here's Fraenkel's quick response. I think, with your kind permission, that we should incorporate this into our *Hamlet* book. Or perhaps that would be running counter to your own plans? Let me know, anyway.

Here's a typed copy for you, as you wanted to have it back again. May I keep the original in red ink? I rather prize it. Have it tacked up on the wall for all and sundry to read as they go out the door.

Mairet seems rather decent. Took a little article of mine—which I had to cut in half for him—on schizophrenia, the Nov. 5th issue. Says he will take more stuff, if I like. *But doesn't pay*. However, if you can enter England by the backdoor, I suppose it's something.

Herbert Read sent me the new book, *Surrealism*, which I am answering immediately with a broadside, in the hope that his gang of English and French surrealists will have the guts to publish it in one of their forthcoming manifestoes or what not. I'll try to send you the carbon copy when I'm through with it. Finished the *Money* pamphlet, 50 pages of hilarious farce meaning absolutely nothing, and think my publisher will bring it out as a cheap pamphlet. More of this anon.

Cordially,

HVM

Dec. 6th, 1936

[Paris]

Dear Durrell:

Am so sunk in correspondence now that I don't quite know where I'm at. For instance, about the book you ask for—from which I quoted. Haven't the faintest idea *what* book. And by *Titus*, you mean the surrealist number? O.K. In a little while. I am just finishing a long article, an attack on them, after reading Herbert Read's new book, *Surrealism*.

Yes, I read Wyndham Lewis' *Time and the Western Man*. I like him as a permanent enemy of the people. Don't always agree with him. Must ask if you ever read Cocteau's essay, "The Laic Mystery"? Just read it because it happened to appear in that anthology from America in which portions of *Black Spring* were reprinted. It's all about Chirico, and you should see it. I like it. It's in English in this volume. Don't imagine the anthology costs much. Write to my friend James Laughlin IV, Robin Hill, Norfolk, Conn., if you want one. Tell him to give you a reduction, that I said so. Laughlin will print you too one day, if you wish. He is doing things over there.

Waiting to see the revised article on *Hamlet*. Hope you won't lose the freshness and spontaneity of the letter. The *N.E.W.* is open to you at all times, I imagine. Perhaps the *Criterion* too. I just wrote Eliot about you, hope it will do you some good. He seems to treat me very gingerly and cavalierly. He means to be warm-hearted, I suppose, but has grown such a crust that it is almost impossible. I just sent him about a hundred pages of the *Hamlet* book (ten letters), saying I know he won't take it, but read it. He almost permitted me to review Saroyan's book —almost. Was extremely apologetic. Anyway I have persuaded the *Nouvelle Revue Française* to translate and publish one of Saroyan's stories. Pretty good, because they won't publish me yet.

Also got the *N.E.W.* to take a seven-page article from the *Hamlet* book, mostly about "Bastard Death." Mairet seems to be pretty decent. That's the trouble, as you damned well put it, they're too decent! I agree with you absolutely. They make it worse for one.

If you care to be translated for *Orbes*—it's small but read by a select critical few—I might again be useful. For Jacques Levesque the maddest stuff you've got. He wants only what the others don't want. Laughlin too, I feel sure, would be interested in your most recent works. Why don't you write him directly and mention my name? Besides his own venture he has friends among the editorial gentry.

Met Lord Beecham at Bricktop's cabaret the other night. (He of liver pill fame?) Anyway, very droll. I was in a big sweater and corduroys—dragged there unexpectedly—and milord was in full dress with a magnum of champagne in front of him and a young Negress beside him—a beauty! Very democratic, the old bugger. He wanted me to sit down with them, but there was a gang with me—all of us looking like hoodlums. Now I just get a letter from Kahane saying "must come to luncheon Tuesday—Countess So and So and Baroness So and So—must come, Henry! Because Somerset Maugham wants to hear all about you." My word! Simon and Schuster write to inform me they are interested in everything I am doing (just saw Laughlin's anthology). When I write a *popular* novel I am to let them know.

Listen, much much better news. I have found an American who thinks he can translate me into *Chinese!* Am corresponding now with several Chinese men of letters. Want to be translated into Chinese above everything else.

Enough! Tired. I would send you a copy of those *Hamlet* pages I submitted to Eliot, but need them for the moment. A little later.

Who were *you* in the photos? You look like a Greek if you're the one I think. Or were you spoofing me?

Cordially,

Henry Miller

c/o Ionian Bank, Corfu

[December 1936]

Dear H.M.:

I am so struck dumb by your generosity that I don't know what to say or how to make a polite bow to you. Villa Seurat I always imagine as an immense factory, rather like the Walt Disney studio, with you in the centre, surrounded by a few hundred active typewriters all making copies of the *Hamlet* essay. It's splendid of you to send me about like this. It's more than Curtis Brown can do for me in years. But I chuckle slightly when I see that you are writing to one of these people about me, because, should you interest one of them in me, they will, at the worst, demand to see some work of mine which justifies your enthusiasm. MY DEAR H.V.M. I HAVE NONE! I have no work, and no typist, and no dictionary. So I always keep what I write in my pocket for fear of losing it. I have no copy of the *Hamlet* essay, for instance. As for Eliot, well, Faber and Faber have put me on a three-novel contract, starting with a cheap romance called *Panic Spring*, which is a leprous distillment, BUT REFUSED THE POEMS, which are not at all bad for a small boy like me. Actually

32

I am up against the wall properly now, just finishing a *Black Book* which Fabers will reject and rupture the contract, because it is good— (I AM TERRIFIED OF IT IT IS SO GOOD IN LITTLE FLASHES) —BUT NOT POPULAR. I need a few months' revision on it. But there again I am shy of sending it to anyone because I have no copy. I really must grow up and buy carbons. But as I write straight on to the machine and am lazy, I have chosen as my motto: EVERY COPY A FAIR COPY. Needless to say this only works once in every five pages. As for work, why, I have only grown up in the last year or so, and so have hardly anything to show. But I'll send you a little prose-song called "Ionian Profile" when I rewrite it in a day or two. Maybe it will interest Laughlin enough to print it. Go easy on me, will you, because I don't want to let down your golden opinions of me, which I value above everything else. I am going quietly mad in this book and feel very sore and strained. So far no one has seen it, I am so jealous of it. The curse is that I must submit it to Faber for rejection. They have been very decent to me and are editing the romance, parts of which I must rewrite, wince I never so much. It's a filthy trick to publish a writer before he's grown up. Am starting to realise that. I WANT TO BE IN YOUR HAMLET BOOK LIKE HELL. ARE YOU JOKING OR SERIOUS? A nice letter from Fraenkel from Bruges. Is he in New York now? Have planned the heraldic book, but lack reference books on psychology, the pathology of childhood, cretinism, genius, etc. LET US KILL THE LITERARY MEN ONCE AND FOR ALL AND *force* THEM TO A PHILOSOPHIC ADMISSION OF THE *mystery*. ONWARD. ONWARD. HAVE YOU READ CYRIL TOURNEUR?

Did I tell you about Zarian? All yesterday he kept rushing into my room with "Bastard Death" in his hands,

his silver mane flying, his glasses on his forehead, saying:
"How is possible this? HOW IS POSSIBLE? I wrote all these
things in Armenian and here . . . the same phrases
. . . same words . . . Meeler writes of the Middle
Ages . . . and I wrote it." He is immensely thrilled
with the letter. "It's in the air," he says, "in the air these
ideas." He is a great friend of Saroyan and wants to write
you a letter about God, so I said go ahead. *Tropic* worried
him a bit, and he said it was destructive, but *Black Spring*
has him by the sash. Is writing an immense trilogy in
Armenian. We were on the point of starting a quarterly
calendar called *Eos*, for which we were going to ask you
and Fraenkel and Saroyan and others for material, but
the fascists intervened with a comic economic law which
doesn't permit you to send books outside the country unless you receive them back! The Greeks are amazing in
this way. Pity, we had the best poets and writers of everywhere, including Greece. Owing to this law I can't even
print the bloody poems which are festering on my shelf.

I am delighted at the breaks which are coming your
way, but I knew it was only a question of time. By the
way, tell your publisher to see that you are represented
in the British Museum Reading Room. It'll be very useful in any cases of piracy, or copyright troubles in England. Apart from the fact that your readers will increase.
It's the mistake D. H. Lawrence made when printing
abroad, and got pirated. I say, don't bother about payment if you ever land anything of mine. I'd be delirious
with just a copy of it. As for French, I don't care myself.
Dislike the literary set-up of that nation, so it wouldn't
shake me to be translated. But congratulations on the
Chinese translations. God knows how it will sound, but
congrats anyway. There's a kind of evocative surrealism
in the idea of a mandarin dozing under the plantains,

fanned by eunuchs, and reading *Tropic* quietly and in-
scrutably. I must ask my wife to make a picture of it for
you.

Sincerely,

L. Durrell

How about a trip down south for a month or two next
summer? If you are interested, if the idea is at all near
the bone, let me know and I'll make enquiries, etc.

Fête day for me. I've finished *The Black Book*. I'm in
love with it. Hurrah!

Tuesday

[Paris, December 1936]

Dear Durrell:

Your letter this morning interests me profoundly. Especially about the magazine which you have abandoned.
Supposing you can't print from Greece, why not from
Bruges, or Paris? You could still edit from Greece and
have the printing and distribution taken care of elsewhere. I myself would hate to undertake the distribution,
but I might find some one here to do it for you, some one
like Sylvia Beach, perhaps. Anyway, here is a suggestion,
a few of them, for you:

Why not make the contributors to the review pay for
the printing and mailing, etc.? Say about 250 francs
apiece—about $12.50. No avant-garde magazine can
hope to make money. Not today. But one might clear all
expenses, and if by chance any money is made it could
be returned to the contributors—both what they coughed
up and a proportion of the profits. The first thing to do
would be to write the potential contributors and see if
they were willing. I have a few people in mind who I
think would respond, with good contributions and with
money. To wit:

35

Fraenkel, Lowenfels, Saroyan, Laughlin, Anais Nin, James Stern, Van Heeckeren—possibly Hilaire Hiler and Mayo for drawings. Stern is a young Irish writer, who wrote a book of excellent short stories on Africa. Van Heeckeren might give us something about China—he is an adventurer. Mayo is a Greek painter whose drawings are almost made to illustrate my books. Hiler is a painter and a good friend of mine, now in Hollywood. There may be others—I think of these at random. The point is that the magazine, or anthology, or whatever you wish, should be fairly inexpensive. One could use both English and French, I imagine. Perlès could then come in with some of his marvellous passages from the *Quatuor*. You have your friends. Zarian sounds interesting. Make him write that letter, by all means! I would give you something from *Capricorn*, something beyond either *Tropic* or *Black Spring*, or something from *Hamlet*, or a long short story called "Max," which I am sure you would like. Or "The Universe of Death," from the Lawrence book. Anyway, there would be no dearth of material.

The thing is the expense and how to get it out. I am a bad business man. Don't count on me for that. But I have a host of friends and connections, and I have a good list of about 250 names to circularize. There should be a bang-up announcement, stating the truth about the situation, and asking for no quarter. I do think one could make ends meet. I see no profits. Well, think it over. It's just an idea, but one that has been in my crop a long time.

About yourself. First of all, order! Why not put in a carbon when you write? What's to prevent it? You will find that you save time and energy. Another little thing, if you don't mind. Why should you compromise? You have a little income. You can afford to speak your mind, do as you please. You will save ten years of sweat and anguish if you do it now, and not later. Of course, doing

36

as you please also involves a certain kind of anguish, but it's different, and more tolerable. The other eats you out and leaves you dry. Doing as you please either kills you or strengthens you. Naturally I surmised that you hadn't a great deal to show. How could you, at your age? But— just assume that people are going to ask you for something. Start now and give it from the guts. No matter what you do to please the editors it will never please them. Better please yourself and trust in God! So many good men had to print their books themselves first. Walt Whitman peddled his own book from door to door, believe it or not.

Sure, I intend putting you in the *Hamlet* book. I am suggesting to Fraenkel that we put your essay in the appendix. Just sent a copy off to the *Southern Review*, Baton Rouge, La. You may hear from them direct. Am expecting a reply from Levesque, of *Orbes*, any day now. And something more definite from Lundkvist. Don't be too grateful. I did what I did because it was worth doing. I never do anything that is not worth while.

You speak of the factory. Yes, this is a sort of factory, but without assistants. I do everything myself, and I'm half dead. I have had to retype over two hundred pages of stuff in the last few weeks, besides doing fresh things, and carrying on my Gargantuan correspondence. And reading the books that are sent me. But I'm in the plenitude of my powers now and one has to make hay while the sun shines. I can hardly sleep at night for the ideas that are surging in my brain. A little more dough, a little assistance, and I would be another Victor Hugo or a Balzac, so far as output goes.

Today I see Stuart Gilbert who has the copies of the ten *Hamlet* letters I sent to Eliot recently. Perhaps I will forward them to you to give you an idea of the substance of the book—especially now that I realize you are going to stay in Corfu.

And about a trip. Yes, I think it might be possible early in the spring. I am going to be fagged out. Pooped out, I might say. Going at a terrific pace the last few months. And no sunshine ever. Sleep between moist cold sheets, the walls wet, the heat almost nil, etc. Beastly climate, Paris. My dream has always been to see Constantinople. You will laugh, but I got that way reading Pierre Loti years ago. Never forget *Disenchantment*, even though it's old hat and sentimental now. As for the Greeks, as for Athens, I am no great admirer of that venerable civilization. But just the same, the sun, the water, the resined wine, the little blue islands. Listen, could we possibly see the isle of Lesbos, or Corinth, or *Crete?* I would give a lot to see the labyrinth at Knossus. Read all about Sir Arthur Evans' work years ago. Am crazy about that stuff. But I know no Greek and I know nothing of the classics—practically nothing. I am ignorant. Even about English literature. But I want to read *The White Devil* some time. John Ford, is it? I saw his *'Tis a Pity She's a Whore* in French. Made a great impression on me.

Sending you a copy of *House of Incest*, to keep. Must let me know what your wife thinks. So long.

HVM

And Merry Christmas to you all! You ought at least to give me your wife's name!

Corfu, Greece, etc.

[December 1936]

Dear H.M.

Very many thanks. You can't stop me. I'm delirious about that essay. Particularly the *Hamlet* which is my private piece of fame. When I do it in the long version

I shall offer it to you on a platter if any one wants to print it. *The Black Book*, by the way, is not bad, unless you're extra fastidious. I've revived it. Just rewriting it, trying to demillerise as I go along. Unhealthy influence you are, whatever virtues you have. Sticks like fluff.

About order, yes. And again, yes. And a third time. Of course it's a kind of pregnancy tic my loathing for carbons, their foul soft blurred print and the soapy feel of the type-heads against them. I lack faith, that's all. But I will be good. And it's only decent to offer to pay the typing fees on the article. Couldn't have been sweller if I'd sent you the original *Hamlet* instead of just a note about it. Skoal. Yes, Ford is fine. You would like the Elizabethans, I know you would. If you haven't struck Webster and Tourneur, there's a treat in store. Best seen or read aloud. And Nash's prose is one long dysentery of delight. Middleton, Dekker, Greville, Marlowe. Very rich age.

As for compromise. You are perfectly right if you think you are addressing St. Lawrence. But if you are talking to me I say : yes, but I'm going to have my cake and eat it. I have no hesitation about what to write any more. I am discovering what I am. Only it's a bit painful because I started in another direction, and being forced to write what I'm going to will estrange me dreadfully. It's inevitable, but I shed a few pious tears now, at the beginning of the trip, so that I can be dry as cork and controlled when we put out to sea. Sometimes I wonder whether it wouldn't be better to leave both trails and enter a bank. I'm writing about all that now with great charity. It's good in spite of the drops. Send you *The Black Book* on its way through to Fabers for a rejection. It's an ave atque vale for me. Maybe a laugh or two or a good image for you, or an action for plagiarism.

Hope you're serious about the spring. If you keep me

posted I'll get the new house finished in time and you can live here for a month or so and go quietly blind. We could be a spring-board for any trip you want to make. Don't need Greek except a few phrases like, "You are a liar" and "Give me that wallet back, it's mine" and "Fetch a policeman." Also any invitation here extends to any of your mysterious, plangent, etc. wives—unless you're a travelling Bluebeard, which would strain the exchequer beyond repair. (Evans is puzzled by the number of them in your books. Not to mention children. Sends greetings.) Myself, I'm going to see Crete properly as soon as I've consolidated my home base. I'm not a nomad at heart. I must have a landing somewhere to be happy. Hudsons say they're coming back next year, so if you're gregarious you couldn't wish for more agitated, unbalanced, enthusiastic, charming people. Even if Barclay is a comic behaviorist. I must get an engine for the Van Norden so we can take trips into the wilderness.

As for Constantinople. Why destroy your illusions by going there? You'll get those unspotted memories mixed up with spit and scrofula and mosaic and pellagra and offal. As for scholarship, we'll try not to show our erudition. It doesn't exist. Shall I send you a nice piece of the Tiberius' summer villa ruin above Kassopi? Or the date of the battle of Salamis?

Post-prandial

Knossus, now that's a dream, with the blue hills and the saffron and the women's clothes. If Evans was there it would be easy to call on him. I believe Knossus is on his own private property. He bought it.

I have finished *The House of Incest* at last. What a silly title, but I like it, in spite of the technique. It's the first book in this mode that I've read that is alive. In spite of the method. Dream minus reality. It's really alive, God help my soul, with a queer kind of poignance about it.

Like sudden dazzling tears. Who is Anais Nin? I remember Barclay saying something about her. And the introduction to *Tropic* of course. What else has she written? It's a queer name, has a sort of Oriental flavor. But this wasn't written by a sleek soot-black Cleo with a vermilion cigarette-holder, I'm sure. Nancy (my wife) is reading it and seems to like it. Those first two poems are grand. "Choked in its sails," etc. *The House of Incest* is a bad title. It sounds stale and a bit wormy, whereas the book is fresh and sweet and squeezes itself into sudden malleable shapes and colours. Nice. I think your review didn't do it justice quite. Or is this where I get a smack in the neck?

For the time addio. Don't write. I know how busy you are and am glad. Onwards into a new season. Capricornus, Capricornus, for you this must be where even the dream ends and the spirit comes through the rind, clean as a bone. I'm eager to see it. Up Capricorn!

Sincerely,

Lawrence Durrell

About the journal: we were set with the manifestoes from you and other prophets. And what better than an island as a centre? But the latest Greek fascist law is this: books sent out of the country are the same as MONEY. One has to make it good to the Bank of Greece whether one gets the returns or not, or face jail. Unhealthy position for an editor. So one has in effect to issue the book and buy up the whole issue oneself before you can send it into the world. Even with the cheap printing and free contributions we couldn't do that. I think Bruges is a good idea, but the printing rates are enormous. And we wanted (as we had here) a printer under our thumb, a fount of our own type, and a feeling of personalness about the business. Also cheap good printing. And here the quotations

41

were a third of English or French or Italian quotes. Alas for Lycidas! Zarian was going to carry through from Vienna where he goes in a week, but again the printing costs a lot. I'm no business man either.

CHRISTMAS 1936—JANUARY 1937
(Durrell in Corfu—Miller in Paris)

———◆———

THE correspondence going full spate now, Durrell professes the most extravagant admiration, Miller offers every kind of encouragement, and both now send their manuscripts to one another. For Christmas Durrell sends Miller his latest prose poem (eventually published as "Asylum in the Snow," and together with a companion piece, "Zero," privately printed by Durrell on Rhodes, 1946). Miller, tremendously enthusiastic, undertakes to get it published in half a dozen different countries through his spiderweb of literary connections. Next Miller sends the first ten *Hamlet* letters. Durrell's reply, beginning "No one will print them," provides a pretty good description of the Miller-Fraenkel correspondence; as "Hamlet, Prince of China," Durrell's second *Hamlet* letter is published in *Delta* two years later, with only minor changes, almost as it rolled off the machine. Miller, overcome, capitulates to a greater letter-writer than himself, prepares to retire from his epistolary career, and goes on for six more pages. His *apologia pro vita sua* elicits Durrell's autobiography in reply—a beautiful letter in red ink with characteristic Durrell doodles. This exchange of self-portraits establishes their close personal affinity for life. The correspondence is prodigal on both sides at this time, enough to fill a small volume; indeed for sheer bulk, 1937 is the biggest year of the correspondence.

*   *

[Corfu, Christmas 1936]

Dear Henry Miller:

With a Merry Christmas I enclose this carol which happened to me last night. I don't want to look at it any more so I send it to you. Perhaps you might think it promising. Anyway, I know that you will not hesitate to say what you feel. If you like it and contemplate sending it to the anthology you mentioned, let me put a small "To Henry Miller" on it. As after all you are doing for me I feel I want to dedicate some little thing to you. Punctilio, don't you know. A salute of one toy cannon passing your enormous broadsides. Or a squib to celebrate your victories over the infidel.

If you don't like it, then send it back because I have no copy, and I'll offer you better food at a slightly later date. I feel I'm very near now.

Much good wishes, and a verry merry christmas, if the damned event means anything to you.

Heraldically yours,
Lawrence Durrell

Jan. 3, 1937

[Paris]

Dear Durrell,

The "Christmas Carol" flabbergasts me! It's so damned perfect that it makes me green with jealousy. You will begin to think I have lost my critical faculties altogether. But not so. Whether you realize it or not you have done a masterpiece, the most perfect thing of its kind that I have ever read. Not only that, I should like to add that it is the sort of thing I have always wanted to do myself—and never could. This puts you in a class with Léon-Paul Fargue. It's far superior to Breton or to Dylan Thomas.

I read it in the dentist's office, waiting for him to go to work on me. Almost got hysterical over it.

This is just an acknowledgment. I will have more to say about it later, after I read it over a few times.

What am I going to do about it? Well, I have already written Laughlin about it, asking him if he wants it for the next issue of his anthology. Haven't sent him a copy of it as I am perplexed. It's this. I have a little scheme of my own—another!—which I want to propose to you. Perhaps we can do both—adopt my plan and have Laughlin take it also. I am thinking of investing in a machine, a sort of mimeograph machine which enables one to make innumerable copies from an original typewritten sheet in any colored ink one wants. I have been wondering if, instead of a magazine, with all the difficulties it entails, we could not do better by bringing out one thing at a time, after this process. We would put a thin paper cover around it with the title printed on it—by the same process—or else each one separately, in Chinese ink or something like that. We would send the thing to a select list of people who we think might be interested. Put no price on it, but suggest that they pay what they like towards the expense, if it appeals to them. I haven't solved all the technical problems involved yet, nor have I the dough immediately. But all that can be solved all right, in a little time.

Now I thought, if the idea appealed to you, that we might bring out your "Christmas Carol" first. You would still have the right, I believe, to sell it to a magazine or publisher, if you could get one. In this instance I frankly think it to be difficult because it's too damned good and too unusual and too uncategorizable. Laughlin, however, ought to fall for it, unless I am greatly mistaken.

If you have any ideas, practical ones, shoot them. I am the most impracticable, unhandy fellow in the world. The idea is, as I see it, to do the thing as simply as possible,

45

and yet not have it look commercial. The postage is a big item—depending, of course, on the list. The rest is labor, that's all. And the advantage lies in placing them where one wants.

I am sending you tomorrow the ten letters from the *Hamlet* which I sent Eliot and which of course he has just turned down, with a mildly sarcastic letter about it being more suitable for my "admirers" and not calculated to "widen my public." Perhaps soon I'll be able to send you a carbon of "The Universe of Death" thing. The woman who translated *The Crown* (of Lawrence) is now reading it, likes it very much, and intends showing it to Louis Gillet here who in turn may present it to the *Revue des Deux Mondes*. I am about to get another review—in the *Cahiers du Sud*. That means I have made every important French review now, excepting *Mercure de France*, which is about on a par with the *Criterion*. And did I say that Kahane got a letter from the translator of *Ulysses*, asking for the translation rights to both books in German? That doesn't mean it will be published immediately, but it's a step in the right direction. 1936 was not a bad year for me at all.

Of course, I am going to see what I can do about the "Carol" with the French, and possibly the Scandinavians. By the way, was the *Hamlet* essay printed in the *New English Weekly?* I haven't heard a word from Mairet recently.

And now here's a little excerpt from my Lawrence book which I think applies to you, to your work. "The poem is the dream made flesh, in a two-fold sense: as work of art, and as life itself, which is a work of art. When man becomes fully conscious of his powers, his role, his destiny, he is an artist and he ceases his struggle with reality. *He becomes a traitor to the human race*. He creates war because he has become permanently out of step with the rest

46

of humanity. He sits on the doorstep of his mother's womb with his race memories and his incestuous longings and he refuses to budge. He lives out his dream of Paradise. He transmutes his real experience of life into spiritual equations. He scorns the ordinary alphabet which yields at most only a grammar of thought, and adopts the symbol, the metaphor, the ideograph. *He writes Chinese.* He creates an impossible world out of an incomprehensible language, a lie that enchants and enslaves men."

Chinese! That reminds me. In the last issue of *Life and Letters Today* there is a notice about a Chinese review, which is printed in English, at Shanghai. Appears there was an article in the last number concerning Shakespeare as a Taoist! I have written for a copy of it. Also to inquire if they take contributions from Europeans. Must be a queer assortment of fish.

You asked me about Cyril Tourneur. The same day I saw Stuart Gilbert and he asked me the same question! No, I never even heard of him. I'm ignorant, I tell you. Know scarcely anything of the Elizabethan literature. Practically nothing, I should say. Alors, inform me.

Well, greetings and profound thanks. More anon. You're a stinking genius!

HVM

[Corfu, January 1937]

Dear H.M.

Your absolute generosity makes me slightly delirious. I have been walking all over the town in the rain with many cigarettes softening in my mouth, buying wool and reading your marvellous letter. It has been raining all over your letter. I went and stood at counters in shops, repeating "stinking genius." Consequently I stagger a little as I walk and feel three stories high, and still going up.

I never knew what I wrote in the "Carol" thing, because I couldn't tell. I never can. Hurrah! Only I know that some things radiate (no, irradiate) a whole day for me. "Carol" made me luminous for one whole day, so I sent it in all good faith. I'm glad you like it. I give you full permission to print sell edit burn eat anything you like with it. I don't own the damn thing, if you see what I mean. I am delighted but I shake my head. I don't own it. I haven't even got a copy of it. Hurrah! Stinking genius. And if you can get hysterical IN A DENTIST'S WAITING ROOM. . . . No higher praise.

About the mimeograph. The last one I saw was at school. They did the exam papers on it. I used to help print it on parole not to look at the texts. Needless to say . . . I was a clever lad. Well, you could get the colours off all right, but for some reason the actual "takes" were very smudgy. As if you washed each sheet in soap and water. However, that may be a personal fault. I mean not all machines diseased in the same way. Perhaps the platen was weak or something. But why are you people in need of ink? Doesn't the Siana Series do you on hand-made paper at a guinea a time? Why shouldn't the Obelisk hatch a brood of little obelisks, à la *Criterion* pamphlets? Let me know what you feel. I'm with you, with many honoured bows, whatever you say. How much does the machine cost, and how does it write?

I like that bit you quote about writing Chinese. Sounds marvellous. But these people never understand. They finger their spats and suck their eyeglass, but they never understand. Fuck the whole trade. I don't want to write, I don't want to write. I want to "stand still and dance inside." You should see how nice the publishers are about a beautiful romance I wrote for them. They say I may be a Book Society choice one day. Onward. Onward. If I am we'll bloody well print our heads off with the money and

48

a fig for momus. I think the Elizabethans are your meat if you can get inside the language before you get bored.

Another thing : Nancy says that "Carol" is not a patch on *The Black Book*. NOT A BLOODY PATCH. See? This frightens me a little. I don't think it's quite true. I've been rereading *Black Book* with a blue pencil marking all the echoes of you. It's terrible heartbreaking work. You have no idea. A sort of queer cadence. A Henry Valentine hangover which disgusts my numerous admirers. Very well, I am rewriting. The great thing is to sprawl on the pages and let no one have a look-in. Exclusive. And pray, sir, at what age may a young man cease being influenced?

Derivatively yours,

Lawrence Durrell

Your encouragement has driven me crazy almost. I'm working like a beaver on *The Black Book*, a chronicle of the English Death which I was hinting at in the end of the *Hamlet* essay. It's young of course—everything I write seems disfigured by an adolescent hangover. But I think it's coming away clean and fresh from me now, after all this hesitation. Like a peeled stick. Mark my words, one of these days you will wake up and find that I've earned the magnificent adjectives in your letter.

Skoal,

Lawrence Durrell

c/o Ionian Bank

[Corfu, January 1937]

Dear H.M. :

No one will print them. I'll tell you why. You choose a title with the word *Hamlet* and ring an old psychic chord in the cranium. You excite the critics (damn the critics) in your first letter by some real death-rays on the subject, immensely profound; then you begin roughnecking and capering the theme round in your second; and then suddenly the whole arena shifts round and empties for a duel between you and Fraenkel. Your last letter is magnificent. It's all magnificent, but why kill the book by calling it *Hamlet?* Because somehow it's so unexpected, this tissue of mirth and magnificence. It's all HENRY MILLER, PRINCE OF DENMARK. When I said in that letter that Hamlet's major problems you had solved for yourself, I was nearer the mark than I realised. You cannot write anything about *Hamlet* because the place it occupies in the Heraldic pattern is below you. There is only going up, not down. This peculiar English death which is epitomised in the play is foreign to you. I say foreign, and I mean by that China, the stratosphere. It was a stratosphere that Shakespeare inhabited, but only wrote about by accident. Your whole propensity is set towards the recording of the flora and fauna of that stratosphere. You have penetrated it further, and at a higher level. This is not Shakespeare's fault. It was the fault of the damning literary formulae of his age. If he had faced the world as it is now, he would have written things greater than you can imagine. When I say this I am not patting you on the back for being a better writer than Shakespeare, qua writer. I am saying that you have realised yourself as a man more fully. Also this important thing : in our age we have reached a point in writing when it is possible for the writer to be himself on paper. It's more than possible. It's inevitable and necessary. But for the Elizabethans writing was separated entirely from living. The self you put on paper was recognisable by a few mannerisms, a style of moral thought, etc. But it no more corresponded to the author than Hamlet corresponds to you. The virtue of the Elizabethans was this : their exuberance was so enormous, so volatile, so pest-ridden, so aching and vile and repentant and spew-struck, that here and there, by glorious mistakes, they transcended the canon. But their critical apparatus was interested only in the narration. Was it good Seneca or wasn't it? If you look at the state of criticism now, you will find a whole terminology of mysticism has entered it. Even the critic has been trying to accustom himself to the disturbing factor, which all this new ego-writing has brought to light. Lawrence is bad Seneca, Ben Jonson would have said, and meant it. The man can write, but having opinions about oneself is not enough. He lacks art. Off with his head.

I like what Fraenkel says about you being at a critical pass in your writing. I feel that too. The next few years will show me whether you can support the theory of the ego-protagonist indefinitely. I rather think you can't. I was surprised by *Hamlet*, because I thought that it was going to be a sort of opus; but Fraenkel has reduced it a little by introducing personalities. Its value therefore will be documentary. I am amazed at the Pacific Ocean which you keep in your nib. The fertility. The immensely fructuous energy. The paper seems quite used up when once you have written something on it. That is why I'm impatient. These are letters from high latitudes, but the drama —that's coming as yet, the drama that you have up your sleeve. It scares me a bit. But it's coming. I have an idea that if any man can bust open the void and figure it out in a new dazzling mythology, you can.

I don't think the others understand properly. Fraenkel accuses you of such trivialities and frills that I don't understand what you are doing in such poor literary company. I hope you don't mind me talking like this, but it alarms me when I see how little your own friends and contemporaries understand you. But his letters are such poor stuff, really. Their only purpose is to goad you into some of the most magnificent pieces of prose you've ever written. But *Hamlet?* *Hamlet* is going to be the title of this drama of yours. *Hamlet* squared, *Hamlet* cubed, *Hamlet* in an atmosphere which gives trigonometry cold fingers, and logic blunt thumbs. Shakespeare and Lawrence and Co. have been crippled from the start by being unable to realise themselves. Consequently the final drama, the *Hamlet*, when they wrote it, was entangled in their diseases, held down by them. But you it seems to me are going into this final contortion with the purest mind we have yet had, by what propitious circumstances, social, literary, and personal, God only knows. What I saw is this: you can write *Hamlet*, but in this book so far, you have only written about *Hamlet*.

I'm tired. Your praise of "Carol" has set me working so hard that it hurts. *The Black Book* is shaping for a minor eclipse. I wish I could grow up a bit. Proofs of the *Hamlet* essay today. No news. Lovely weather, but I've got a dour Cornish mist in my belly and the hump generally. Why does one bother? If only the summer would come. Destroy this letter please. I wouldn't like to hurt Fraenkel's feelings, because he has been nice and friendly to me, and because he suffers as we all suffer, and that's a bond, even if one is poles apart. Well, yours ever, as this machine is to you, Hamlet.

Sincerely, Lawrence Durrell

Leave the title. When you do your own opus I hope you call it *Hamlet, Prince of China!*

Next day

[Corfu, January 1937]

Dear H.M.:

These letters disturbed me profoundly. I was awake a long time last night reading them over a few times carefully and brooding on the subjects they throw up. Particularly the subject of the artist. I was reading pieces of

Black Spring and *Tropic of Cancer* and trying to isolate a few of the megrims that Fraenkel was trying to lay. It seems he has spotted a disease but diagnosed it wrongly. But I feel he is right when he says there is yet a battle to be fought. Last night I felt it, but I had no idea what it was. Then a shrewd remark of Nancy's started the fuse going, and I was grubbing about among books and notes to try and lay it. The mechanism which Jung calls the guilt-responsibility, which you quoted. The germ of it is in there. I was thinking of Cézanne's fear that society would get the grappins on him, of Gauguin's insistence on what a hell of a fine billiards player he was, of Lawrence fervidly knitting, knitting, and trying to forget *Sons and Lovers*. AND OF YOU EATING! Here are numberless types of the same ambiguous desire on the part of the artist to renounce his destiny. To spit on it. O Lord, if it be thy will, let this cup be taken from me. But in your books there are also numerous full larders. You say in big strident tones: I AM A MAN. THAT IS ENOUGH. Because you know that an artist can hardly taste his food he is so weak with virtue. If it were possible you would like to go on saying I AM A MAN ad lib in order to hide the more terrible stage whisper I AM AN ARTIST and from there to the ultimate blinding conclusion IAMGOD!!! It is this role which confuses you by its limitless scope. And it is in this area of the soul that that germ of the final thunderclap is breeding.

These letters are going to be very valuable as the log of that ultimate journey. I can feel the first peeled statements breaking from them. If only the issues could be cleared and instead of fighting Fraenkel's obsolete battles for him, you had time to concentrate on your own, which is more important, I'd be happier. I was thinking all night about HAMLET, PRINCE OF CHINA, and the colonising of that empty territory out there, beyond Ararat and the

Gobi and Tibet and Ecuador. It tires me, this terrible subject. I have to keep going and having a snack and repeating to myself the magic incantation: I AM A MAN. THAT IS ENOUGH. For me, it will be enough, I hope, if I ever am. My ambitions are hedge-hopping and clipped of wing. As for you, you are about to do something NEW. No one as yet has been what you are in the mammalian sense. The question is QUO VADIS? Father and Son in all their glory. There remains only the ghost. YOUR HAMLET'S GHOST. Then, and only then will it be laid. I am writing this letter extremely solemnly and passionately as a salute to you AS YOU ENTER THE INFERNAL REGIONS.

Sincerely,

Lawrence Durrell

P.S.   I suppose you haven't a full face photograph of yourself? Reading Kretschmer and would like to see whether you resemble the pycniks or the leptosomes.

Jan. 20, 1937

[Paris]

Dear Durrell,

Your last letter about *Hamlet* is the finest letter I ever received in my life. I hope that means something to you. Heretofore I have been on the sending end; for the first time in my life some one bobs up who is more than a match for me. My letter-writing days are almost over, I fear. I am harassed. It is a great pity because you deserve the fullest response. Unfortunately I gave in the past of my best to my old friends in America who never really understood me, not deep down anyway, and now I am so possessed by the work in hand that I haven't the energy to give myself in letters. But I want you to know that even if I deal out a meager response I am deeply appreciative —not only that, but touched, almost overwhelmed. I say

54

almost because, entre nous, I can honestly say I deserve it. (Without egotism or vanity.) We get back in the measure that we give. That's the sort of poetic justice which rules the world and there is no other I recognize. Now the tide is turning for me. I have definitely gotten a foothold, a grip on the world. I have made them stop and listen, I feel, and perhaps a little later it will be a terrible avalanche. I am almost afraid of it—of what the future holds.

Not long ago, as you will surmise when you read the "Max" story, I read the correspondence between Georg Brandes and Nietzsche. It was Fraenkel who lent it to me. I came to a startling conclusion about his insanity. Something like this. That he, Nietzsche, was all right so long as he took a fighting stance, so long as he was fighting the world. What took the pins from under him was Brandes' wholehearted acceptance and admiration. Against that he was powerless. He fell over backwards. It's an amazing correspondence and worth reading. I think you will see what I mean if you ever get to it.

I mention this because you say something about madness. There was a time in my life when it seemed as though I might go mad. That was between 20 and 25 years of age. I hadn't written anything, couldn't write anything, and yet felt myself all-powerful, able to cope with anything, able to do anything. I was in a ridiculous position, as regards everything. I had to do something desperate, something active in the world of men, or go nuts. I did it. Every move I made I burned my bridges behind me. Despair, desperation, megalomania. I rolled up such an experience of life that if I live to be a hundred years old it will never be fully told. I know literally thousands of people. I know hundreds intimately. I saw what few men have seen without losing their faith or their balance. (All this, by the way, I discover recently from my astrologic acquaintances, is decreed in the horoscope.

And further, that I would either go mad or accomplish something tremendous.) I have had innumerable crises. Well, I am alive, gay, energetic, optimistic in a crazy unoptimistic way. I have taken the world in and now I am spewing it out. Mairet writes me an incredible letter the other day, anent *Tropic*, which he just read, to the effect that it is a chaos and incredible and so on and so forth. But if I ever told him the truth, the whole story, what would he say? He would call me a monster, no doubt. This is a prelude. What amazes me in you is your intuition, your very genuine and vital understanding. May I say that I honestly believe that there is not a man in England who is thinking as you are thinking? I believe that absolutely. I believe that if in your creative work you will show anything like the penetration and insight which you reveal in your letters and the fragments you have shown me of your work you will be the foremost writer in England. (You said you had some Indian blood, and that seems to explain a great deal to me. Tell me more about it, more about yourself, your upbringing, your ancestry, etc. I believe in stock. In race, in blood, in the ancestral horde.)

What you say about "realizing yourself as an artist, i.e. God," struck me as one of the most profound things you've written. The very core of the matter. No, I do realize it all. I came to the most tremendous decision in New York, the voyage before last. Shattering realizations. Above all, the determination to be absolutely responsible myself for everything. I really have no fight any longer with the world. I accept the world, in the ultimate sense. Yes, I fight and I bellyache now, but it's rather old habit-patterns than anything real in me. The fight is over— I mean that fight which sank Lawrence, and maybe Shakespeare too, as you infer. And that is how I interpret your Chinese allusions. Am I right? One enters a new dimension, certainly non-English, non-American, non-European.

Oddly enough, I too have felt that the great opus lies ahead, and in somewhat the manner indicated. Not *Capricorn*, which will be tremendous enough, I can assure you. No, something of a wholly different order. Something to put beside *Quixote*, *Gargantua*, *Satyricon*, etc. A classic for the 21st or 22nd century. First all this Brobdingnagian experience must be vomited forth. I must clear the decks of vital experience. It bumps around inside like huge stones. When I have turned completely inside out the new work will shine forth of itself. I fear nothing. I will simply show my new skin. And, if you won't laugh, I think that is what the astrologers are trying to say, though they haven't invented a language for it yet. They need a flesh and blood language instead of this stratospheric algebra or logarithmic junk which they spout. That is why I listen to them. I don't give a fuck about what they predict. I do my own predicting. Or rather, I act and let the predictions take care of themselves. But, in another way, crudely, it's something like this, I think : that we are all working towards the realization of the potential. The man who realizes it most, in no matter what field, floors the world. Has the world by the balls. Just as man. I'm trying to say that over and over again in the Lawrence book. That is why I can make absurd cracks about the man 20,000 years hence. I see man passing in long waves like that. Pithecanthropus erectus . . . Neanderthal . . . Cro-Magnon . . . Maybe we are about 10,000 years or so along in our cycle of development. Maybe it will take 15,000 more years for us to show all we've got. Then out! Out like a flash! And another brand-new race, new ideas, new taboos. Not higher necessarily. No, but totally different. Totally. Gloriously different. That's always in the back of my head—the new man to come who won't even know how to read our relics.

Well, in the meantime . . . Today, tomorrow, next year, ten years hence . . . I've got ideas, more and more of them. I'm hatching them fast. Latest is to bring out an anthology, of the things *I* like. Live and dead ones. Call it maybe "The Quick and the Dead." I want to put your "Christmas Carol" in it surely. (Hoping Laughlin won't want it, or will grant me the right to use it again, which I think is possible.) I have, for one thing, a piece of reportage on the famine and pestilence in China which I think is the most horrible and most honest and most poignant thing I ever read. That alone should stop all silly talk about War, Communism, Bread and Butter, Idealism, etc. It blots out all known pain and suffering by its scale. One just can't take it in. That's China! (Yes, "Prince of China," by all means!) I have about fifteen selections in mind, the most heterogeneous imaginable. Including Rabelais' "How to Rebuild the Walls of Paris." And Kirillov's speech to Stavrogin in *The Possessed*. Searching for a cheap printer—in Estonia first. Searching for contributors who will help me put it out. This may even be successful from a financial standpoint. It's not been done before, not that I know of. Knopf's just issued a colossal one, but old hat, sure fire. This one will be like poison gas dropping from above.

Anyway, I'm tired, done in. I'm going to Copenhagen for a short stay about the middle of February. Will see Lundkvist, the Swedish poet, there. Have a swell letter from him about the books and MSS I sent him. He's doing things for me up there. And for you too, I believe. Said so, anyway. I'll come back and work some more, and then, towards late spring try to get down to Corfu, and to Crete. *Must see the labyrinth!* An obsession since the last fifteen years. Read Evans years and years ago it seems. Knocked cold. Same for Schliemann or whatever his name is about Troy.

Well, more later. Going to bed. Fagged.

HVM

c/o Ionian Bank, Corfu, Greece

[January 1937]

Dear H.M.

I was born 27th February, 1912, at one o'clock of the morning. The Indian blood must have been a mistake. I'm Irish mother, English father. God-fearing, lusty, chapel-going Mutiny stock. My grandma sat up on the verandah of her house with a shotgun across her knee waiting for the Mutiny gang; but when they saw her face they went another way. Hence the family face. I may have a touch of Indian in me, who knows? I'm one of the world's expatriates anyhow. It's lonely being cut off from one's race. So much of England I loved and hated so much. The language clings. I try and wipe it off my tongue but it clings. O what the hell, I was born to be Hamlet's little godchild. The horoscopes can't touch me, I'm already mad!

Yours sincerely,
Larry Durrell

This morning I feel better. Much better. I shall take a stroll with the gun later on and shoot a couple of snipe to give my courage a flip. I read "Max" today in bed before breakfast. It's terrifying—and the "Eye of Paris" too. Are these recent? How can you stay in the ant-heap? Myself, I shall go lonelier and lonelier ultimately—to some white Parian little island with nothing but a set of clean togas and a few brainless flute-girls for company. I shall not teach or heal or anything. Just eat watermelons and fondle the second from the left, and learn the flute maybe. Please H.M., don't crack up *The Black Book* until you see it yourself, will you? Because I don't want to let you down, and the book mightn't be so good after all. One is so familiar with the story of the young author no great man will help that when you are so damn generous I feel an obligation to live up to your opinion of me, that's all. You shall have it the second it's done.

My birth and upbringing? I was born in India. Went to school there—under the Himalayas. The most wonderful memories, a brief dream of Tibet until I was eleven. Then that mean, shabby little island up there wrung my guts out of me and tried to destroy anything singular and unique in me. My so-called upbringing was quite an uproar. I have always broken stable when I was unhappy. The list of schools I've been to would be a yard long. I failed every known civil service exam. I hymned and whored in London—playing jazz in a night-club, composing jazz songs, working in real estate. Never really starved, but I wonder whether thin rations are not another degree of starvation. I met Nancy in an equally precarious position and we struck up an incongruous partnership: a dream of broken bottles, sputum, tinned food, rancid meat, urinals, the smell of the lock hospitals. And so . . . well, we did a bit of drinking and dying. The second lesson according to St. Paul. Ran a photographic studio together. It crashed. Tried posters, short stories, journalism, everything short of selling our bottoms to a clergyman. I wrote a cheap novel. Sold it. Well, that altered things. Here was a stable profession for me to follow. Art for money's sake. I began. My second I finished when we reached here. After that, the deluge. All this epic *Iliad* of course took about three or four years. Feels like a million.

Well, there it is. My life is like a chopped worm. Until

eleven marvellous memories. White white the Himalayas from the dormitory windows. The gentle black Jesuits praying to Our Lady and outside on the frontier roads the Chinese walking stiffly and Tibetans playing cards on the ground, the blue fissures in the hills—God, what a dream—the passes into Lhasa blue with ice and thawing softly towards the holy forbidden city. I think Tibet is for me what China is to you. I lived on the edge of it with a kind of nursery-rhyme happiness. I wanted to go one summer into the passes. They promised to take me. But I left without going—alamort—it is a kind of unreasoning disease when I think of it. I am illogical again like a child. I whimper. I pant. And so on.

And now, illustrious, came the day when *Tropic* opened a pit in my brain. It freed me immediately. I had such a marvellous sense of absolution, freedom from guilt, I thought I'd drop you a note.

Tropic taught me one valuable thing. To write about people I knew something about. Imagine it! I had this collection of grotesques sitting inside and I hadn't written a line about them—only about heroic Englishmen and dove-like girls, etc. (7/6 a volume). The whole collection of men and women opened up for me like a razor. I borrowed the historic present and sat down to it. You mustn't judge this book from very high standards. It's only a beginning. But I can feel it all beginning to unroll inside me at last. I am entering into my autistic self without responsibility. The rest should follow. I tell you two years ago God couldn't have prophesied more than a Hugh Walpole income for me. Now I don't know. Rimbaud's solution is always in the air. If there's a war now, I suppose I'll be among the killers.

I send you a few pamphlets that might amuse you. One poem about the night-club I worked in. I send you also a copy of an early volume of poems. With good will and apologies for poor quality. I have atoned since by one or two real poems.

Don't bother to write. I know how fagged you must be. Just a postcard if anything crops up.

Sincerely,
Lawrence Durrell

FOR some time Durrell has been making gingerly, hopeful, premonitory allusions to a work in progress. Now as it nears completion, he mentions it with increasing assurance and misgiving in almost every letter. Finally a month or so after a full-scale blurb, he holds his breath and sends the manuscript—a unique copy—to its muse. No need to have worried. Miller, delighted and dazzled by *The Black Book*, hails Durrell as genius and fellow-outlaw. One of Miller's several appreciative cadenzas goes on for five single-spaced pages. Letters often overlap here because the mails take as long as a week between Corfu and Paris. Betweentimes Durrell tries to induce Miller to visit Greece by describing the idyllic life of *Prospero's Cell*. Miller, though tempted, nevertheless values the distance between them: "I'm glad in a way that you live in Corfu and not around the corner. It's like writing to a brother monk in Ultima Thule. Did you ever see Rabelais' letters to the scholars and confreres of his day? You can feel the distance and the patience and the quiet dignity and the grip on the inner substance which refuses to be dissipated."

* *

[February 1937]

Honoured and illustrious:

First it's your output that staggers me. As for the way you crack me up to these people, gratitude is a poor word. I should say FRIGHT. Supposing I ain't? And as for *The Black Book*, poor thing, the position with regard to it is this: I am a proud father of a cheap romance, wishy-washy stuff. Sheer lochia. But Faber and Faber, on the strength of it, gave me a three-volume contract, not realising, poor people, what a phoenix lurked under the lamb's evening-clothes. I wrote them recently and said: I am writing one of the most amazing books ever completed outside an asylum. It is, though mild, unprintable in England. What will you do? They have the option on it, you see. They replied decently enough, that it was O.K. with them, so long as they got the first offer, where it was printed. Accordingly I am bound to them firmly, until they give *The Black Book* the K.O. I don't think they could do anything but refuse. It is so short (70,000 words) that it won't stand castration. Myself, I don't know. I like it, frankly. It's a good little chronicle of the English death, done in a sort of hamstrung tempo, with bursts of applause here and there. I think it's a book Huxley could have written if he were a mixture of Lawrence and Shakespeare. It dates from that insomniac day when I felt a sort of malaise, and began to wonder if I would really be content as a best-selling novelist (once my ideal). Very little is censorable in the ego of the book. Nothing in fact. I had to go easy on the ego because a twenty-four-year-old ego is a dull thing to contemplate. But there is an irrepressible dying diarist called Gregory, and a quite unprintable person called Tarquin. These two are slightly libellous: very, in fact. I am going to send it to you to read first when it's done because technically it's very influenced by you. But after millions of anxious nights Nancy says she sees a distinct personality in it which is not Miller. This must be a comfort to you. In order to destroy time I use the historic present a great deal, not to mention the gnomic aorist. It is not too risky, but here and there it was necessary, when dealing with Tarquin, who is (if he lives yet) something of a frontal sarcoma, a fairly wide excavation, not to mention a spot of oblique traction. And once the foetus is really man-handled in a sort of Church of England fashion. For the rest, you might like passages.

About heraldic: my pet is in a very muddled state just at the moment. A new book on the anatomy of the brain has set me wondering whether there isn't a distinct locali-sation of the two recorders, anterior and posterior, as it were, reason and unreason. Whether the whole germ of humanity's struggle isn't seated in the brain cancer, the slowly bulging frontal lobes which over-balance the ver-tebrae, and set us a censor to canalise the findings of the sensory mechanism. I've written cute notes to a couple of brain specialists, asking them what they think they're playing at, localising a fantastic terminology of words, which mean nothing. Don't know whether I'll get an answer. But if anything comes of this theory, I'll write a book which might indicate the locality of the system. Of course one starts with that damning premise of Lao-tse: the Tao that is the subject of discussion is not the true Tao. But it's good to see that the doctors are at the end of their hook. They are waiting around for "discovery of genius without which it is impossible to proceed." I propose later on, as a mere by the way, to hand it them on a plate. Always wanted to be a doctor. Young enough to be as yet. Maybe in a year or two.

And what do you think of this as a curiosity: ALL ART

IN THE GERM IS CURATIVE! Of course I'm hopelessly ill-read and jump to conclusions wildly. Mostly other people's conclusions I find afterwards. The heraldic universe is just this side of China, where it touches Ethiopia and the Dead Sea. O, it's a frightful mess. I've just ordered *The Meaning of Meaning*.

You see, H.M., I know what I mean, but I must try and make sure, when I start expounding it, that you see what I mean, behind the rather squashy vague sounds of an idiom. By the way, thanks for the photograph. I see you're a pycnik. All great artists seem to be. As for the development of the frontal lobes, my sincere congratulations. This puts you in the running alongside Shakespeare, who had the cutest frontal ever popularised by Kretschmer. The temporals seem well-developed, over-developed in fact, which points to mania of a depressive kind, with alternating slices of fragile homicide. But this may be due simply to the phagomania which enlarges the tendons of the jaw-bone, and covers the temples with schists, bosses, nugs, and snags. Otherwise you look remarkably normal and VERY PROFESSORIAL. What degrees have you? Nancy promises to frame the painting if you send it. A long time ago Barclay Hudson said your water-colours were splendid, so I'm all agog. And the method you analysed in *Black Spring* seems full of promise.

Looks like war again, don't it? If only Europe would just look at the curative properties of art for a second. Well, hail. I've another seventy pages to do before the chopper falls. At a page a day, that makes fine progress, as you can imagine. How do you do it?

Sincerely,

Lawrence Durrell

[February 1937]

Dear H.M.

Perhaps if our plans don't chime now they'll chime in the autumn. But the situation is this. For certain I'll be in Venice for the first two weeks of May, either by the Yugoslav steamer or by Max's yacht, if it materialises. He is negotiating for it now. I've asked him, and he says if he likes you, and if someone sleeps on deck they might arrange the down trip for you. I'm paying a little for food, etc. But much cheaper than the steamer to be sure. And what a trip, staying as long as one likes anywhere!

Now, the cast-iron good weather begins in June. We are moving out of here in that month, boarding the Van Norden and moving to the sea-coast of the island, where all the long sand-beaches are, Myrtiotissa, Peleka, Sinarades, etc. Evans and my brother are coming in the smaller boat, and we are all going to camp down the other side, sleeping on board. As a base we are using Koster's house in Paleocastrizza. His wife is leaving for Norway, and he was telling me yesterday that he's got half the house free to offer anyone—was thinking of Perlès. If you liked to come, not on a wild few-day trip, but for a couple of months or so, I expect we could fix you a room with him where you could do some of that pressing work, and spend the rest of your time with us, bathing and going blind with sand. June, July, August are wonderful months. In the boat we could make a few longish trips to the islands at the north and south with you, Paxo, Rhoda, etc. Incidentally, once you got here, there would be NO EXPENSES to shoulder. The rent of the house is free, and I do all the catering. Anyway, as I say, don't feel rushed into anything at all, will you?

Pity you're leaving for Copenhagen. I am sending you

The Black Book next Tuesday for a look over. I'm depressed over it, but feel written out completely after it. Rather like having a stroke, all soft and numb and pole-axed. You must see what you think. It's honest as I can write as yet, but the affectations and literary flapdoodle stick a bit. Shall I send it you first or wait until you return? Get it over with Fabers?

As to the poetry, I'm rather inclined to agree with you. That was juvenile stuff I sent you. Much better since. But I reserve verse these days for those tiny bitter mosaics which you can't do in prose; tight as diamonds and very brightly coloured. Things like this economical lyric.

ETHIOPIA

Soften in my arms, my sugar,
Nigger nevermore release
Till the gold day-lion pounce
Strike my Nubian with white paw.
We are such whose fate is fleece.
We explore,
Evermore,
Ethiopia ounce by ounce!

I don't think you can *concentrate* so immensely in prose as this, with its visceral rhythms which are not in the scansion but the word values, and the transition of colours from Nubia to lions to Ethiopia being weighed out in ounces, like fleece. It's the only real poem I've ever written, I think. Poetry to me seems more and more to be a pill, a number nine. I hardly write any these days. But the best example of what I mean is that stroke of genius, so economical in its touch, so deft, so bland, so unique. I wonder if you know it?

Out of the gorse
Came a homosexual horse!

Nothing else. Just that. I wish I knew who the author was. Just read *Black Spring* again. You know, it is bigger writing than *Tropic*, much bigger and bolder in design. But it's not symphonic in the same degree. It's more a suite of magnificent organ-notes. It should be read in pieces to get the full value, not all at once. Also re-read the *Hamlet* letters. I take back my pert criticism. They are ENORMOUS, your letters, enormous. Just re-read Webster. What an analogy with Eliot. Much more gifted and lucky in age, but what a literary man. I prefer Tourneur and Co., they had balls and tears and the real principle of love in their guts. I send you another postcard of the Gorgon here in Corfu museum with a note about it. Tell me whether to send *The Black Book*, will you?

Best wishes on the northward trip,
LDurrell

[Paris, February–March 1937]

Dear Durrell—

Am just getting up out of bed after an attack of the grippe. In my present mood am unable to decide anything about the future, about vacations especially. I do appreciate extremely all that you propose doing for me down there. But I'm non-plussed for the moment.

I shan't be going to Copenhagen either. No money. Just finishing with the dentist. A long, gruelling, expensive affair. Thank the Lord I'm through, for the time being. All this because of malnutrition.

The photos are very enticing. What sunlight! I think I got ill because of the incessant rains, the damp mold of the walls, the courants d'air, as they say here. Foul weather in Paris in the winter. And now am just a bit afraid of the sun—a fear of disintegration, through real relaxation. I have never really relaxed these last years. A constant drive, an obsession to get it out of my system. And I never will finish. I am doomed to write perpetually. However, all this may change. I should like to see you all and the great Mediterranean basin too.

I have just finished the chapter on my aborted trip to London, "Via Dieppe-Newhaven." Will try to send a copy soon. I think you will enjoy it. Another forty-page story!

Do you want more water-colors? I did a few more recently while ill.

HVM

c/o Ionian Bank, etc.

[March 1937]

Dear H.M.

Many thanks for the note and I'm sorry you're low. Listen, there is absolutely NO OBLIGATION to come down here unless and until you want to. I say this because when I get exuberant and make plans you may feel bad about refusing to fall in with them. So don't. If I can't see you this summer I'll meet you in Paris next winter en route for England. On the other hand if you feel the need of spending a few months in the sun this summer I want you to know that we will always have a little room for you in a shady house with a bed and a table in it. So if you feel you can't leave your work, why BRING IT.

The technique of reintegration-lapse is more difficult in a town, I've found. When there's nothing to do one works. I have that awful contamination of restlessness too. But in the summer here there's a fresh trip to make every day and a siesta to take regardless of where you are. Myself, I put a straw hat on and sleep in the sea usually. It's astonishing how after a week or two the sun stops disintegrating one and begins to fill one out. The warmth instead of eating you ripens you. Everything falls into the sea, even the publishers' lists.

The Van Norden is being painted. Photos later. Are you in low financial straits? Let me just pay the workmen and buy the engine and maybe I'll have a few pounds to offer at the shrine of St. Valentine. I hope you don't get sore at all this talk of money. Nancy winces and prefers to send cash under a plain cover with "anonymous" on it. That's an English habit of thinking of money as unclean. But if I can help I will.

Sent you *The Black Book* last week. Today "Zero" for Anaïs Nin if she'll accept it—with my gratitude and good wishes.

More in a moment when I get back to the machine. In town now for lunch. I transcribe a quote from Zarian's letter overleaf.

Now, I do hope you'll feel better soon and not be worried.

Yours, etc.

L. Durrell

From Zarian: "Say to Miller that I like him; not always his intelligence of which he has too much, but his SOUL: that I understand, that I feel in the circle of my own soul. And you too, my dear Durrell," etc. A trinity, what!

March 8, 1937

[Paris]

Dear Durrell,

The Black Book came and I have opened it and I read goggle-eyed, with terror, admiration and amazement. I am still reading it—slowing up because I want to savor each morsel, each line, each word. You are *the* master of the English language. Stupendous reaches, too grand al-

71

most for any book. Breaks the boundaries of books, spills over and creates a deluge which is no longer a book but a river of language, the Verb broken into its component elements and running amok. You have written things in this book which nobody has dared to write. It's brutal, obsessive, cruel, devastating, appalling. I'm bewildered still. So this is no criticism. And did you want criticism? No, this is a salute to the master! I will tell you more calmly, when I get finished, when I reread and sponge it up more thoroughly. Now it's an onslaught.

Of course I don't expect to see Faber and Faber publishing it. Did you? No English or American publisher would dare print it. We must find the men for it! I am pondering it over already. And right here a problem presents itself. You say this is the only copy there is. You frighten the life out of me. I can, of course, send it on to Faber registered and all that, but even so, I wouldn't rest easy putting it into the mails. Before I do anything, tell me if you don't think I had better have a copy made, several, in fact? I could arrange it, if you like, with someone I know I can trust. It's a big job—I don't know how many pages, because you didn't number your pages. But, if you deem it advisable, I will go ahead with it and defray all expenses. You could square that off, if you so wished, against my indebtedness to you. On the other hand, you may wish to get it to Faber's in a hurry. So let me know pronto what to do.

My dear Durrell, you'll never do something more to their liking, as you put it in your note. You've crossed the equator. Your commercial career is finished. From now on you're an outlaw, and I congratulate you with all the breath in my body. I seriously think that you truly are "the first Englishman!" This is way beyond Lawrence and the whole tribe. You are out among the asteroids— for good and all, I hope.

The whole thing is a poem, a colossal poem. Why you should ever want to write little finished poems I don't know. Anything you write as poem can only be a whiff, after this. *This is the poem*. It's like the Black Death, by Jesus. I'm stunned. My only adverse reaction is that it's too colossally colossal. You have to be Gargantua himself to take it all in.

It seems to me, at the moment, that Kahane would be the only man to do it. Possibly Fraenkel. That's why I'd like to have extra copies of it. No commercial, legitimate publisher can possibly bring it out. I can see them fainting as they read it. Unfortunately Kahane, my publisher, is rather set against you. Very unfortunately, and partly my fault. Seems he doesn't like any one who admires me too much. Curious thing that, but a fact. Sort of professional jealousy. He writes too, you know, under the name Cecil Barr. Vile, vile crap, the vilest of the vile, and he admits it, but with that English insouciance that makes my blood creep. But, if you assent, I will try him. I will wheedle and cajole and jig for him, if necessary, because I believe in it wholeheartedly. And I see no one else on the horizon. Only Fraenkel. Again we will be up against the professional problem. Fraenkel, however, is more capable of being objective, capable of admiring something he could not do himself. He has the money and the press. Has he the courage, the initiative? Perhaps it could be brought out in a deluxe edition, through subscription. All this I must think about.

Anyway, now I understand the Himalayan background. You should thank your lucky stars you were born there at the gateway to Tibet. There's a new dimension in your book which could only have come from such a place. It's like we're out among new constellations. How long, for Christ's sake, did it take you to write this? I can understand that you must be exhausted. It's a tour de force.

Well, more when I finish. And salute!

HVM

[Corfu, March 1937]

Dear Miller:

I'm dumb of course. Don't know what the hell to say. I knew it was good, of course, but the extravagance of your praise frightened me. In bed. Grippe. 103° and all that stuff. Had a nice letter from the reader at Fabers who has heard whispers of the book and wrote to ask after its health. Very nice people. I told them you were holding it to make copies and would send it on post-haste when you had made them. Much thanks for the idea. I know no typist who would do it for me in England, that was why it was alone. As for Kahane, tell me, where do I compete with *Daffodil?* And as your publisher isn't he happy to find his taste corroborated? Sounds a bit of a shit to me. However, no hurry. Slowly, slowly. Let me get back on my feet again and I'll let you know further. In the meantime your praise rings in my ear like the silver hammers of quinine, and I'm covered in sweat and glory.

Evans and Nan and Co. reading Anaïs Nin out loud and going crazy over those passages in *House of Incest.* Wow, motile silk! Now I know. It was written during the grippe.

Best wishes, and pray God you still like the bloody tome when you shut it up. Personally I find a lot wrong with it. I'll do better. May even rewrite here and there.

Alors,

Lawrence Durrell

74

MARCH—MAY 1937
(Durrell in Corfu—Miller in Paris)

———————◆———————

DURRELL now decides to take Miller's public relations in hand with a scheme to lift the American censorship ban on *Tropic of Cancer* and *Black Spring*. Their discussions of strategy are detailed and exhaustive; only a sampling is included here. As a matter of fact, Miller is more absorbed in Durrell's *Black Book*, which he is busy copying; every letter during this period expresses his enthusiasm. Later, when Durrell revises *The Black Book*, Miller finds he has cut it too drastically, feels as though it were his own flesh.

Another subject now enters the correspondence, as they begin to exchange water colors. Here again, Miller assumes the role of mentor, for he is an old master while Durrell has only recently started painting—though his wife Nancy Myers is an artist. Hans Reichel, the Villa Seurat painter Miller mentions, is the subject of his discourse on painting, "The Cosmological Eye." Both Miller and Durrell have remained water-colorists to this day—amateurs in every good sense of the word.

*   *

[March 1937]

Dear H.M.

This occurred to me. Have you got a typescript copy of all the letters written you about *Tropic of Cancer?* Or even a list of names of the people, chiefly the well-known people? Why not anthologise them? Get the writers' permission. I thought of making an anthology called "The Banned Book." Get two writers, well-known ones, to discuss the problem that the modern publisher is faced with, the reasons for it, a little essay as a preface, and the correspondence as an answer.

If you like, I can write and ask both Curtis Brown, and John Gawsworth, a friend of mine who is a marvel at placing stuff, what the chances of such a book would be. But if you have a typescript of the letters can I look them over, so as to write with more authority on the subject? I imagine the collection has enough names in it to be a publisher's draw. What do you think?

Among them have you such signatures as Aldington, Lewis, Campbell, Huxley, possibly Shaw and Morgan? Their names would count and some of them are good-hearted and would be keen to see the ban on real literature lifted. If Campbell and Lewis have not seen the book, will you let me circularise them on the subject? They are always yelling about the obscenity laws and might do you the introductory essay. Also Stein, Joyce, Pound, Carlos Williams.

Hope this doesn't bore you. But if the idea suits you let me know. I can do little enough actual string-pulling, but it seems the strings you've got are pretty long and tough anyway. Let me know.

Yours, etc.,

Lawrence Durrell

P.S.   Were you ever influenced by Gauguin's Journal?

[Paris]

Dear Durrell:

One of the best evidences of the great merit of your book is this, that I haven't yet finished it! This is not flippant paradox. I mean sincerely that your book has caused such an upheaval, has had such a fecundating power, that the discussion of it outstrips the reading. I myself am deliberately prolonging the achèvement. Even I, voracious and gluttonous as I am, find it too rich and savory to gulp down quickly. I don't even feel like saying much about it until I have read it several times. And part of my desire to have copies made is to keep one on hand for ready reference, to bite into it now and again or show it to others.

This evening, suffering from a bit of a hangover, I was in bed when my friend Edgar knocked at the door. I told him to glance at the part about the womb. We sat on the bed and dived right into the schizophrenic zone. Time to eat. Walking down the Villa Seurat towards the restaurant we are still discussing the book. Now it is after midnight. We have been talking Durrell for five hours, and yesterday it was almost the same. In the midst of the discussion we were going to send you a telegram. We were going to ask you a vital question. What the question was I forbear to tell you, as it would take too long to explain what led up to it. But anyway, I felt constrained to remark that it was a great pity you weren't here to listen to what we had to say.

There are whole blocks in your book which are nothing short of miraculous. Gracie, Miss Smith, the womb, for example, to mention just a few. You seem to have expressed the ultimate. The demonic quality of the writing comes from a super-consciousness which is simply a mystery. How you attained it God only knows. You are absolutely one with the writing. Edgar thinks you must be living on this plane of significance. I myself can't believe it. You would almost be God if you were. At any rate, you're an apocalyptic writer.

The reading of your book was an event in my life. I had the impression of having finished a simply colossal work, something of two or three thousand pages. Partly due to the form in which you cast it, a form rigidly imposed upon you by the very nature of the book, and partly by the poetic significance, the symbolic nature of the work. It is a modern poem of the first dimension, something that not only frees you from the Ego and the Id but the reader also. The few readers there will be! For this is a book for the initiated only, and how many are there at present in the world? It is a surgical operation, a self-birth: the navel string is definitely cut. No going back from this point. You are now out in the wide world, the world of your own creation in which you will be very much alone. A terrorizing prospect if it were not for the fact that you know what it is all about, that you reveal a supreme awareness, a super-consciousness. The theme is death and rebirth, the Dionysian theme which I predicted in the Lawrence book must be the theme for the writers to come—the only theme permissible, or possible. Your rebirth is the most violent act of destruction. A positive one, just the opposite to the surrealist movement. Superficially there are analogies between your technique and theirs, but only superficially. The real difference is vast, a chasm veritably. And that is precisely because of your wisdom, your ability, after terrific struggle, to effect a synthesis. The book, though outwardly chaotic and confused, a sort of monotonous avalanche, is really structurally solid and formal as a diamond. It happens that instead of using the mineralogical material of the form-worshippers you were employing the live, plastic material of the womb. Edgar would have it that you have performed the astounding feat of following the schizophrenic trend to its logical, consummate solution, that instead of the retrogressive neurotic swing back to the womb—womb being the unattainable, the Paradise of the Ideal, the Godhood business—you have expanded the womb-feeling until it includes the whole universe. All is womb, hence you are constantly with God. Hence, like God, a thorough out-and-out schizoid, able to move creatively, easily, freely in all directions and all dimensions. In my charts, when trying to solve the problem of the Lawrence book, I was obsessed with a similar idea. I felt that the return to the womb feeling was a right one, but untenable simply because impossible (only the insane achieve it!). But the process of transformation, metamorphosis, symbolization, if you will, is this same return to the womb tendency, only in reverse. You die out utterly, as you did in your book, in order to achieve a life on a thoroughly new plane of reality. This is so clear in your book, so exhaustively and definitively written out, that it makes one dance inside to follow you.

O High and Mighty Lama, how did you come by your great wisdom? Give us a tangible, personal statement of the condition of your soul today. Are you still standing there on the top-most tip of Mt. Everest? Does the snow still dazzle you? Have you passed out of snow and into the blue? What is the favorite color now? What is the password?

In replying send a new and unabridged volume of Funk and Wagnall's Dictionary. I am beginning to relearn the English language. *Aboulia, masma, floccus!* When you finally felt the Ark grounding on Mt. Ararat what a consolation it must have been to find that all your marvellous words were also rescued from the Flood! The

Picassos on the wall! Yes, and with it floccus, masma, aboulia, alexia, aphasia, amusia, anoi, and Miss Smith's red coon slit, her conk, her poll, her carnivorous ant-eating laughter, her Chaucerian Africa with Freudian fauna and flora, with Chamberlain's agraphia, Chamberlain hanging on a hook by his own navel-string, listening with dead mastoid to the Ninth Symphony of fluked-fin futility. I must read it all again a hundred times. I sit here with a bag of dynamite and fear to mail it out. I wait for the command. It must be retyped. More carbons, more personal readers, more alexia, more aboulia, more iconography, more snow, more coon slits and coon-slatted laughter. Immense. Colossal. *Kolossal!* Alors, zero hour! God the Illogical lost in the schizophrenic rush. Alors, up with the womb and hail to the divine osmosis!

About the letters for the "Banned Book." Am sending you them under separate cover. Another batch will follow when I get back from Kahane the ones he has. Look them over and see what you think. There are not so many big names as there might be. And most of the big names have written idiotically—which is rather good, from one standpoint, if we can secure their permission to quote. I was trying to bring them out myself—all the letters as is, and the reviews too, in a brochure. Without a word of explanation. Send them out gratis to all the periodicals, newspapers, critics, publishers throughout the world. Your idea may be even better, more practical. All my ideas are halted for the time being because of *no money*. Hamstrung.

In answer to your questions, however, about the "Banned Book." No, I don't know Aldington, Campbell, Lewis—you mean Wyndham Lewis? Wrote the first and last named, care of their publishers, but never heard from them. Shaw I deemed hopeless, as I would H. G. Wells.

You have in the enclosures letters from Pound, Stein and Williams, the first two absolutely imbecilic, as also are Dos Passos, Dreiser and Max Eastman. I like Lowenfels' long essay and your own, nothing much outside of that.

I shall probably have more to say about *The Black Book*. The most stimulating thing I have read in years and years. Leaves me wide open. Nothing pre-natal about it. The pre- is finished. *Now it* is. And so, once again, salute, and a round salvo of 59 guns!

Yours,
HVM

c/o Ionian Bank, Corfu, Greece

[April 1937]

Dear H.M.

The magnitude of my achievement deafens me. At least your letters anent it do. Well, if we are not to bluff or become mock-modest, I knew it was a good book. I felt that virtue had passed out of me. But so good . . . ? This is a discovery which has illuminated today, yesterday and the day before. I am inclined to say: "Good. Destroy it. If YOU like it, then hardly anyone else will understand it."

AS FOR THE GRAND LAMA, I'M IN A SLIGHT COMA, SOMA, OR TRAUMA ABOUT YOUR LETTER. I'm tremendously grateful you find so much meat in the book. It is rather a mystery, I suppose. I don't pretend to solve it. I look at myself in the mirror from time to time—no clue whatever. A short fat obelisk with the features of a good-natured cattle driver. I am 25 but I feel much older. Zarian has just sent me a huge Viennese briar pipe and I have been making Nancy photograph me at all angles, with it in me. Perhaps some clue will emerge from the subsequent photographs. I'll send you one. The state of my soul is shaky just now. I've come down several thousand feet below snowline, and intend to stay as long as I can. Buoyancy does me no good. I get over-emotional and shaky and liable to rages and fears and psychological tics—all due to this damned writing. I used to be so healthy and full of a sort of gawkish je m'en foutisme. The summer inaction will bring it back. Am planning a monastic summer. Boxing at dawn with Capt. McGibbon. Diving. Swimming. No smoking. Actually the thing which will heal me is a visit to Calypso's grotto on the lonely island north of us. As soon as the boat's ready we go. No more books, no more writers, no more anything. I WANT A GOOD STEADY JOB WITH A LITTLE HOUSE LOTS OF CHILDREN A LAWN MOWER A BANK ACCOUNT A LITTLE CAR AND THE RESPECT OF THE MAN NEXT DOOR.

The Black Book took about 18 months to write: 4 re-writes: altogether in quantity I wrote about four times the amount, but it's a very short book. I'm afraid it's over-packed with lard. Well, that's a technical problem. I admire the effortless way you butter your bread, not too much, not too little. Myself, I'm so scared of the butter not showing or being mistaken for mere margarine that I over-cloy the works. A sense of proportion will come, however.

It is when I face the author of the original deluge that my real modesty begins. Anything positive I have as a writer I owe to your books—my stance, a new emotional attitude, the way I hold my gloves up at the world. As for the wisdom—my God—it is all a question of induction, convection, you might say contagion. I shall do better yet, I hope. Don't lose sight of the ardent disciple in me, and mistake a fledgling for a full-grown phoenix. It's a point I labour because the influence is there—rather more than I would care to admit to a jury! What affects me most is the complete selfless generosity which you all shower on me. I fatten on it. Gratitude is no reply. You shall have a book, if possible, a bigger book. Dedicated to Miller, Edgar, and Nin, Inc., Paris, specialists in plasm, germ-plasm, mind-plasm, ectoplasm, soul-plasm. I have planned AN AGON, A PATHOS, AN ANAGNORISIS. If I write them they should be The Black Book, The Book of Miracles, The Book of the Dead. Perhaps I shan't write them.

As for my vocabulary, mea culpa. Words I carry in my pocket, where they breed like white mice. But there isn't a single neologism in the whole book. Every word IS. Aboulia and Co. are from brain-surgery manuals. Words belonging to trades stick to my tongue. I'm a fiendish reader for mere syllables. Anoia, alexia and Co.

I'm afraid you can't talk, because you have the same assimilative power.

More anon.

Yours sincerely and excitedly,
Larry Durrell

I've moved my machine out on to the terrace under the vine leaves. Uneasy blue sea. Lizards sucking in warmth on the wall. Spring opening quietly. It is impossible to think of writing—my writing that is. Been reading you again lately without so much fear of contamination. Growing up, I suppose. Feel a bit jaded, but pleased as hell you like that little book of mine. I carry the letters around with me chewing them over slowly and smiling to myself. I feel so exclusive with that book; no one will understand a word of it. One thing I've hammered home is that there is no word-coining in it. The vocabulary may be Elizabethan, Middle-English, Dutch, etc., but EVERYTHING MEANS SOMETHING. I don't like neologism except used as an occasional hand-grenade. That is why Laughlin's dream-writing contributors bore me stiff with their "wingle wangle obfuscating inspissate hunger-marching shitshat." Come, we demand more than chewing-gum. WE ARE HUNGRY.

Perhaps this fall we can meet and arrange some sort of campaign to take the skin off the public's behind. Another thought struck me: you see, it must be water-tight —like those ads you read. An eminent doctor says: "I always take *Tropic of Cancer* in a glass of water before going to bed. A marked tonic effect." A famous divine writes: "Sire, I have used *Black Spring* now for a number of years and find it good for swollen joints. My wife's arthritis, for many years crippling, has vanished after a single application." In my quiet, annoying, knowing, pious little way I have been doing some quiet crusading. The one livid paradox which starts up from your writing I have been at great pains to express to my correspondents. None of them see it. Religion, I mean. *Tropic of Cancer* and *B.S.* as the most religious books written since the Authorised Bible. Must keep these people red hot. Alan Thomas, a friend and an influential bookshop owner in England, is another man I'm laying for. He doesn't like your stuff yet, but he will.

I'm still stunned by your letter. I can't help feeling a bit of a fraud, because the book DOES seem damn good, and what I personally have to do with it is a mystery. You will shriek with laughter when we meet. It's so curious, after all. That the thing should have been dictated to ME of all people. I get slightly hysterical when I think of it. How soon will you have a copy? Never mind if nobody wants it. It's a written fact and I feel shriven by it, absolved, free. And so happy you people were moved by it, and excited. I suppose I am with God, but only during consulting hours, not all the time, tell Edgar. The surgery has a white door with the hours of attendance painted on it. At the moment everything that is me is breaking up. The spring opens up today and I open up with it—Durrell the novelty, whatever that means. Leave for Athens Saturday to buy a tent, etc. Then the black sleek douce Van Norden will be launched and off we go. In June Alan Thomas comes down here. I'll send your MSS back to you by hand with him. Safer. New Fascist restrictions open everything up and scatter it about, and you can't afford to lose originals. Send you photos of our trips this summer. Plan to leave for England in the fall, stop off a day or two in Paris and meet you and have a meeting of soul-shareholders.

April 5, 1937

[Paris]

Dear Durrell :

There's so much to answer in your last two letters that I am tackling it piecemeal, as I reread them. All this is far more interesting to me than dealing with the English. You can understand. I say they are clean daffy, all of them. I don't understand them, their language, their attitude towards life, literature, death, any fucking thing you say. So it is very difficult for me to deal with them— more and more so as time goes on. I just don't know any more how to frame a simple letter to them. I say "hay" and they say "cheese" for answer. And after having written so damned many letters (hundreds, I should say) I am a little fed up. I've lost that prime spontaneity which after all brought about a few feeble reactions. It's a drain on me. I am perfectly willing to give you carte blanche in the matter, if you want to waste any effort on it. I feel I can trust you implicitly—whereas I wouldn't trust Fraenkel et alia who are all supposed to be my most intimate friends. (At bottom I haven't any *intimate* friends. I'm something of a monster, just as you make yourself out to be in *The Black Book*. They never reach the inmost core of me, these people. They attach themselves and I act like a Chinaman—drop them when I've had enough, and so on. But never hostile. I have no genuine hostility—rather an enormous pity and comprehension. I say this to clarify a bit only. My real friends never write to me, or very seldom. They are fine nobodies, but they are my friends. They are real and I have a bond of affection with them. Beyond literature. They don't know or care much about this side of me. Perhaps I exaggerate here a little, but it's more like that than the reverse.)

As for the financial end—don't worry about that. If you can write the letters I can dig up the books always. Kahane is rather stingy in his Manchester way, but can always be persuaded over the bar where I usually get him. I've already hinted to him that you have a scheme up your sleeve. If he resents things it's only because he wants to do everything and be everything himself. A really impossible fellow, stupid as they make 'em, and yet "sharp," I suppose, in a business way. But gets everything wrong at the start. Suspicious. And really hating himself deep down for having failed to be an artist. You see what a set-up I have. If it were any other man alive I would already have sold your book—with him I have to proceed like a tortoise. I have to get other people to back up my opinion—for he is like a weathercock and has no opinion of his own at all. I don't give him the least bit of credit for having published me. He was forced into it!! But he's forgotten that already. So mull it over—there's time—and let me know what you propose. Count on me for little, except the books and moral support. Maybe later I'll swing into it—but it's embarrassing, to say the least. And time is working in my favor always. I have no inner doubts about things. It seems clear as a bell, what will happen eventually. And now I am eating every day—occasional lapses which don't count any more—and so things are quite quite rosy. I have only had one serious problem all my life, you know, since I came of age : FOOD. And I'm very glad it was only that.

If I seem to ignore a lot of things you ask about forgive me, it's only because of the hectic everyday living. About coming down there now. You've asked me so magnificently and so many times. What can I say? Honestly? I don't know. Why I don't know is probably because I hate to separate myself from my daily activities. My life has become a very smooth machine-like affair—in the good sense—in which writing, eating, drinking, etc., all move naturally on one level. Sort of earthly rotation. And this is quite a big thing for me to have achieved, because it wasn't always thus. So in a real way I never have need of vacations. I get a little off now and then, but just a good sleep puts things right again. Just plain loafing, in bed. I see no reason to move from this very spot. Yes, I'd like to see the world. Sure. Who wouldn't? But if I don't nothing much is lost. I've got the world inside me, so to speak. I am a man who is really content, really happy to be doing what he's doing and not doing something else. Does that explain it somewhat? As for you, to meet you would be quite an event—I'd like nothing better. And sometimes I think, well, I ought to stir myself and go as far as Venice, for example. Reunion in Venice. Sounds good. And maybe something like that will happen one day. Understand, I am not timid, nor awkward, nor any of those difficult things. But I am content where I am and how I am. And if it's in the cards I suppose we'll meet. But if we don't, why I'll feel that we met anyhow in some other way. I see my friend Fraenkel trotting his legs off searching for the right place and never finding it. Lowenfels too, always seeking, seeking. They make me laugh. I feel sorry for them. I went through all that years ago. I went through everything—that's how I feel.

Sounds pretentious, but believe me I am quite serious when I say this. To top it off, let me tell you that I gave a lecture the other night, in French, to a few of my friends here at my place. Just to prove to myself that I could do it. In a way it was a fiasco. In another way it was excellent. Subject: "La Vie Intégrale." I must send you the little chart I made for it—as a souvenir.

I also enclose some circulars, as you requested. Don't use them if you think they will damage the cause. They are pretty horrible. I always did want to bring out a brochure of the letters and reviews—to use as publicity. Just mail them gratuitously to every publisher, editor and reviewer throughout the world. Just a quiet sort of megalomania. But you can see what an effect it might have. The virtue of these letters, from such a standpoint, is in their contradictoriness. It's a grand hodge-podge, and in a subtle way, a testimonial to the value of the books. I wonder do you see. Because, had I been a regular guy—à la Huxley, Gide, etc.—it would be another story. There wouldn't be any such letters.

Glad to know it took you eighteen months to write *The Black Book*. I was a little worried—for fear you'd say, "Oh, about six or eight weeks." That would have given me a real anxiety. Because you are capable almost of doing such a thing. You have genius, there's no doubt about it. You *are* a genius. And I don't say that easily.

Yours,
HVM

Corfu

[April 1937]

Dear H.M.

YOU MAKE ME LAUGH LIKE HELL. Of course the English are arsey versey. I get quite weak with laughter. You need an English manager, because you are much too human to do anything with the buggers except make them feel uncomfortable. The idea is to take a self-deprecating stance, somewhere between faith, hope, and charity, and speak in loud treacly tones. If you cover your head with a tea-cozy, so much the better. The voice is muffled, and the indeterminate buzzing MIGHT be an author speaking, and it might be just gnats. That's what the English like. A compromise, neither here nor there, shilly-shally, niminy-piminy. All this I can do almost as well as a Jew. I part my hair in the middle, adjust the horn-rimmed lenses and settle like a Catholic homosexual at the master's feet.

You see, H.M., the front on which I propose to attack has almost nothing to do with you. The question is A CAUSE! Are we to support the growth of free speech in art when we get the chance or not? In my letters I shall be as wily as the fox. I shall say that regardless of personal reactions, with this promise held out by the American censor, it would be churlish to refuse one's support . . . and so on. I aim not so much at getting testimonials as simply getting names. Almost a petition as it were. This is cute national psychology, because many a man who wouldn't follow you would follow a GENERAL CAUSE to lift the censorship ban anywhere anyhow. It's a sore point with all writers nearly.

As to the books, I shall husband them carefully. Buggers who won't help will get their copies taken away from them again. No nonsense even from G.B.S.! One copy will tour around until its reader comes across with his help and a request to keep it. That's the idea. I shall slowly draft the letters, send you out carbons, and when Alan Thomas comes he can take them back with him to post. I am assuming that no one would bother to answer letters from Corfu. Tell me one thing: would you prefer a round robin, a petition? I could circulate a printed form which would look sort of semi-official, less personal, almost as if the censorship department in New York were trying itself to appeal against itself! And it's easier to sign your name under the PRINTED NAMES of Huxley, MacCarthy, Eliot and Co. than bother about wording a fresh blurb. Tell me what you think. I think the more like a cause it looks the better the chances. You could put a little cracker motto on it thus:

> In the opinion of the undersigned the work of Mr. Henry Miller is impressive enough to deserve a wider public than he has yet been able to get; and for this reason, the lifting of the censorship ban on such books as *Tropic of Cancer* and *Black Spring* would be a valuable step in the right direction. It is just to add that these works could by no standards of criticism be considered as merely pornographic.

I added Yeats and Santayana of course because, though dead, they are, in their way, national monuments. You would weigh in with a couple of French signatories too with the English. Céline, Cocteau—the more internationally known, the better—Cendrars would be fine.

Of course I have no ultimate fear for you. Who could? You do not need effort. The books will generate all you need by themselves. Only the sooner the day, the happier I'll be. I'd like you to make America. What a revolution! The whole national psyche shocked to the roots by a 1000-volt charge, a shudder, and then the curative adjustment slowly. I believe in artists as healers. And you are not an artist, but a new nation, really, whatever you say! (By the way, in telling anyone about myself these days, I always say I'm the first writer to be fertilized by H.M. I think that's awfully true.) You wait and see what your books are going to do to literature. Just you wait!

I am resting. I am assembling the pieces slowly in this spring. It is a very hallowed process. Soon the sunshine.

When you say "genius" it has a funny ring, exciting me. I feel a fraud, really. *The Black Book* is epileptic, a fit. WHY? Was I a monster? I tried to say what I was, but of course with my talent for covering myself in confetti made out a hell of an epic. I wanted to write myself so miserable and wormy and frightened as I was. NUMB, really. That terrible English provincial numbness, the English death infecting my poor little colonial soul and so on. Instead you say monster! I wish it were true. But I have yet to find which is the theatre, which the mask. Time. I tell myself, give it time. I'm too young to go fucking about with a typewriter in this dangerous way. For the present I'm wrung out. Yet there is another book THERE!

Salute, O world, salute,

Larry Durrell

May 3, 1937

[Paris]

Dear Durrell—

It's very hard to know what to answer you about this business of campaigning for *Tropic*. Letters perhaps would be better than petitions. I hate all the cheap publicity that goes with these things. I really don't want to have anything to do with the matter. I leave it to you. And I think too that if you decide on anything you might better write the censor yourself. Write him formally and he will answer you officially. But don't play any tricks on him, please. Shoot straight wherever possible, that's my motto. Especially when a man is friendlily disposed, as he is.

If I had been able to raise the money for printing I would have done this—simply publish the letters as is, and not a blooming word about censorship or obscenity.

No brief, no petition, no appeal. Just see that the book of letters and reviews was widely disseminated—and gratis. I may be a poor business man, but I think with that method I should achieve the result I wanted—attention.

My books, oddly enough, are not creating mortal antagonisms. Even the old farts seem to admit enjoying them. And *Black Spring* has not been officially barred from the States yet. Perhaps because the Customs have not yet seized a copy. Very very few have been mailed to America. The joke is that the censor has asked me to get him some extra copies of the books so that he can show them around to the critics. But I daren't mail them to him!

I have already written him about your intentions. To date I have heard nothing. Answering you officially, as he will, he will doubtless be cagey—naturally. You will have to read between the lines. I can only repeat that so far as the law goes there is nothing to prevent my books being admitted into America. The republishing of them there, the circulation through the mails, the passing of them from one state to another—these are all separate matters. There's the whole situation. And add to that the fact that no publisher over there seems sufficiently interested in me to risk starting a hullabaloo. Entre nous, time will solve everything. The books *will* gradually make their own way, there is no doubt of that. Brentano's here in Paris now displays them openly in the shop window. That in itself is a big step forward, for they are still very conservative.

As for *The Black Book* I am in the act of proofreading the typed copies preparatory to distributing them according to your instructions. I would suggest now, when you receive your copy, that you reread with an eye to reducing the verbiage. Having read it over three times I feel sure that it would be improved by pruning. Your elaboration is excellent in the vital places, but there are passages of minor importance where you elaborate for no good reason—perhaps because the machine was geared up and you couldn't apply the brakes. Throw a cold searchlight on it. You will lose nothing by cutting. If you find that you agree with my opinion, let me know and I shall hold up the copy I intended giving to Kahane until you have altered it. But the copy to Alan Thomas I shall send "irregardless," as they say in New York now. (Also, if it means anything to you, the opinion of several of my friends whose judgment I respect is pretty much d'accord. They complain of fatigue, of preciosity, while admitting to the power and beauty of your language. But *language*, a little too much of it!) This is a common enough phenomenon, so don't let it worry you. You have simply overshot your wad. Hitting the right stride is always a matter of getting beyond language, don't you think? Of being immediate. You sometimes talk too much about and around. Move in closer and deliver good body blows. Aim for the solar plexus, always. If you deliver a foul now and then you will be forgiven—because your intentions were good. But don't pull your punches—that's unforgivable.

So, mind you, I don't say rewrite the book—simply prune and trim, as the guy says in his letter to the Park Commissioner. "More light, more air, more natural light, more beauty, more safety to the pedestrians and to the general surroundings along by all parts of Queens County, etc."

Anyway, cheerio!
HVM

[May 1937]

Dear H.M.

Many thanks for the letters. I am replying at once on the subject of the verbiage. Will you tell me the parts you think are too heavy. And of course language is my problem. Why I am your most ardent admirer is because of the way you use everything and are used by nothing—in writing, I mean. I set out on a voyage to find myself—and find language. A vicious thing good writing is. I wish I wrote worse—in the good sense. But I think that is partly to be overcome by an experienced technique. Also by being somebody. In *The Black Book* there was nothing for me to be, really. I'm still nobody. But I think I will be. Then I can show myself without the cocoon, the arty kimono. In the meantime any advice is accepted with gratitude—I might say relief. Your first letters were so damned uncritical I was getting quite frightened. Seriously thinking of leaving for Ethiopia to join Rimbaud. Now that I know there is verbiage about I have something to clean up. It does me good to be sat on. Thanks a lot.

As a matter of fact I can't remember a damn thing about that book, except little Gregory in book III. My own part of the diary is where the trouble lies, is it not? I locate it somewhere in the second book. Too much fruit and whipped cream. Never mind. I learn from every fresh thing I do, thank God. I hope you'll mark the MSS you send me. I'd treasure it, specially if it's my own typed copy which I'm giving to my darling Nancy who has nearly been driven mad by me while I was writing it. Any pencil marks from the hand of the immortal Henry M. would be just about enough to thrill her.

Anent petitions: I'm writing to the censor chap right away. No, have no fear—I won't do the dirty on him.

At the worst it does no harm in a letter to say something mild and ambiguous like "there seem to be definite indications that the public are ready for Miller." I understand how you feel. Writing the books was your job; now it's up to buggers like us to get it about.

I lend *Tropic* about hopefully. Your public pushes out. The latest, a rather sweet little fairy, wants to be a writer, met Connolly in France, who recommended you heartily to him. I lent him *Tropic*. His only comment so far: "Mai *deere*."

More later. And thanks for your niceness over the *B.B.* I do appreciate it immensely. And if I can write a really good book I'd like to dedicate it to you and Co. with a flourish. Means a lot to me, this contact.

Send you my latest abortions. So restful splashing colour. Light your pipe with them.

To a cinder,
Ldurrell

Monday, 5/10/37

[Paris]

Dear Durrell:

Just got your latest letter and latest water color. And with it a lot of interesting mail from near and far. Send you herewith a few copies. Note the one from the censor, and my answer. That leaves you a clear field. Think you ought to write him and be absolutely sincere and on the level with him. He seems like a damned decent chap— more and more so, I am coming to believe. Could you ever expect that of an English censor? I wonder?

Here's an excerpt which concerns you from a recent letter from Mr. Wen Yuan-ning, editor-in-chief of the *T'ien Hsia Monthly* (of which you'll get a copy one day, with that article on "Shakespeare as a Taoist," lost now somewhere in Siberia). He says: "The manuscript of an essay on 'The Prince and Hamlet' by your friend, Lawrence Durrell, I enjoyed reading very much, but I regret that I can't make use of it as it has already appeared in some other magazine before. Our rule is never to publish anything which has already appeared elsewhere. Otherwise, I would have been glad to print it in *T'ien Hsia*. . . ." That does not prevent you from sending other things.

Capricorn is not done yet, me lad. But it comes out definitely in January, 1938. I'll probably be able to send you a copy before then, or at least portions of it, enough to get the flavor of it. Am calling in my excerpts now. But still lots to write. So don't send any cash. Anyway, don't ever. You're on my free list for all my works to come.

Probably you confuse *Capricorn* with *Max and the White Phagocytes*, which is done. I have sent you a couple of things from it, and will probably rake up more copies soon. As I told you, Kahane doesn't want that published before the first volume of *Capricorn*. However, that would not prevent an American or English firm publishing it, if they wanted it. In a way it's good because it's a cross section of me—very diverse things in it. I say it's finished, and so it is. But I may still add more things to it as time goes on. I wouldn't mind adding a few more stories. Though it's plenty long enough as is.

Glad you really liked the Tibet water color. It was a bit faked, as you see, but that doesn't matter vitally. Not in my eyes, anyway. Give it a generous mat, and cut it down close so that you have nothing but a solid body of color. Listen, about these damned things. Do you realize something? You must go slowly with them—not fast, as people ordinarily imagine. I wish you could see my friend Reichel's work. Reichel is a genius, the poet of the water colors. And how slowly and lovingly and patiently he works. It's enough to make you weep. At any rate, I am certain you never saw anything like them in your life. He's the man I should love to help materially.

Anyway, do this next time. Sit before the paper, ponder long, put a little spot down on the big white sheet. Think about it. Move on to another area, slowly, quietly, very quietly—like a mouse. Get up and talk to yourself a bit. Look out the window. Go back. Let it dry a while. Put it away until the morrow. Take it out, look at it at the breakfast table. Think what it is you want to paint. Don't try to paint that, but what you are thinking and feeling only. For instance, that landscape—was it the landscape, or was it a color in the sky you wanted? Or were you thinking of spring coming on? Or of the "mallards"? Or perhaps it is aboulia and amusia and anoia you would like to serve up. Get that "about" feeling and fuck the what-is-it business. And a good paper and brush is important. But it's like chess, me lad. Once you go at it earnestly, you're hipped for good. Don't dabble in it. A good water color is like precious ointment. I am putting them up, your things, in my bedroom where the light comes in under the black curtains and makes them glow. That's Corfu, is it? I ask myself. Well, O.K. Corfu, then, and here's to a good sound nap!

I must write you a whole special letter about things Tibetan : the film *Lost Horizon*, your magic book on Tibet, the book *I Ging*, which I am still burrowing for, "the most extraordinary book in the history of world literature," says Keyserling. And more, please, about the first twelve years of your life there in the passes. It drives me nuts. If I go anywhere from here it will be there. Maybe I shall be the next Dalai Lama—from America sent! This is one of my quiet megalomaniac days. I believe anything is possible.

Listen, where did you get that "KONX OMPAX"? Marvellous. That and Miss Smith's conk and poll! And Hilda and the Womb. I sent you and Alan Thomas by registered mail the copies of *Black Book* the other day. Now I shall send my copy, the third one, and ask you to be kind enough to correct it against yours, as it was inconvenient for me to correct three at once. Will you mail it back soon as possible? A half dozen people are clamoring to read it. Remember, I wait to show it to Kahane until hearing whether you will make emendations or not.

Let me add another word or two on the subject. You see, writing you don't need to worry about. You are a writer—at present, almost too much of a one. You need only to become more and more yourself, in life and on paper.

I am impressed by your "double" nature. The man you reveal in *The Black Book* is not the same man who writes me from Corfu. Perhaps Corfu is nearer to your *climatic source*. Anyway, had you remained in England you would have been done for. There was one curious touch I omitted to mention. A most strange use of the impersonal, "One said to her while fucking her," or something like that, it went. Was that deliberately done—for some caromed irony, or what? Or was it an English locution, a relapse? I enjoyed the strangeness of it, but did you mean it to be so strange? Almost like the speech of a Houyhnhnm.

The most terrible, damning line in the whole book is that remark of Chamberlain's: "Look, do you think it would damage our relationship if I sucked you off?" That almost tells the whole story of England! Since Drake and Frobisher! And there are, as in the womb passages, marvellous crazy things which beat all the French surrealists stiff. "With that knowing look I always imagine the spermatozoa . . . etc." Or "send out to the clitoris for an ice."

I wish you would make a copy of the five or six pages on the womb. I can't find them now in my haste. But it comes about where you have made a footnote on the "return to the womb complex." Send it to Laughlin, please. I feel certain he will use it. That is to my mind magnificent, incomparable. Well, enough.

Yours in the "gnomic aorist,"

HVM

P.S.   I also sent the other day the big water color "The Ego and his Yid."

Corfu

[May 1937]

Dear H.M.

I am sitting here in a peasant house on the north point, where we have come in the Van Norden—huge seas and spray. Your letter has just come by the bus. I think your criticism of *The Black Book* is the best thing anyone has said about me yet. Believe me, the root of the struggle which on paper looks like the struggle to write is really the struggle to live. All artistic dislocations and failings go right back to the author. Hence my disgust when rereading the book from the copy you sent me. Jesus, I can do better than this! Let me kill the "artist" in me and the man will appear—if there is a man. The copy is being bound at present. I plan to take out whole pieces in the 2nd and 3rd books, just phrases in 1st book which seems fresher. See what you think. If there's anything you don't like afterwards, help yourself. I loathe the little book today. I'd rewrite if I could stand the strain.

About the watercolours—don't hang them up, they're too bloody. I'll send you some of Nancy's on the sly. They're good, solid, well-behaved. I loved the "Ego and Yid" one. When I do a good one I'll send it you with a notice—*to hang*.

I suppose Fabers have the *B.B.* by now. Waiting for the

noise of breaking literary crockery! When I wrote "one says this," and "one says that," it was the sort of ironic impersonal fish-like tone which the clever, superior Englishman uses to belittle himself and his experiences. Perhaps you've never met a Gregory!

Yours in the Gnomic Aorist,

Larry Durrell

(Durrell in Corfu and Paris—Miller in Paris)

———◆———

"A CABLE FROM FABERS CONGRATULATING ME ON A FINE BOOK," Durrell writes in a state of agitation. When Fabers' letters follow, he reports their stipulation—an expurgated edition. It develops that Durrell has been leading a schizophrenic literary life, though he has scarcely told Miller of his second novel published earlier in the year under the pseudonym Charles Norden—*Panic Spring*—regarding it contemptuously as a potboiler. Now he is prepared to expurgate *The Black Book* until Miller tells him flatly no. The ensuing correspondence gets right down to the bone on the issue of integrity versus success. After this exchange the correspondence lapses for a month or so while Durrell is on the move. Finally in mid-September, after more than two years' intensive correspondence, they meet. Alfred Perlès describes that momentous encounter in *My Friend Henry Miller*. No letter records the event, merely an exchange of notes between upstairs and downstairs at 18 Villa Seurat where Miller has arranged temporary quarters. On Miller's reply concerning garbage and God, Durrell writes this memorandum, "Preserve it in my file. This kind of correspondence is worth volumes of Pascal."

* *

c/o Ionian Bank, Corfu, Greece

[July 1937]

Dear Miller:

Bombardment from the directors of Fabers. Enthusiastic letters from Morley and Pringle and a typical "kind letter" from Eliot. In short they want an altered English edition. I have replied that provided it does not stand in the way of the Paris unexpurgated, I don't mind. It will be advertisement, I suppose. Will you, however, immediately ask Kahane whether he would like to do the book in its full-dress uniform regardless of Faber? An English and American edition would contain enough jewelry to give the Paris edition réclame and movement. On the other hand if Kahane wanted exclusive rights I could fob off Fabers. I feel the unexpurgated edition is more important. Let me know what you think, will you? If you care to, hand Kahane the MS and explain that I am not free as yet to offer it to him. But ask him how he feels about it all. Will he take it? If not I'd better castrate for Faber and wait until I have money enough to do the full version myself. It's rather a fix. If I refuse Faber and then this "weathercock" refuses me, I'll be left with my first real book on my hands. No money. No edition. Nowt.

Lawrence Durrell

July 15, 1937

[Paris]

Dear Durrell:

Just got the red ink letter about Faber's and Kahane. I am getting in touch with him at once, Kahane, and will let him have my copy to read if he wants. I also will write you in the next few days about the corrections you made —I haven't had a chance to tell you about that. Some ought not to have been made, I feel.

102

Frankly, I am not in accord with you about accepting Faber's plan, just because it is a pis aller. No, with that logic, that attitude, you'll always be fucked good and proper. Don't you see, according to *their* logic, you *must* conform—because they control the situation. But the moment you say to hell with that and decide to do as you damn please *you find the man* to sponsor you. But, anyway, whether you lose out permanently with Faber or not, all that is beside the point—that is *their* affair. Yours is with your own conscience. On that grain of faith on which you built your book you must rest. You stand firm and let the world come round. No, it won't be Faber's and so on, but always someone, something unexpected, something from the blue. It may even be me! In other words, forgive my advice, but I would say you can't look two ways. You've got to accept the responsibility for your actions.

Notice that one always thinks he must do something because he must earn that money which was involved. But that is nearly always a clever excuse we make to ourselves. We usually can do very well—even better—without that money. The only thing that truly nourishes is the doing what one wants to do. I tell you, everything else is crap, and futility, and waste. Let the angel be your watermark. If no publisher exists for you we will have to create one!

More soon,
HVM

[1937]

Dear H.M.

I think you are the most diabolically honest man I have ever met. And of course I should take the stand on my own dunghill. I am always making a brave face and then diving down the nearest man-hole. As for looking both ways at once, yes. It can't be done. But I'll tell you one reason—the only one which made me want to deal with Faber, apart from their extreme niceness. It was not that I cared a fuck either way ULTIMATELY whether the *B.B.* was cut in England. I KNOW THAT SOONER OR LATER IT WILL COME INTO ITS LITTLE OWN UNEXPURGATED. But there's another thing. My double Amicus Nordensis. He is a double I need—not for money or any of the fake reasons I'm always giving—but simply for a contact with the human world. I am so alone really that I'm a bit scared of going crazy. Norden would keep me in touch with the commonplace world which will never understand my personal struggle. Very well. When I submitted *B.B.* to Faber I was prepared to have it rejected without favour. But when they showed they were keen and willing to fly as near the wind as possible, I suddenly thought: if they print the *B.B.* in whatever form, it will destroy Amicus Nordensis and keep all my work together under one banner. This was sheer weakness. But the spectacle of going on splitting like an amoeba, each new book a new name, never getting anywhere, was a bit terrifying. I am a little more sober now. You see, I CAN'T WRITE REAL BOOKS ALL THE TIME. It's like an electric current: increase the dose very gradually. Already the *B.B.* has played havoc with me. What I want is this, frankly. Once every three years or more I shall try to compose for full orchestra. The rest of the time I shall do essays, travel-books, perhaps one more novel under Charles Norden. I shall naturally not try to write badly or things I don't want to; but a lot of things I want to write don't come into the same class as *The Black Book* at all. I consider that resting. Travel essays about Greece, literary essays, Hamletry, and all that. This kind of literary gardening will soothe me and stop me fretting myself. In the meantime my *B.B.* will come out, and be followed by the Book of the Dead, the Book of Miracles, etc. Under my own sweet name. I think you will probably feel this is traitorous or something, but you must understand that I need my friend Norden in order to keep my peace of mind and be happy a little and love. It is not good to fly so violently. I am too young to cut myself off altogether, and not strong enough as yet. The carapace will come. In the meantime I have asked Faber, in curiosity, to post me the specimen cuts of the book. I think it's useless in England, really.

Whether Kahane wants it or not, the book is an act in itself and I would be glad to put it in a drawer. No one can alter my having WRITTEN it. On the other hand there was only the question of réclame for a Paris edition if there was one. You think it's bad to expurgate? Perhaps you're right. But you know, for an artist of your calibre it is rather different. Nietzsche COULD stand aside and let the world come to him. So can you because you HAVE a world to offer. But as yet I have no great positive body of work and thought to offer. The *B.B.* is a goodish beginning. But it is not quite adult yet. I can do better if I lose my fear. For you there is this powerful total world unrolling itself; you are so deep in it that there is no time for anything else. With me it is different. The little world, the heraldic universe, is a cyclic, periodic thing in me—like a bout of drinking. I am not a permanent inhabitant—only on Wednesdays by invitation. I enter and leave—and presto, the ordinary individual is born, the Jekyll. In the bottom of my soul where I have some faith in myself I always know it doesn't matter. Why all this agony over paper and ink and words, when life is running away like a greyhound, and everything is felt much too poignantly and passionately to try and write it down? Then I take the Van Norden, run up wings, and swerve off from myself. I wonder if you understand. But of course you do. You understand everything, otherwise you wouldn't be the giant you are.

Anyway, let us see what Kahane thinks. Tell him there has been point blank refusal to print the book in England in its present form. Always feel apologetic for the amount of my irons you put in the fire. 1,000,000 thanks.

If you COULD find us a place to live in we would be grateful as hell. Just having a fearful row with *Night and Day*; they have rewritten one of my articles and printed it under the name of another man. Nancy has just lifted five quid for a comic drawing and is quite unbearably aloof today. And I have found a goddess in the flesh. Nausicaa. I feel I want to buy her and keep her with me, framed, but nothing doing. She is 17 and going to be an archeologist, and I am dying of old age in my twenty-fifth year. Eheu! I think the innocence afflicts me. Not a single stain of experience on her. So fresh and waiting for life—like a clean knife. Her hands are in her lap and she looks at men with the impersonal mindless way that cattle look at trees. I adore her for that. I hate to think of such a mindless world being smudged afterwards. What a shame!

> Love's not so pure and abstract as they use
> To say who have no mistress but their Muse!

Pity me,
Larry Durrell

[Paris, July 1937]

Dear Durrell :

Kahane is now reading *The Black Book* and promises
to tell me soon what he thinks. The letters from Curtis
Brown and Harold Strauss are masterpieces of idiocy, no?
Though it is marvellous the esteem you are in already.
That is a good omen. I think you are born under a lucky
star. But listen, *Panic Spring* can't be such a damned bad
book as you would have me believe. Why don't you send
me a copy? I'll risk it!

Alors, "I want to begin here and now to talk about your
future work" . . . (Ahem)

Don't, my good Durrell, take the schizophrenic route.
If there are just a half dozen people in the world, like
myself, who believe in you, that should more than out-
weigh the other considerations. The danger is to the
psyche—believe it or not. You are young, happily married, full of encouragement, praised to the skies, healthy,
not hungry, not penniless, befriended, surrounded with
congratulations, with what not, a boat to boot, be Jesus!,
the Ionian skies, isolation (which I would give my shirt
to have), and so on. Now don't, my dear good Durrell,
ask me to weep with you because you are *alone*. You
ought to be proud of that. That's in your favor. You can't
be alone and be with the herd too. You can't write good
and bad books. Not for long. Show me examples, if you
know any. The toll is disintegration. You must stand or
fall either as Charles Norden or as Lawrence Durrell. I
would choose Lawrence Durrell, if I were you. And what
is the penalty, after all? What can they do to you—THEY?
Nothing, really. You will soon have them hog-tied. The
man who sticks to his guns has the world at his feet. That's
why I prefer Mussolini a thousand times, much as I despise
his program, to the whole British Empire. Mussolini's

politics is real-politik. That's something in a world of cagey bastards, of pussy-footers, and stinking hypocrites. For me it's simple. None of this stuff for me. Tao, me lad, and more and more of it. I'm wallowing in it. It's exactly my philosophy, every inch of it, even to the contradictions, precisely the contradictions. It's in my blood, and I am scouting about now to discover if I haven't really some Tibetan, some Mongolian blood somewhere in the line.

If, as you say, you can't write REAL books all the time, then don't write. Don't write anything, I mean. Lie fallow. Hold it in. Let it accumulate. Let it explode inside you. I can understand the phrase, Homer nodding. But that is different from Homer pseudonyming, what? A man can fall down, can undo himself, can go haywire. But he ought not to deliberately incarnate a lesser self, a ghost, a substitute. The whole thing is a question of responsibility and willingness to accept one's fate, one's punishment, as well as one's reward. I think that is only too painfully clear, if you ask yourself. You want Charles Norden to be the scapegoat. But in the end it will be L.D. who will be obliged to kill Charles Norden. That's the "double" theme. By the way, do read Dostoievski's *The Double*, if you have never done so. And even *Aaron's Rod* is a good book, on this score—Lawrence suffered from it too. And he knew it. It was a little different, but fundamentally the same problem. Not accepting oneself in toto. Not integrating.

And why couldn't you write all the other books you wish as L.D.? Why can't L.D. be the author of travel books, etc.? What's to hinder it? And it's wrong to think you are cutting yourself off. On the contrary, you are muscling in. The other way is the way to cut yourself off. Soon enough you are found out and the smell is a bad one. The rotting part of you will stink to high heaven, believe me. Better to let that rotten part, if it is rotten, die off naturally. Better to acknowledge your weaknesses. You can't put perfection in one scale and imperfection in the other that way. We are imperfect through and through— thank heaven. I hate perfect books and perfect beings. Where are they, d'ailleurs?

Note, too, how you write to me and how you write to *them*. With them you're strong, with me you're weak. Well, drive the center-board down a little deeper. An even keel, me lad. You're a sailor wot ought to know. An even keel. And no catamarans. No life-saving belts. Believe me, it's the only solution. I don't elect for the cross, and I think it's largely poppycock, the cross business, it's only self-pity, weakness. But if it must be the cross, then let it be the cross. Shit, that's an honorable way out. It brings relief—besides the gall and vinegar. But really, the cross is a myth. If you develop your powers you will find that it is, when all is said and done, *a gay life*. I think you're a gay bird, despite all the raving, despite *The Black Book*. Of course it's a fine jolly book, *The Black Book*. I allus said so, and everybody agrees with me too. Sling it over the counter and make no bones about it. Do your damndest and take what's coming to you.

Well, enough of that. Think it over. And remember I'm with you to the last ditch.

My friend Fred Perlès is just being given a sort of white elephant in the way of a lousy magazine, owned by the American Country Club, and called *The Booster*. The President of the Club wants to make him a present of the magazine. There is good advertising, enough to pay all expenses, for the moment at least. Fred is thinking of running it—has to keep the same name and also devote two pages to the activities of the Club—that's the price. But he will make it gradually into a literary magazine. I am going to aid him, of course, and sink some of my drivel into it. We may draw up a list of contributing editors and make a drive for subscriptions and more ads. It would be a means for Fred to live. He has none at present—his job is finished. He is down to his last cent, as usual. Would you like to be a contributing editor—contributing gratis? Do you think, if we got it into some decent shape, that we could sell it here and there, in England? About five francs a copy, 50 francs for a year's subscription. 500 francs will buy a life's subscription! How does it sound? Now it looks like bloody hell, the worst imaginable shit, and it will look like that for a month or two to come. We have only twenty pages, of which nearly half is advertising. We think to put some of the crazy ads (like Johnny Walker, Hanan Shoes, etc.) right in the middle of a page of serious writing. And we are going to boost the shit out of everybody and everything. We are going to take an optimistic turn for the sheer devil of it. Alors, your advice, doctor.

Signing off,
HVM

[Paris, September 1937]

Dear Miller:

Two questions:

(1) What do you do with the garbage?

AND (TWO)

(2) When you say "to be with God" do you identify yourself with God? Or do you regard the God-stuff reality as something extraneous towards which we yearn?

Durrell

[Paris, September 1937]

My dear Durrell—

The first question is easier to answer than the second. The garbage you put in a little can under the sink and about sundown, or thereafter, you deposit it in front of your door, in the street. The noise you hear about 7 :30 in the morning is the noise made by Madame the Garbage Collector who rolls her little truck out of the little hut at the end of the street—illuminated by a cross at night.

As for the second question, being rather pressed for time, and slightly jocund at the moment, I should say blithely sometimes you approach and sometimes you become. Gottfried Benn answers it nicely (via Storch) in an issue of *transition* which I will dig up for you and show you. I could discuss it better over the table. When do I eat with you downstairs? I am free for dinner this evening, if that says anything. May have to do a stitch of work after dinner, but no great hurry about it.

How are you? Did you find clean sheets, etc.?

HVM

———◆———

From September through the following April Durrell is in Paris most of the time. This is their first and longest period together, and the talk, as Perlès reports in *My Friend Henry Miller*, flows like wine. "Don't talk me under the table!" Miller has written earlier. "I hear you are *marvellous*. It must be that Irish gift of gab." Apart from brief notes arranging rendezvous, there are only a dozen letters written during this period—while Durrell is away—all concerned with the business of publishing the most hilarious of little magazines. In September Durrell makes his first visit to England in over two years. Despite his horror of the "English death," he finds himself in his element in the London literary world, getting along swimmingly with such national monuments as Havelock Ellis and T. S. Eliot, and with other members of Faber and Faber. He returns to London three months later, then goes from there to Austria at Christmas.

By this time three issues of *The Booster* have appeared under new management; the President of the American Country Club has repudiated his Frankenstein; and only one number is yet to appear—belated and shrunk to half size—the "Air-Conditioned Womb Number." Hereafter the magazine appears three times as *Delta:* the poetry number edited by Durrell in April 1938; the "Peace and Dismemberment Number with Jitterbug-Shag Requiem" at Christmas; and another poetry number, Easter 1939.

The magazine is largely a vehicle for the Miller-Durrell-Perlès triumvirate. Among the contributors are Gerald Durrell, aged twelve; Henry Miller, Earl of Selvage, fashion editor (for men only); Charles Norden, sports editor; and Nancy Myers, wife to Lawrence Durrell and Charles Norden. Durrell's pseudonym, by the way, derives from one of the more unsavory characters in *Tropic of Cancer*. His boat, the *Van Norden*, was christened with Miller's blessing.

The next venture, a more sober undertaking, is the Villa Seurat Library—subsidized by Nancy Durrell, edited by Henry Miller, published by Jack Kahane of the Obelisk Press. Printing costs are guaranteed for the first three titles—needless to say, the only three to appear—Durrell's *Black Book*, Miller's *Max and the White Phagocytes*, and Anaïs Nin's *Winter of Artifice*. The Villa Seurat Series is to be a major preoccupation and a thorn in Miller's flesh for the rest of his stay in Paris.

*   *

[Paris, September 1937]   Saturday

Dear Durrell—

Beginning to wonder if you are ill. Or is it that you are discouraged and disgusted with England? Seems strange not to hear from you. Ominous. As for us, things are going forward. *The Booster* is progressing. We are getting subscriptions in driblets but from fairly good sources.

Betty returned from Belgrade with three subscriptions —Jugoslavian—and expects to round up a half dozen more, including Consuelo de St. Exupéry! We landed, through Edgar, the Princess di San Faustino, of Rapallo, and expect she will do things for us. *The Booster* will be out by the end of next week—everything quite well done.

This morning I got a letter from Curtis Brown, inspired by you. I will answer later. I suppose you missed Eliot—no? Isn't he going on vacation? Write us, anyway. We are dying for news of you. And Nancy? What is she doing in London? It must be quite horrible.

Betty was delighted to know you had been living in her place and looks forward with great pleasure to meeting you all. When will that be, have you any idea?

And don't worry about the money. "Remember, we are *boosters* first and foremost!" We need subscriptions. But really, I see now that we are getting them, and that we will get more. I think it's a go.

Fred asks me to send you both his warmest regards. He misses you both. We all do. You left a vacuum behind you.

                                             Henry

[Enclosed]

Booster Placard
THE BOOSTER

is a non-successful, non-political, non-cultural review published in English and French from Paris once a month under the direction of the celebrated literary quartet:

First Violin	Alfred Perlès
Also First Violin	William Saroyan
Viola	Lawrence Durrell
'Cello and Traps	Henry Miller

18 Villa Seurat, Paris (xiv)

ON SALE HERE

5 francs   1 shilling   25 cents

———•••———

WE ARE

For	*Against*
Food	Peace
Pocket Battleships	Poison Gas
Depressions	Fair Play
Plagues	Hygiene
Token payments	Moderation
Epilepsy	Rheumatism and Arthritis
Taking the lead	All isms
Shangri-la	Schizophrenia

c/o J. A. Allen, Bookseller, 53 Woburn Place,
Russell Square, London W.C.

[September–October 1937]

Henry,

I'm sorry I haven't written. Fuck the English, eh? Henry, the English are everywhere, all around me, like mutilated black beetles. Eliot and Pringle are away but met Frank Morley, a man after your own heart. Huge, great, slow brigand with a sense of humour. Admires you greatly. Hopes to be able to do *Max*. If it's humanly pos-

116

sible I know he will. Meeting Eliot and Pringle on Thursday. More talk then. Listen, I went down and bearded Havelock. I should say rather that he bearded me. Magnificent beard. He is covered with hair like a wild boar. Likes your work and promises to write you in detail about the books. Hasn't finished them yet. Disagrees with you about urination!! Lovely old man. As yet haven't rung up Rebecca West. Will do so if I have time. I hate England. Hope to leave next Sunday for somewhere civilized. Will telegraph. I've got two coats, a light velveteen and a Scotch tweed. Everything very expensive. So far no pink shirts. Two more subscriptions for *The Booster*. Orwell promised one.

Been to the Café Royal a lot and confirmed the opinion I always had of English writers. Henry, fuck the English. Listen, don't get angry if I don't write as I'm snowed under with things—proofs, engagements, work in the British Museum. *Money* was sent today.

Things are beginning, only just beginning. Why not come over for the afternoon? Choose a Sunday afternoon. See London at its best.

PFUI!

Larry Durrell

c/o J. A. Allen, 53 Woburn Place,
Russell Square, London W.C.

[September–October 1937]

Dear Henry :

Wonderful *The Booster* is going so very well. I have got in the following items to submit for future numbers :

(1) An article by Potocki proving that Bach was a Potocki.

(2) An Urdu poem by Mulk Raj Anand, famous Indian novelist who says if you will send him your

books he will review them for *Life and Letters*.
Very keen to see your stuff. A good man.

(3) A poem in Zulu and one in Swahili by Holland.

(4) Written Zarian for an Armenian poem, also Stephanides for a Greek one.

I have met Eliot who is a very charming person, believe it or not. Had an impertinent note from Shaw saying that *Tropic* must wait its turn—which may be months. Alors, I wrote and asked him to return the one copy to me, the old bugger. Seeing MacCarthy on Wednesday, about *Tropic*—hasn't yet read it, by the way. Pringle reading *Max*.

Ellis and Eliot said they thought it a little premature to fight a test-case for another 5 years over *Tropic*—in case you lost.

More later,
Larry

STOP PRESS. Plan to return next Friday. Sending Potocki MSS today to you. Will bring other stuff with me. Everyone keen on *The Booster* here. Eliot offers me his help. Hurrah! We are all opening fire now on different fronts. Boom, Boom! Great puffs of prose. The battle is on.

c/o Hotel Goldener Adler, Innsbruck, Austria

[Christmas 1937]

Dear Good Henry :

We are poised here on a fucking Alp with acute tonsillitis and swollen gums. I have written Eliot for a poem, but doubt exceedingly. Reavey will send some, Gawsworth will also send some, Blakeston will find some. You wire Evans for some new stuff, will you? I wrote an impudent letter some time back to Kininmonth and have not heard since; they use me as a sort of seismograph to record their aesthetic tremors, and occasionally I revolt. Will write to David Gascoyne today also. Dylan Thomas has no poems, he says. As for Porteus, I meant to ask him for something but forgot. I would like something of Roger Burford's printed; I think *Poems and Documents* is a good book and deserves a boost. With the next number Joe said we should have a column dealing with the books we like in thumbnail reviews, a few lines about them regardless of when they were published or whatnot. I would like to do the Burford book and Amanda Ros too sometime.

The general opinion about *The Booster* in London is that it has fallen between two stools. The clowning is regarded with distaste, and the serious part of it is so snowballed in mysteries that people excuse themselves hurriedly and make a wry mouth. I made myself the sheathed sword of the outfit, and pictured you and Alf as a couple of insane and incorrigible cherubims running everything into the ground as hard and fast as possible. WILL the next number appear? I wasn't sure so I lay mum and said we had run it off the rails.

Shall I draft a little bit of spurious advertising for the Villa Seurat Library? Not a ripple of a smile on the face of the pond, the bland and lidless protozoic eye of the commercial man dealing with Art. This of course is our Big Bertha; if it doesn't go off nothing will. Let me know what new schemes hatch.

You know, it's good to be able to get twenty paces away from you people and take a good look at you all in perspective. I see that from now on you will have to rely on me a great deal as PUBLIC OPINION. Because you have created such a bubble around yourselves there in Villa Seurat, talk such a personal and strange language, that you cannot even conceive the bewilderment of people who sit outside in London, for example, and listen.

The people I met I liked awfully, specially REAVEY, BUTCHART, BLAKESTON, PORTEUS.

We must widen out and print everybody, good or bad. Then in exchange they will print us for better or for worse. Then we shall get into all the anthologies and finally into Westminster Abbey, so help us.

Cheers chaps,
L.G.D.

18 Villa Seurat, Paris (14ᵉ)
Monday

[January 1938]

Dear Nancy and Larry,

I'm enclosing herewith Kahane's agreement for you (Nancy) to sign. It means, as you may make out from his two letters also enclosed, that after some correspondence about the subject, you will get a shade more than the figure I previously gave you. In any case, you are sharing equally what remains after all legitimate deductions have been made. I think the agreement quite all right to sign, unless you find some flaw which I don't see. The main thing now is to get the money so that I may hand him back the script. It will be February until it's out, in any event. And I hope you will forgive me for not tackling the script alone. In proof you can do a lot, though it will cost you a bit extra. It's too grave a responsibility to entrust such work even to your best friend. Even if no cuts are made, *The Black Book* stands O.K. with me. And the more time which intervenes the better. That final moment, when it is about to go to press *forever*, suddenly wakes one up to everything. So leave it that way, won't you?

Have just redrafted your prospectus, with very slight changes, and forwarded it to Kahane. Herewith a copy. I

120

hope you find it all right. I think it's good. We'll see how Kahane feels about it. As to the frontispiece, I really don't know. Generally I dislike books with photos in front. Maybe I'm a little afraid to show my mug—yours is attractive, you know. However, that's something to settle later. *You* think about it some more. Think of the books you've seen with the author's mug in front.

I feel weighed down with all the responsibilities that I seem somehow to have assumed. Beginning to overwhelm me. We have another idea for *The Booster*—the last, probably. (While waiting for the womb number and with what to pay it.) Supposing we refused to distribute it openly, even in Montparnasse, but made it absolutely a private affair for subscribers only, raising the price of subscription to 100 francs here and five dollars for America. Mailing them out in sealed envelopes without return address, and only, to begin with, to those on our list of whom we are absolutely sure. Cutting out all dead wood, all or most of the gratis ones, and the few American Country Club members who might get us into trouble. Letting all such-like think that the magazine is dead. It seems to me no one has ever tried doing this before with a magazine. We would print much less, and print on even cheaper paper, cheaper cover, etc. Making it an affair of *contents*, and also making it difficult to get hold of. Perhaps this little Chinese policy would do the trick? I feel we *have* fallen between two stools, as you hint. We might come out quite irregularly, but guaranteeing 12 issues to each subscriber. I feel that trying to get ads, distribution, etc. brings about the compromise which is hurting us. I really disagree strongly with you about accepting poor things because the chap is good for us or likeable, or this or that. I think it's a mistake, and gets one deeper and deeper into the mire.

I had another wonderful session with Reichel—something I will tell you about in person when you get back. But I feel depressed somehow, suicidal. However, that may be only an astrological set-up. Everything is bright on the surface, and promising, but underneath it feels dark. Do let me know when you're getting back, the two of you, and don't run off to Tahiti immediately, will you?

                                                        Henry

MAY—OCTOBER 1938

(Durrell in Corfu—Miller in Paris and points south)

———◆———

D URRELL returns to Prospero's island and again tries
to lure Miller away from Paris for the summer. Again
unsuccessfully, for Miller is too absorbed in work at the
Villa Seurat, first seeing *The Black Book* through the
press, then finishing *Tropic of Capricorn.* For some time
there have been rumors of war in the background. In
September, as Chamberlain goes to Munich, war impends.
Miller settles his affairs in Paris, considers Corfu, decides
the outlook is too uncertain down that way, and ends up
stranded in Bordeaux. Durrell promptly comes through
with money but can do little to dispel Miller's mood of
black despair. In due course the Munich crisis passes, war
is postponed a year, Miller returns to Paris, but with
thoughts now of leaving, perhaps of returning to
America. His dream of finding a Tibetan retreat somewhere presages Big Sur. However, he writes Durrell in
early November, "I will be here yet a while and hope to
see you passing through."

*   *

[May 1938]

My dear Henry:

Just a swift shot in your direction to thank you all for your sweetness to me and help, and to tell you I'm thinking of you. Tomorrow we leave for Ithaca to spy out the land. Had a lousy journey down, enormous seas running, and had to run for shelter at the Forty Saints. Still waiting for my machine, with which to open fire on you all about God and olive trees and blue sea. The good weather is slowly starting. Figs budding, etc. No news of Kahane, have written him. I'm writing poetry a lot, and quite good stuff.

It was wonderfully sad seeing me off at the station, the sweetest of gestures. This summer I really hope you button up your overcoats and come down south. The sea will sledge you and the aching blue. Will have two boats with any luck: the Van Norden and also a small speed runabout for short trips, shopping, etc. I am seriously thinking to start a medical training in England next winter. It will fill a gap of several years and absolve me of this tedious task of putting words together for Faber to sell like meat.

Much love to you all,

Larry

Enclose some photographs, a suite entitled "Birth of a Tibetan." Keep them, will you?

18 Villa Seurat, Paris XIV ͤ

[June 1938]

Dear Larry—

Just rereading for 6th and final time the *B.B.* Pages had to be re-set and so I had to read every line—like a new book. I write you this, first to assure you it is progressing, second, to *re*assure you that the book is magnificent. After so many readings one gets tired of even a good book. But yours improves with each reading, and that speaks wonders for it. Alors, send out to the clitoris for an ice! Or empty the womb like a bucket of mush—into the silence! And the kingcups shining! I can't get this image out of my head—marvellous. The whole thing glows. It's the fucking "hypaethral" universe all right, all right! I salute you, O Son of Jupiter! You will soon be crowned. Anyway, now the book should be out in July sometime. There may be errors here and there, but I think they will be microscopic. It won't be my fault anyway—I've done everything possible. You had the worst printer, unfortunately.

I won't be leaving for a couple of weeks, that's certain. I fell from the top of the ladder (in studio) in the dark a few nights ago. Had to be taken to hospital to be stitched up here and there. Full of glass. But recovering nicely now. No broken bones, just cuts and bruises. So I am resting on my oars a bit for the moment. Naturally I have the best of attention. It's like a vacation with all expenses paid for. I always enjoy these little mishaps.

How is the climate in summer on the island of Lesbos? What do you know about Lesbos—*physiognomically?* Love to Nancy!

Henry

Ionian Bank, Corfu, Greece

[July 1938]

Henry,

What a devil you are. We have been all agog and on tip-toe, having the boats systematically watched from all over the place, and every day rushing out of harbour to

125

see if you were on the Italian boat which passes through these narrow straits. Yesterday I had a presentiment that you were on the boat—but it was just your letter which I got today.

I feel so bad about all the trouble over *The Black Book;* I feel it really should be dedicated to you. You have done everything for it, except actually write it. Sun is terrific. Lie all day and bathe. This is the life. Henry, I didn't write before because I thought you'd left, but really it is madness to try to get to Crete in this weather. As far as Corfu O.K., vegetation, a certain coolness; after that STONE, ROCK, GULLS, HOLM-OAK, SHEEP, nothing else : it would be your forty days in the wilderness.

If you are coming down, dear Henry, please be wise about it and choose your weather. September is the best time now that you have left it so late. Why not come down and stay towards the end of September, and use Corfu as your base? I can fix any trip you want to take and be of use generally. But I think in the cooler weather you'd be happier; not here but down south.

I send you two little watercolours I did. One a portrait of you which is bad colour but an accidental likeness, the other called "Imitation of Reichel." Nancy has done one or two good things but is so busy feeding us that she has no time to work. Also the house and garden are being built with fury around us. At the end of this coming month we should be well fixed up down here.

I have stopped being a doctor this week. Full moon. We bathe in a little half-moon of green water under the tiny shrine to St. Arsenius : clean pebbles like baby's hands; sheer straited limestone metamorphic up to ceiling; water so warm it is like silk; hornets; silence; ache of noon-blue heat. And yesterday we discovered a cave with an underwater entrance, in which we are going to build a shrine, not to Pan or some such, but to THE UNKNOWN GOD

126

within each of us. His symbol is bull, fish, and scorpion. More later. I am writing it out: a society of secret worshippers. Perhaps, Henry, you would write a prayer for the initiate, about this style and length:

TO THEE, TWO-HORNED IONIAN PAN, I DEDICATE THIS OFFERING IN RETURN FOR MANY DAYS OF BLUE BAPTISM IN THESE YOUR WATERS.

Henry, they are shaking the fruit down; must run; and we have two magpies very tame called Romeo and Juliet. Here, I hand you a chunk of this warm sunny nothing we have all become.

To the last drop,
Larry

Corfu

[August 1938]

Henry:

It's so quiet today, and the sea so blue, and now the garden wall is built and the floors a little polished, so we are getting a little settled.

I was thinking: you must come about the tenth of September; it will be very quiet and quite new to you. Drop everything and leave someone in charge of your mail. Just wrap *Capricorn* in a red wool shawl and bring your portable along with you. I can give you a deep cool room with two windows over the sea, bright rugs on the floor, a desk and some books, an encyclopaedia and dictionary. Bring a woman too with you; that would make it an even keel for the days which come and go quite silently. We could sail and bathe in the mornings, have a fine sunny lunch with wine, then a long afternoon siesta, bathe before tea and then four hours' work in a slow rich evening. Even if you did not touch *Capricorn* I think you would profit; the thing would be there and the invisible chisel would be jockeying it about as you slept. Get well set on an even base, and come to terms with the scenery. Then in the middle of October you could start lashing out for Crete, Lesbos and so on.

It is perhaps not so primitive. There is a lavatory, for example, and we might have a bath put in by that time; anyway we could motor into town every week and have a bath at the hotel there. No mosquitoes, or any vermin: your work-room would be as flyless as Villa Seurat; bathing in the sea; trips into prehistory. And I think all this, a lull in your streamlined life, might just provide the shifting of the stance that *Capricorn* demands; because after all one only lets people and things impose if one wants them to; and if things intervene it really means that the Roman Road to *Capricorn*, your biggest and most dazzling child, runs not so straight.

After contemplating the circle for a week I have evolved one or two new speculative ideas on the nature of classical art: as DETACHMENT not being synonymous with objectivity; as in writers every new effort being vitiated by rationalisation—whereas in sculpture you find your way sensually through your fingertips and leave the critical debris to Herb Read; as the next phase is a CLASSICAL phase, a form of diathermy, a writing on the womb-plasm with the curette. You see, today all writing is pretending to be Classical (Eliot, Hemingway, Stein) whereas the origins of it are really ROMANTIC. Compare *Waste Land* with Baudelaire, Stein with Alfred de Musset.

Never mind. Cut it all out. It's too hot. But in *Capricorn* your new attitude will be definable (surely not) as CLASSICAL, in the sense that a circle is classical.

Listen, the British fleet is in: two huge grey monsters, really beautiful to look at. War is really a fine art, I feel, when you think of this flawlessness of ingenuity spent on steel to twist and rivet and smooth it. Guns like great pricks, sliding in and out and coiling on themselves. And little men like lice running about in groups by arithmetic. It's wonderful. One side of us responds to the aggregates: when you see these flawless dummies you feel it. No responsibility. The idiots dream of an ant world where giant pricks slide in and out and vomit steel semen, and a regiment could be licked off the walls of this tower and leave not even a blob of pus behind.

Now Henry, no more dilly-dallying. Tell me, shall it be definitely in September? I don't think you'll regret it for a second.

Skoal to Capricorn,

Larry

Ionian Bank, Corfu, Greece

[August 1938]

Dear Henry:

I wanted to write before, but we have been away on the other coast of the island camping on a sand beach, and I had nothing to write with, nor felt anything to write, except that I feel so much in tempo always with you that it is almost unnecessary to correspond with you. We talk about you incessantly, and yesterday from morning to night we sat on the balcony and read *Tropic* aloud from beginning to end, and sat up a long time discussing the strange human being you are. We have some young people staying with us here for a while who are profoundly thrilled and excited by *Tropic*. But on other scores, my dear Henry, the effect you have is a terrible one. I enclose a letter from a young man I met, which is intended to be an imitation of you. I hope it makes you wince aloud as it did me. Ach, but it's hopeless; they will take nothing from you except an attitude. The real essence they spit upon.

Well, this weather which is so full of omens and portents brings us really closer together. The screw tightens a bit, the stresses increase. These days I am not happy in myself but going through a kind of internal strangulation. The writing has gone suddenly sharp and matt, not fluid any more. I have the sensation of writing with little hard crystals of something—renal calculi. "The Aquarians" has been left for a month or so now. It is all there, but I feel powerless to continue it. What I have to say seems such a barren waste of self-questioning and argument that I go bathing instead, or write poems. I have cast it into a strange and novel form, that of a Euclidean proposition: first a letter from God to me explaining and enunciating the theorem; then an analysis of the theorem; then a letter from me to God explaining who I am and what I have tried to do. I think the strange humility of this book will make you smile a bit. I have lost revolution and anarchy now and am swimming through hundreds of compass points towards myself. It is difficult and horrifying.

Well, everything lies and rots in a drawer: all my mail, bills, cheques. I don't lift a finger but sit with my feet crossed and feel the ceiling closing in on me. In Paris we made something, by God. There was a good, firm freemasonry laid there between us all. And now when I am alone in myself and forcing my hysteria back against the wall, I think of those days like comets, and the good warm contact of wills. This is an interval in which we have to bear up under the malignant opposition of the stars. Later it will all lift.

Ach, what if the doom does seem to close in a bit and the portents loom thick? I feel there is another strange meeting lying ahead of us all. Let us eat our way through this dying section of European time and the wonders will begin again. I am like a man with a cheque for a million in my pocket but no legs to walk to the bank; I go painfully on my amputated trolley propelled by my arms. A little while and the miracle will happen again; I shall rise up on my stumps and run like a hare.

In the meantime, my darlings, let us revise our allegiances and make all new, tight, sealed, caulked, and polished. Can Spring, I ask you, can Spring, can Spring be far behind?

Larry

18 Villa Seurat, Paris 14, France
23rd August

[1938]

Dear Larry and Nancy,

Suppose you've received *The Black Book* by this time, no? Here are two clippings from the *Herald Tribune*, Paris. All review copies sent out. Just got your fine letter on blue paper, will write decently a little later. Just to announce that I finished *Capricorn*—a little work of revision now in store, that's all. About 450 pages. And I'm damned well pleased with it. I accomplished it. So maybe I'll be taking a vacation soon—maybe we'll see each other down there. I hope so.

I'm O.K., except for fatigue. I'm reeling with ideas. But I can't sit at the machine any more. It's too bloody foolish to work your balls off this way, what? Listen, I have new terminologies for you. I can almost hear the two of you talking sometimes. I'll write you a letter very soon. This is just to let you know about the *B.B.* Hope it doesn't look too bad to you. I think the cover is all right, what?

Cairns writes me that there will positively be a watercolor show for me in Washington this winter. Wonder if you ever found "The Ego and His Yid"? I like that, despite everything, and would like to include it in the show if possible. You could send it direct to him, putting your name and address on the back for safe return, if you find it.

I ended up *Capricorn*—that is, the part before the "Envoi"—with a few wonderful phrases on music and on the happy rock and the ocean of consciousness. Here's a line from towards the very end : "Music is the noiseless sound made by the swimmer in the ocean of his own consciousness."

Henry

Hôtel Majestic, 2, Rue de Condé, Bordeaux
Sunday, 25th September

[1938]

Dear Larry and Nancy—

I left Paris a few days ago to take a vacation after finishing *Capricorn* and having my teeth fixed. Found the country too dull and came on here just as things began to look really bad. Before leaving Paris I packed all my belongings carefully. Gave Kahane MS of *Capricorn* to put in vault of his bank. Have carbon copy with me, also *Hamlet* MS.

I have been in a very bad state up until last night when things looked so bad that I could begin to think of action. Sending you this by air mail, hope it will reach you before declaration of war. I am stuck here—no use returning to Paris because city will be evacuated. Can't go anywhere from here as I haven't the money. If an American gun boat comes along I may have to take it.

I'd like to know what you intend doing—stay in Corfu or return to England to be drafted? Could you send me a telegram to the above address? Communications are already poor, interrupted. I am here with just enough to last about a week. I won't budge from here, if I can help it. There's no place to go to! Have written Kahane for an advance on royalties due, but doubt if he'll come across, he's such a tight bugger. I may be stranded here in this bloody awful place where I don't know a soul and never intended to be. No doubt I shall pull out all right—Jupiter always looks after me—but I'd like a word or two from you. Maybe I might find a way to get to Corfu—if it's safe there? If you don't reach me here, try Kahane. I have two valises with me, cane (bequeathed by Moricand) and a typewriter. If necessary I'll throw it all overboard and swim for it.

If I need some dough in an emergency, if I have to make a break for it somewhere, can I depend on you for anything? I won't ask unless I'm absolutely up against the wall. I'm already on a war basis, ferreting about like an animal, not a thought in my head except to keep alive by hook or crook. The worse it gets the keener I will be. It's the tension, the inaction, the pourparlers, that get me. Five minutes alone with Hitler and I could have solved the whole damned problem. They don't know how to deal with the guy. He's temperamental—and terribly in earnest. Somebody has to make him laugh, or we're all lost. Haven't spoken to a soul since I left Paris. Just walk around, eat, drink, smoke, rest, shave, read papers. I'm an automaton. Fred was still at the Impasse Rouet, not called for yet. And without a cent as usual. If you lose track of me, if Paris is bombed and Obelisk wiped out, write to my friend Emil Schnellock—c/o Mrs. L. B. Grey, Orange, Va., U.S.A.

Henry

[1938]

Dear Larry—

Got your telegram and your air mail letter to Bordeaux, letter only today. I telegraphed you asking if you had sent money only because I wanted to return it to you. The enclosed notice from Post Office here suggests that Bordeaux has no record of receiving cabled money from you for me. So you had better send this on to your bank in England and advise them to recover the money. Anyway, a thousand thanks for coming to the rescue so promptly. It's not your fault that I didn't receive it in time. Where was I sailing to? To America, of course, or South America, or Mexico, anywhere out of reach of the bombs. Kahane sent me 3,000 francs, but that was not enough for boat fare. I thought of Corfu naturally, but feared I'd never get there if the Italians went with Germany. You see, they don't really want to fight for the Germans. Mussolini was devilishly clever this time. In fact, the two of them are just too clever for the English and the French. A marvellous pair of brigands. Perfect team work.

I don't know where I go from here. Am waiting around for $200 by cable from Laughlin. He cabled me, offering this sum as advance royalties on all American rights to past and future books. I cabled yes, send money immediately. No answer yet. If it doesn't arrive by Monday morning I blow "disregardless."

Am completely schizophrenic now. Change my mind from hour to hour, or minute to minute. Nothing seems any good or worth while. Zero hour. I am completely eclipsed. I am sadder and blacker now than I was at 21 years of age. Maybe it's a change of life!

So don't write me here. Address me care of Kahane. I

notify him from time to time of my whereabouts. I have seen a lot of towns and people. It all stinks to me. I imagine Corfu would stink too, maybe even you. You can't imagine to what a low point I have sunk. A black-out, as they say. If I were younger I would commit suicide again. But I am too old for that. I must live like a bedbug for a while—away from human society.

What licks me, to put it simply, is this: how can people resume life after an experience such as we went through? How can they have the faith and the courage to take up their tasks? This event was only a little warning. Nothing will stop the onward march of these crazy German bastards. They will sweep over all Europe, like the Huns before them. They may even take Russia and China. That's my deep conviction.

No, if I can, I will go to America, to visit certain places I always longed to see: Mobile, Alabama; New Orleans; Jackson, Mississippi; Arizona; Nevada. After that—?? I will probably have to return to Villa Seurat to repack what things I want to keep—which is damned little. I am going to unload ferociously. One needs so little really. *No books!* I could live the rest of my life without ever opening another book. I am going on with your little book on Jupiter. But slowly, sadly, blackly. You will see. Anyway, love to you and Nancy, and cheerio! Ho ho! Always a cheerio!

Henry

P.S.   Eliot is peeved with Kahane for not getting proofs of the *B.B.* in time. Says he just read review of it in the *New English Weekly*.

P.P.S.   If I write pessimistically about the world situation it's because I know the Germans so well. You may expect no mercy from them. And no light and no joy. Only *order* and *cleanliness* and *efficiency*. It gives me the horrors.

[October 1938]

Dear Henry:

It's sad to see you so black and grum. Myself, when I look outside this house to Europe I can't help feeling that all you say is right. The cataclysm looms. It is only that this bay settles every night into black silk so that one's panic can ride at anchor. You can see deep fungus and the cypresses turned upside down like paint brushes in it, and a surface which would record the scratching of a fingernail on it.

I am alone for the time. Nancy has gone to Athens. I speak nothing but Greek, so I don't even read or write for breaking the spell of being a foreigner, a complete foreigner for once. Somehow nice tight paragraphs seem null when the bottomless pit is opening to swallow. I wish I could mail you over a bit of the hallowed sangfroid I have felt today sailing the boat over to town and back. I am not a person who can usually stay alone, but for the last two days I have been happier than ever before in my life. Like a bright web of sunlight drawn over everything. At night sliding into sleep like the water sliding over the pebbles. This is a period in my life, like a milestone, and no bombs can stop it. Hurrah! Now tonight I have an even more crazy idea. In another two hours we shall have the ravaged horn of the moon. I have filled the engine and stowed some blankets in the boat. I am going to set out for the Bay of Fauns, just this side of the Albanian frontier, and sleep the night there. Tomorrow? Gomenitsa or Meurte. I am taking with me an *Odyssey*, rewritten in simple Greek for schoolchildren, which I can follow easily. The language tastes sweet and sinewy. Also dictionary and some food, my revolver in case Albanians stray over into the bay. And my new mood; it is like a keen knife which I want to try on the weather. Perhaps even a fountain pen. I may write you a little poem in the very bay, what?

Cheer up, Henry, keep the little raft of hope floating. The worse it gets the more keenly we'll store the seconds. A shaky future makes the present radiant. I taste each second, believe me, like a fine drop of Grecian oil, matured and pressed. And damn the Germans.

Well, cheero, what? And do keep the ensign waving. You know we are cherishing you and sending waves of comfort in spite of the distance.

Love,
Larry

Ionian Bank, Corfu, Greece
October, 1938

Henry:

This is bad news, you going to America all of a sudden. War? Why not go to England, it would be an easy stepping-off place for U.S.A.? Listen, have you got a great package of MSS and letters belonging to me, in a brown paper folder? Could you leave them somewhere where we could pick them up on our way north this winter? I need my British Museum ticket which is in among them.

Moore is thrilled with "Zero" and "Asylum" and will print them in *Seven*. Someone is attacking the *B.B.* in this number. I've told them to open a correspondence column so I can defend myself at length. Lawrence Durrell and his art. What is good about it. And so on. Also lots of poems. They are doing me proud. Eliot refused the *B.B.* excerpt—as I said he would long ago, unless he got proofs before publication. It's sad. I was counting on the money. Damn Kahane. And after all the delay the book wasn't perfect. Writing stopped again. It's like April showers

137

with me at the moment. A mere momentary moisture, and then nothing. Not even drip drip drip.

Send me some *Phoenixes*, will you? I want a good laugh to cheer me up in this stinking tomb of civilisation. Also a bit of the body mystical. Greece is beautiful and impoverished. Going to England soon to take a hand for a week or two in literary Life/Death.

Bored to death by uncertainty. Now, of course, Nancy wants to have a child. A little red general with fat legs, to ride into Czechoslovakia on a white horse? What sort of animal-vegetable-mineral is a woman's mind?

We are all caught in the rat-trap and smiles are at a premium. We are no good if, after all we have professed in talk and writing, we cannot laugh NOW, AT THIS MOMENT.

love,
larry

October 25, 1938

[Paris]

Dear Larry—

I don't feel so black any more, because I can work again, and because I am determined in advance to beat it at the first sign of trouble. I *would* like to go to America this winter—to the southern states and to the desert. I'm afraid of the Mediterranean. It all seems so degenerate to me. I don't like olive trees, cypresses, figs, grapes, etc. I want to see Oriental people, ultra-civilized people, decadent, rotten through and through. On the other hand, if I could scrape up the money for an easy trip—and that's the only way I will travel henceforth—I would come down there, and from there to Constantinople and Persia, which I long to see. I even wonder if we shouldn't try to establish a sort of Hindenburg line for ourselves at Corfu? We need to have some place of retreat when the storm breaks. I wouldn't stay in America during a war. I want only to visit certain places there to complete my American picture, do you see?

I discussed with Fred the idea of trying to buy or rent a small house in the south of France, perhaps even Ibiza or even Corfu, where he and Moricand could live dirt cheap, and where we others might go for a rest or in case of necessity. If I found a spot I really liked I would leave Paris for good. I no longer feel obliged to stay here at the Villa Seurat. But when I see the country, peasants, degenerates, the desert of the mind, when I see cows, sheep, trees, all that which means nothing to me, I get panicky. I could live with rocks and mountains or sand, but not with Nature which is cultivated. It makes me feel like a cow myself. I don't need much space or environment. I only need to feel that I don't positively dislike a place. Naturally, if I could get to that Tibetan frontier, either side, if I could live somewhere there in the Himalayas, I haven't the slightest doubt but that I would be content for the rest of my life. Arizona would be excellent—if only it was peopled with another race. Do you get me?

I'm damned glad to know you are doing so well yourself. It sounds wonderful, all you write. You must be a genius! And I think, incidentally, that as I predicted originally, *The Black Book* is going to be recognized and is going to make your reputation. I hope you believe that I did my utmost to make it a decent job. It's heartbreaking to work with an insensitive bastard like Kahane. I can't stomach him. Do you think of going to England still? We sort of look for you all the time. Yesterday I thought I saw you on the street. And give my love to Nancy. Thank her personally for all the trouble she went to. I'm ashamed of myself begging for help all the time. But maybe the tide will turn soon. More shortly. Did Kahane send you a copy of the *Max* book?

Do get hold of Balzac's *Seraphita* in English. It's usually included in a volume called *Etudes Philosophiques*, often with his autobiographical novel called *Louis Lambert*. It is something phenomenal—and it was written with *Louis Lambert* in one month, amidst the most sordid worries, financial and otherwise.

Henry

DECEMBER 1938—MAY 1939
(Durrell in London—Miller in Paris)

———◆———

A FTER a reunion in Paris, Durrell has gone on to London, taking Perlès with him—where he remains to this day, disguised as an Englishman. They invite Miller to join them at Christmas, but he is broke. His pathetic reply is too much for the Durrells; they find money somewhere, and Miller spends Christmas with them in London. Two weeks later, back in Paris, he writes, "You don't know how grateful I am for that trip. It was a real experience—and starts a new and more auspicious cycle of travels, I feel sure."

Miller's letters in this period show the prophet and clown alternating in a variety of moods: contemplating Balzac's achievement with awe, cutting loose in one of his elated jazz cadenzas, down to business planning the Christmas number of *Delta* (the "Peace and Dismemberment Number with Jitterbug-Shag Requiem"), recommending Zen, solemnly resolving to withdraw from publishing ventures and all worldly affairs. Durrell too is moody, depressed by London and worried about war. It is evident, however, that he is getting on in the literary world: publishing poetry, criticism, and travel at a greater rate than any other year before the 1950's, collecting poetry for the Easter *Delta*, covering the Stratford Festival. Though still hailing Miller as the Master, he is no longer the small boy he characterizes in his early letters.

In the spring Corfu calls him back. Once again he

urges Miller to join him in Greece. This time, with *Tropic of Capricorn* finally published after months of infuriating delay, Miller feels suddenly liberated. In a megalomaniac mood he plans another of his endless itineraries and sets off for Tibet via Corfu. The correspondence breaks off here. The narrative continues in Miller's *Colossus of Maroussi*.

*   *

[Paris, December 1938]

Dear Larry,

I am doing research on *Seraphita* these days. Do you know what Balzac's driving idea was? *To put order into life!* That's what he meant when he said: "What Napoleon began with the sword I will finish with the pen!" He said that at the Rue Cassini, after a night with George Sand. It was there he wrote *Seraphita*. That bugger Balzac did the incredible thing of writing forty volumes under a dozen or more pseudonyms before ever coming to himself. In one book, he said, I learned how to write French, in another I learned how to handle character, in another this thing and that and so on. You might think that when he finally did have the courage to sign his name and produce the eighty volumes which have made him famous, that he had learned something of perfection, eh? Not at all. In the opinion of the majority of his critics he was a bad writer—not an artist, they say. Well, you know what I think about that. The man who wrote *Seraphita* was more than an artist. There were forty books he didn't have time to finish! Thank God he didn't waste time in perfecting himself. When I hear him speak to George Sand, that speech in which he tells her what he intends to accomplish, what life means to him, and so on, I get down on my knees to him and I say, old bugger, I'm for you, right or wrong, whether you're a mis-fire genius or a perfectionist. Anything you say or do goes. Do you know what he said to that prick, George Sand? He said: "Literature! but, my dear lady, literature doesn't exist! There is life, of which politics and art are part. And I am a man that's alive, that's all—a man living his life, nothing more."

I went to the Maison Balzac in Passy and I stood reverently in his work-room, gazing at his desk, feeling it, marvelling at it, as though it were a miracle the desk hadn't dissolved under the herculean weight of his labors. The desk ought to have vanished with him, and I feel sure it will in time, that he will have it again, when he needs it, up there in the astral realm or whatever bloody realm he may be occupying. I can still smell the flesh-odor of his labors up there, where I am certain he is still trying "to make order." "I am like the moon and the stars," he said. "I can't prevent myself from giving light." And again: "If I am what I am, and above all what I am going to be, I shall owe it solely to myself and to my will. A man must be great or not be at all." Once again, I feel that with Balzac we discover that genius is the norm, the prerogative of every man. Thus I tread ever more lightly, more deftly and delicately. I feel he will have a long sleep, towards the end of his super-earthly life, and then awake like a thunderbolt and again startle the world. Tomorrow perhaps I shall meet the man who knows more about *Seraphita* than any man alive. The keeper of the Balzac house is a woman of strange features who talked to me about Swedenborg and of the difference between earthly love and divine. She said she knew immediately I entered that I was a mystic. Then I picked up the bronze hand which Balzac left behind on his writing desk and I kissed the hand that had written *Seraphita*. I learn one great lesson, however, from the study of Balzac's life—that is, not to want to write too much. I am learning how to let the pen drop, which Balzac never learned. More anon, when I get the real clue to *Seraphita*.

By the way, that review of the *B.B.* in the *Criterion* seems to me to be the best so far, don't you think? I was amazed, considering the source. You are having a success almost like Dostoievski's early success. May you be spared his tribulations. I read about his funeral the other day. He had the most wonderful funeral any man ever had. He deserved it, poor bugger. They almost lost the coffin in the scramble. Hallucinatingly real!

Henry

Tuesday

[Paris, December 1938]

Dear Larry, Nancy and Fred—

At the present writing it looks dubious about my getting to London for Christmas. Still no dough in sight. My fare back and forth, a visa, pissgeld und trinkgeld, all that would come to over a thousand francs. However, it may be that in the last Christmas mail from America I will find a check, whereupon I rush to the train and come. I would like to go to the roller skating rink and the casinos and Covent Garden and the Café Royal. But thus far in my life I have never passed a jolly Christmas. Every Christmas has found me broke, balked and frustrated. And usually alone. This one promises to be the same.

It is freezing here—sub-glacial weather. Never saw it like this before. Slept under 6 blankets last night, with sweater and bathrobe on, and just about felt cosy. In 2100 A.D. the earth's abstract axis will be pointed towards the star Polaris in Ursa Minor—this will be the end of another 25,000 years epoch—beginning of the real Aquarian Age. Fire, floods, cataclysms, as usual. Perhaps another Ice Age to usher it in.

Sent you a batch of mail and Nancy's horoscope. Tell Fred if I don't come I hope anyway to have enough to pay *Delta* money end of December. That'd be something anyway. I'll write again soon as there's news. Doing some

145

jolly fierce watercolors now to keep warm. How is it in London? Freezing too?

And a very merry Xmas to you, Mister Scrooge! Next year I will receive the Nobel Prize. Patience. Patience.

Henry

The list of works you have in progress sounds incredible! Jesus, you must be full of ants. Whence this dynamic? On what meat, O Caesar? Not beer and skittles? Next I expect you to tell me you will *play* in your own play. You are becoming a Shakspur!

I am just finishing a dummy for my friend Emil—all about the Water Color. And I have done some new ones—an improvement too, I think. One turned out to be Napoleon dripping with gore and quite mad in the eye. And then a couple of lake scenes—without ducks. One has a green bench—one you could really sit on.

So I went to see Rouault's show the other day. Stupendous. He's a feeling butcher. A Seraphitus with an axe. I liked his show, disjointed as it was, infinitely better than Picasso's. The last Picassos would make chocolate box covers. *Very pretty*. They stink. He's feathering his oars—but not in the timeless flux this time. I got myself a pad and some new greasy crayons. Marvellous! And a tube of burnt umber and one of hot sepia. Still more marvellous. And I discovered the color *green*. Green as Ireland's sunny dells. Now concentrating on eyes, noses, lips and ears. Especially ears. To transmute the original cauliflower breed I use.

French Writing Paper—Merde!
Second Post-Prandial Discours.

Enjoying a life of complete solitude. Every night I mount the guillotine and have my head chopped off. And next day I grow a new head—like that! I live among my

146

ideas, not with them or in them. We are friends, for the time being. The machinery roars in my ears, but I am not immune to the jitterbug shag. I do not feign catalepsy or psychopompernalia. I eat well and drink lightly. For lunch today three dozen oysters, a goose, a filet de sole, a maatjes herring, striped and salted, some fancy olives, a grape or two, and a tarte alsacienne. All flip and no proletarian indigestion. Am looking forward to walking the streets of Lhasa, unknown, unheralded, searching for a cheap cinema or a 5 & 10 cent store. The life of a stoat is one thing; the life of a poet is another. Let us gather in His name and eat pretzels. Solitude is the paradise of the over-driven scribes who write their way into Purgatory. Hallelujah! Peace, it's wonderful. What valises?

Henry

Sunday

[Paris, January 1939]

Dear Larry,

May have answered you meagerly by postcard regarding *Delta*. Meant simply to say that you have full rights to do as you please, Fred willing—he's the editor, don't forget. I realize more and more that I must withdraw from all this kind of activity. I don't have the least qualms any more about not being known or recognized. I think I have already done much more in the way of self-advertising than I had any business to do. I'm going to write more and meditate more. This is not meant as an indirect criticism of your enthusiasm, not at all. What's good for you may not be good for me. My time is getting short. I have to utilize my energies in the best possible way. I see very clearly what lies ahead of me to do. And there are many things I don't see, in addition, which I shall prob-

147

ably have to do too. I am getting more and more stripped, travelling with less and less baggage. When I get to the dead center (strange we should say "dead" instead of "live") I will just BE!

In reading proofs on *Capricorn* I am more and more struck by the metaphysical implications with which the book is strewn. In reading Balzac's life I am struck by the futile detour he made of his life after adolescence. (Innumerable analogies between his secret life—and known life too, for that matter—and my own. Really startling, and that's why I shall write about him with certitude.) Every time I pick up a mystical book I am struck again, shuttled back, as it were, to some fundamental truthful realm of my self which has been so much denied in life. A hundred years from now the phrases I let drop here and there, in the books and in the letters, will be studied to prove this and that about me, I know it. But now, even now, I am struck by the prophetic element which is an essential part of me. For example, I haven't the slightest idea what that book I announced for 1942 (*Draco and the Ecliptic*) will be about, but I am absolutely certain that it will create itself in the interim, and that it will be vastly significant, not just for me but for the world to come. I will add just another detail: that I am in that period of grace wherein all my wishes are answered. I have merely to ask and it is given, to knock and the door is opened. From all sides things are mysteriously conjoining and contributing to my development and enrichment. Tonight I pick up a book and take it with me to the café to read. A thin book, in French, on the Rosicrucians. The cardinal idea is so stark and simple, so thoroughly in accord with my own belief as to the way of life, that I am amazed how men can miss it. It is the doctrine of the heart, to be brief.

148

Well, the purport of this was merely to inform you that you have my blessing and full support, should you decide to take over all this activity which I am now dropping.

Cheerio!
Henry

140 Camden Hill Road, Notting Hill Gate

[London, January 1939]

Dear Henry:

It was strange the way your letter curled through the letter-box, so solemn and valedictory, so extra solemn and measured, as if you had written it with great deliberation and care on the wagon-lit en route for Tibet. I think I know how you feel: a sudden new change of internal form, a sort of anaesthetic progression into a new key. It is so uncanny to see these grave rhythms in your letter, but I rejoice, and unpack the machine to salute you forthwith. But don't write these days: just sit and read and smile and unbrace the enthusiasm a little. In *Capricorn* you have marked the latest and largest milestone—in prose that has no more to do with paper and ink than the new Picasso has to do with paint. It is like following the rhythm of flesh with a finger in the dark, tenuous but truly knitted. So take a good deep breath, warrior, and sit under the laurel until the spring days.

I am collecting a slow but strong poetry number. Will you PLEASE FOR ONCE IN YOUR LIFE CONTRIBUTE. Not poems, but little sayings, three or four lines long, taken from your books, notebooks, or written new. Open *Tropic* again at the first few pages and you will see the short poems there. I WANT YOU IN.

Today we stood around in a pub and suddenly drank to the death of Yeats. So funny, the shabby-intelligenced

149

young with all the gut beaten out of them by social credit and monetary yields and workers' rights, so funny to see them shabbily drinking the toast, as if such a gesture of simple homage was foreign to them. And this is England with its bitter beer. By God, a Frenchman can still salute. But we do it like shop-walkers and cretins. Anyhow, the old silver-haired giant would have been pleased, I think, if he could have been there.

I have written nothing but grown in humanity half a cubit. This fen of adders—you should hear the poets talk. Some good cool poems, like little cold pebbles still tasting of the sea. Inside I pine for the island really, the weird premonition of the landscape down there. I would like to see it if the war doesn't intervene. I suppose you had the other war barring your life at about my age last time. It's a sad feeling but makes you give the final ounce to what you do. It sharpens the minute, so that each tick of time going through is time tasted, unbearably sweet even if trivial things and idiots intervene.

A man just passed in the street shouting ENGLAND FACING WAR. Am going to get a paper.

all our love,
larry

Saturday

[Paris, March–April 1939]

Dear Larry,

Glad to have your letter this morning. This morning too several packages of the Easter *Delta* arrived. I was going to write and tell you by all means not to miss the three articles which have already appeared in the *Modern Mystic* by Bernard Bromage—on "Tibetan Yoga." The third one just out, in current number. I wrote him a letter and received this response I enclose just this morning.

Wonder, after you read his stuff, if you would care to look him up for me, and for yourself? His leaflet sounds bad, I admit. But he seems to have the full dope on Tibetan practices. It drives me wild, delirious with joy. Read especially, in third installment, about Milarepa, the poet-saint—wonderful egg! All these great birds of Tibet remind me of the Zen masters, who are up my street. Zen is my idea of life absolutely, the closest thing to what I am unable to formulate in words. I am a Zen addict through and through. Except for the monastic regime, which I don't believe in at all and see no necessity for. But if you want to penetrate Buddhism, read Zen. No intelligent person, no sensitive person, can help but be a Buddhist. It's clear as a bell to me. And of course all these modern mystikers, the whole Austro-Czech outfit of muckers, are stinking caricatures of the doctrine. First there is no evil in them, second no humor, third no magic, fourth no poetry, fifth no life. What is left is moth dust, the furbelows of the mind rotting in the dead sunshine of the dead.

Down to earth. *Capricorn* is due out 10th of April, as I say. Another error on printer's part—printed book without my final O.K. Only one proofreading. We are waiting to see how many errors we will have to list in the errata. Anais' will follow a month later. Yes, accounts are due Monday or Tuesday. Kahane will send you a statement. You will get nothing—you will still owe him money. This, in spite of the five pounds I paid in. Naturally the sales weren't very high, neither for *The Black Book* nor for *Max*. But they are selling slowly all the time. I myself have bought out of my own pocket a number of your books, which friends asked for. And now that the ban is off them, in America, we may get somewhere— through the Gotham Book Mart, at least. The next ten days or so I ought to have some interesting news from them, as I have written them all about the state of affairs. Cairns may not have had time to see you, his boat left the day after he arrived. But he has a high opinion of you and all of us—a staunch fellow, full of integrity, somewhat naif, but on the right side. I count him a good friend and perhaps my best critic in America.

No, Larry, no use trying to reorganize things at present. Business is quite at a standstill now—naturally. People are not buying, nor living, just holding their breath for the expected catastrophe, which I believe will not come off for a long while yet. There is no other man whom we can appeal to, I am sure of it. I am accepting Kahane as one accepts the cross, and trying to understand it, see its meaning. He symbolizes the world for me, and in a way, I think it is better it is concentrated thus in one individual. When the world at large gets their grappling hooks into us it's going to be hell to pay. We are tolerated now, because we are unknown. But when the publicity gets under way, good-bye. I have just been informed by the *N.R.F.* here that they dare not publish my books, *Black Spring* excepted. That's France, the supposedly most liberal country in the world. Perhaps the only translation I shall ever see, during my lifetime, is that Czech edition, which fortunately nobody can read. I have had many a talk with Kahane, good and bad ones, and I see into the whole situation quite realistically, I think. You couldn't do much better yourself. His way, which is the cunning English way of watching and waiting and nibbling off a piece here and there, is perhaps the only way in these times. Nobody wants a man to take over the affairs of the world. While things are going to pot the jackals must reign. After reading Balzac I get the full import of it because what he described as of 1819 is even more true as of 1939. Wait till you see my essay on *Louis Lambert*. It's done, and it's magnificent, I think. And it ends with a peroration against the French, as it should. I made a fine parellelism between Whitman's utterances and prophecies, in *Democratic Vistas*, and Balzac's utterances, in the famous letter to the uncle which Louis writes. Amazing, and nobody would ever have suspected the rapport, the close rapport between these two views of the world, one in 1833, the other in 1870, Old and New Worlds, same thing, same mess, same death. Whitman makes a plea for the poet to arise who will give us "a great poem of death." It's magnificent.

Well, here I am, enjoying full solitude. I am a Zen right here in Paris, and never felt so well, so lucid, so right, so centered. Only a war will drive me out of it.

I wish I could say that I would see you in Greece soon, but I turn towards America, towards the desert particularly. I want so much to see it again, the waste places, the grandiose, the empty spots, where man is nil and where silence reigns. I think I will make it eventually. I must, damn it, before I am drafted in here as "un ami de France." Bastards! Fuck these amis! When they destroy their Maginot lines, physical and cerebral, I will become the real ami de France. Not before. And they must publish me too, damn their bloody quaking souls.

Anyway, read Zen—Suzuki's *Introduction to Zen Buddhism* and Alan Watts' *The Spirit of Zen*. I'll send you a printed slip shortly telling what to read. A little operation for haemorrhoids and payment of back taxes, and perhaps a pair of socks—from the coming royalties.

Henry

[London, April 1939]

Dear Henry:

I meant to write you before but have been away in Warwickshire covering the Stratford Festival for the paper I told you of, *International Post*. I have never been into the County of Warwick before and am COMPLETELY AMAZED. It is beyond words perfect and greener than this paper; the hedges and trees are all curved in a kind of sculptural balance—in fact the whole county is a piece of garden planning by a divinely Palladian architect. I made the pilgrimage I have always been planning, to Shakespeare's places, and contrary to custom was delighted by the publicity and fame that has grown round this fine industry: his county. Trinity Church, where he is buried, is lovely, facing on to the smoothest river in Christendom, on which lucid white swans go suavely up and down with not so much as ruffled feather. We saw *Othello* and *The Comedy of Errors* by a first-class cast in the new red theatre they have built him. I got up early and sneaked up the tiny Church Street to the site of the house where he lived the last few *silent* years. They have made a trim English garden where the house stood, with green lawns, and shining little trees. HERE IS THE KEY TO EVERYTHING HE WROTE. I don't think you can understand the old boy until you sit in this garden, and reflect how for those five years THE REST WAS SILENCE with him, living his small-town burgess life, cut off from the court and the London joys. With the river going like a clock at the end of the road, and the marvellous Warwickshire woods curving up towards Snitterfield where his family lived two generations before him. I tell you, you don't have to *read* him; just visit New Place sometime when you can be alone in it, and sit on a bench in the sunlight, and you get the whole meaning coming through with a radiance and clarity that his verse could never give you. I am still a little blinded by it. They laugh at me because Shakespeare is now an American industry, and 100,000 people come to Stratford every year; but somehow that only added to the charm for me. Everyone was there for the Festival, boys and girls wandering over the green lawns and ferrying the river. And the Americans, I never felt such a kinship with them before. Everybody drawn by the dim alarm in their own lives, to try and find a meaning in the life of a great unknown national man. And in the hunt New Place gets overlooked. You see, there is no house standing there. It was pulled down. Only the little garden and the commemoration stone. But the real key to the secret lies here. I smelled it out at once, and pried the meaning out all in half an hour, fresh and early one morning, when the sun shone bravely and the birds played. YOU MUST GO TO STRATFORD. Mark it en route for Tibet if you must, but you must see it.

Your letter was disturbing. Henry afloat? It sounds queer to me; but I've no doubt you mean it. Listen, when you are at sea in a storm and you don't want to spring a leak dashing the boat forward against the waves, you let yourself out a SEA-ANCHOR: a canvas bell shaped like a French letter but six foot across the mouth. This holds the nose up to the wind and keeps her dead still. Thus

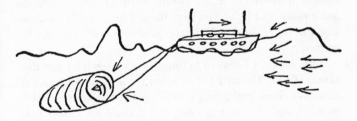

At the moment things look so bad I simply don't know what to do. Return to Corfu with the Italians outside our house? Spend the summer in Cornwall? OR GO TO AMERICA? It would mean a big uprooting, a big turn in the meridian, but I have a sort of feeling that sooner or later I shall take the jump; whether to do so now I don't know.

Working fitfully, in gusts, but no real impetus; little squalls of wind which send me skittering along for twenty yards over the flat surface of a poem or the verse play. Nothing else. Doldrum. I am sorry you are being doctored with a glass ass; next time you invite the world to kiss your ass you will have an uncomfy feeling. What news of the books? And listen, is it any use enticing you to England, if we get a place of our own and have room? Or do you definitely feel NO? I want you to see the cathedral towns, and smiling Stratford. What do you feel?

Love,
Larry

4/27/39

[Paris]

Dear Larry,

A beautiful letter that, about Shakespeare, the river like a clock, the single white swan, etc. Makes my mouth water. I don't want to urge you to do anything whereby you count on me. You know me, a temperamental guy, moody underneath and a tyrant at heart. But if you do get a place and if, as you say, there'd be room for a passing guest, I think it's fairly probable I'd turn up by summer.

I am looking forward to tomorrow's speech by our dictator, Hitler. He will tell us what we may or may not do this year. I am still going on with my treatments—rather painful and depressing now, but I shall be a new man afterwards. It's bad for literature, makes one sober and lucid in a discouraging way. The writer should always be under or above par, I think, not sane and sober. I worked with my diseases quite successfully all these years. But if I am to become a perfectly healthy specimen, I shall come to a full stop. Anyway, it's been good for me—a vacation.

Henry

[Paris, May 1939]

Dear Larry and Nancy—

Just a quick and decisive word to say that if you're willing, I'll go to Corfu first for a bit of a stay with you. I must hang on here till almost the end of the month for various reasons. At the quickest I might get away the 25th or 26th. If that wouldn't be holding you up too long, maybe we could go down together, what? I'm serious. You can count on me this time. You see, I've suddenly realized that I am the freest man in the world. I can do what I please and go where I like and what's to hinder? So Corfu for the first leg, O.K.?

Henry

I thought you were going on with the Book of the Dead? What's happened? Must you *suffer* some more first?

Capricorn due out May 10th—his latest dictum!

18 Villa Seurat, Paris xiv
Saturday

[May 1939]

Dear Larry—

Write me soon as you can about question of mails and censorship in Greece. Do they open both incoming and outgoing mail? Do they lift checks and money orders? Are you allowed to receive money while there? I have written people for dough and some of it may only arrive after I leave. It's important to know. Because if they are going to open my mail I'll tell Kahane to hold letters or open them himself and extract things.

My itinerary is roughly as follows, with allowances for change, if climate etc. is no good for me: Corfu, Monaco,

Athens, Istanbul, Dalmatia, Belgrade, Sofia, Bucharest, Vienna, Warsaw, Paris, London, Devonshire, Cornwall, Wales, Dublin, Killarney, America via New Orleans (seeing Faulkner in Mississippi). America: Mobile, Charleston, Corpus Christi, San Francisco, Hollywood, Reno, Denver, Salt Lake City, North and South Dakota, Butte, Boston, Vermont, New Hampshire, Rhode Island. Then to Bagdad, Teheran, Jerusalem, Bethlehem, Egypt, Fez, Timbuctoo, Singapore, Java, Borneo, Bali, Easter Island, Siam, Indo-China, Rangoon, Ceylon, the whole Indian continent, Darjeeling, China, Tibet—punkt!

Capricorn has had an advance sale of about 800 volumes! "Not so bad for an unintelligent work," as Balzac said of his *Livre Mystique*. But my good friend Cendrars says only one third of it is good: magnifique et sain, the sex and adventure, documentaire stuff. The rest bores the shit out of him. Ho ho! So I have become the public emmerdeur No. 1. Hurrah!

Henry

FEBRUARY—NOVEMBER 1940

(Durrell in Athens and Kalamata)

————◆————

From August to the end of 1939 Miller is in Greece with Durrell. *The Colossus of Maroussi* gives a lively account of their adventures together and of the characters mentioned frequently in the correspondence hereafter, notably George Katsimbalis, the colossus, and George Seferiades, alias Seferis, the poet. Only ten letters survive from the period between May 1939 and March 1941, all Durrell's; presumably Miller's are captured by the Germans when Durrell flees from Crete by caique. During most of this time Durrell is teaching at the British Institute in Athens and later in Kalamata. The letter written August 10 on shipboard as he leaves Athens is published as an appendix to Miller's *Colossus*. Indeed all the letters of this time reverberate with the good times, the travels and good companions of their last visit together before war closes in. This marks the end of an era for them as for Europe; they are not to meet again for almost 20 years.

*   *

[February 1940]

Dear Henry:

Just a line to spell out congratulations for the belated celebrity; we went out to Katsimbalis last week where your postcard was being passed from hand to hand like a totem. It is about time they woke up and noticed you. For the last few weeks we have had strange spells of lovely spring weather, with branches of almond-blossom being carried and sold in the streets; and today a sudden wild fall of snow which melted as it touched the ground. Can you imagine the Acropolis covered in snow? And in one stroke the hills drew themselves in against the sky, with a strange heather-coloured pointillism, like stubble appearing on a chin. Carnival began this week with clowns and harlequins (rather squalid as to clothes, but full of form) parading the streets, singing, skipping, yelling, and beating heavy pig-skin drums to a peculiar rhythm. The shine is off carnival this year because the government has forbidden masks, suspecting that seditious words would be said from behind them. Soon I get a week's holiday on full pay and am off to the islands with Tonio, the captain. I wish you were here to come on another trip with us. Max gets back on March 1st from a rest cure and in the meantime I have his car. For the rest the same dull routine at the school and the general boredom, lack of international news, and rumours.

Had long insane American letters from Simon and Schuster, and *Creative Writing* and a man who invites me to walk in a wheat field and throw my excrement at the stars, while he will put a freshly killed lamb at the rectory. I don't know what to say to people who write you long poetical-lyrical letters, unless they are women. To indulge in this kind of metaphoric barn-dancing with men makes me feel rather dated, obscurely ridiculous, like a morris dancer who had entered a rotary club by mistake. The letter, of course, is a gem. I am sending it to Eliot to make him jealous. Well, dear Henry, all the best for your American adventure. May everything please you, customs, marvels, anomalies, chance meetings, meaningless fornications, meals and music. Do come back next year if we are any of us left next year to welcome you. Love to everyone.

L.

[Athens, Spring 1940]

Dear Henry:

It was wonderful to receive your letter in the midst of this bad imitation of bohemian life. It was a much needed corrective to hear you audibly suffering among the streamlined cuspidors west by west of us, mewed in Athens like kestrel's chicks. And I was getting so bored with the spurious provincialism of the town and the hard rubbery touch of the faithful virgins. Last night I ran into Katsimbalis, sitting huddled over an ouzo in a dirty little hole-in-the-wall kind of a café which he at once pronounced the best bar in Greece and so on. We had an awful blind; or rather I did. Pouring drink into him is like pouring nitroglycerine into a safe; he stands with his calves pressed out behind and his belly in front gently resting on the world, while his eyes race back and forth over the puzzling face of the universe like bats. After his thirtieth or so he will light up, a small blue bud of flame inside his waistcoat, and his eyes will become suave and kind and no longer frightened; then he will begin telling his Wagnerian cycle of stories. For a week after getting news of you or a letter from you he is quite unquenchably not himself. You seem to stand in the relation of a half-analyst because he develops this mock-colossus, like a mock-turtle out of nowhere. Then he begins to stagger and lurch and boast and swear; and every story he tells he says: "I forgot to tell Miller that one." Or "Miller would have enjoyed that one, eh?" Some of the stories are so manifestly neither funny, elevating or even commonly humane, that one winces for him and wonders why. But he goes on roaring and washing the air with his long flat dead-looking hands, trying to carve out this mythical personality for himself from the rubble of language. It's funny. He is the truest Greek I know, and a real Irishman to boot, not to mention a poet. The others are all lukewarm compared to old K. Last night he was in a dreadful state of unfulfilled suicide; he was going to blow up the hotel, set fire to Maroussi, going to drink poison, shoot himself, jump off a high-stool, strangle his wife, ring for the fire-engine. There was nothing that would really wake him up; he was running through his ideas like mezedes for a jaded palate; but whatever he does he cannot get his Flemish body with its oriental curves to cooperate; it lies on top of him like the transpontine marsh, and he's sinking daily, while his little black eyes signal more and more frantically and his laughter comes out of the clouds. Now that he hears you are writing about him he is more unreal than ever; no more restless sitter ever sat and fidgeted in front of the photographer than George C. Katsimbalis in his black transpontine business suit and his chain-mail underwear.

I think he visits Aram regularly, and he has already been to an analyst—with what result I don't know. I haven't been myself as yet. My future doesn't bear dwelling upon. I have finally got Corfu, where we shall retire in May to lose the world I hope and be lost to it. Barring accidents I should be more or less O.K. But I'm in exile now; my age has been called, and I can't go home for fear of being called out. I like the feeling; like Livy or Suetonius or one of those unfortunates exiled beside the Siberian lakes; only an inverse exile, northerner to a southern landscape. Whether I shall write ten books of histories remains to be seen. Last Sunday we went south again. It was like our selves becoming metamorphosed or something into swallows; after Corinth the cold scented spring air came out of the valleys, crushed scents of mint and thyme, and the whole Argive plain rose up like a green shield as we hit the rim of the pass. It was like something biblical and exilic, like the buckler of Jonathan or Gideon's valley of milk and honey. Mycenae, you should just see her now: gone all the Roman cruelty and ferocity of the stone walls against the winterscape; every little tump of ground was on a bias, softly goldened and greened by barley, and little wild anemones. The whole procession of medieval green hills fell away to a still dead blue gulf behind Nauplia. For me it goes too deep really for tears; such a matchless and impeccable land lying there, washed clean in the first spring rain, and hallowed, like a round soft Easter egg. I was afraid to go on to Epidaurus where he sits in his humane valleys eastward; we sat on the top floors of Tiryns and watched the sea for a trace of movement. The inner walls are quite infirm and abscessed like big molars, and even asphodels jut out from holes like discoloured tongues. I'm glad you rumbled to all my réclames: liking Greece, and after Greece the spirit of Greece in Niki and George and Seferis and Antoniou and all the funny painful men. I shall be back in Corfu by May; why not get an assignment from some imaginary paper and get permits to come back this summer? Probably it will be quiet; and certainly you can always dodge bricks as USA citizens. We could fix the visas from this end I'm sure. WHY NOT? We could live like princes on my salary and bathe and cogitate and plan the new world.

Perhaps we could run a little review from Corfu: just a little thing to tell the world, and give it away. Try and get back. Things look brighter in the Mediterranean. Probably no war.

Love.

NA 28 16 CABLE RELAY VIA NR NY=ATHENS JUN 17=18 1940
NLT HENRY MILLER:
=GOTHAM BOOK MART=137 EAST 54ST NEWYORK=
URGENTLY NEED DOUGH CABLED=

LAWRENCE DURRELL

40 Anagnostopoulou, Athens

[June–July 1940]

Dear Henry:

I don't know whether you'll get this, but I wanted to thank you for the speed and size of the cheque. It saved our lives. All communications have broken down and I am busy trying to persuade my bank to telegraph money. I still don't know what the situation is; the school has stopped here, and with it my dough; and I'm supposed to get to Cyprus and start up there in September but at the moment there is no connection. Theodore passed through last week, with a commission in the army heading for Cyprus via Turkey. I expect we will have to do the same. Beirut to Cyprus is only fishing boats, they say, and difficult trailing a baby. O by the way, it's a girl! Penelope Berengaria Durrell. A voice like a siren, a nose like a syren, and a skin like a saurian. I'm very pleased but don't know quite what to do with it; I mean in this world the domestic virtues seem rather an anachronism, household gods at a discount. I may have to touch you once more perhaps, but I can pay back from the British Council work from September when I shall be a man of substance, so fear not, brother mole.

I wish I could give you a crumb of hope about Europe, but I can't. The situation is such a fatal balls-up, so fine a flower of our mutton-headed craven-hearted policy that one can only puke and look away.

Now I'm afraid it does mean war with a vengeance. There was always a hope that the damage of a year or two's war could be patched up, but this is going to be a war of famines. Already in Belgium . . . It's such a pity we allowed sheep-ticks dressed in starched collars to lead us instead of men of tenderness and gristle. The material is so wonderful, you know, the English infantry man. I've been talking to some people who were mixed up in the Dunkirk affair; the Guards can fight, he said, "with a ferocious tenderness: their fierceness comes from an obliterating shame at violence." Which is rather a subtle dissociation for a man who is not a poet, and for the Guards themselves who are only a quarter human at the best of times. Enough of politics. I wonder when this chapter of treacheries is going to cease. Without the offensive spirit we are lost I feel; and I don't see a trace of it in the Mediterranean. Read *Troilus and Cressida* and you will see how we Balkan peoples feel. "Wars and lechery!" We still meet, Seferis and G.K., but it's like the meeting of ancients; we exchange silences rather and pipe smoke; and the weather is impervious to it all, smiling and green.

I do hope this letter gets through, but everything is so uncertain. Anyway, be as happy as you can on your peaceful continent because no one knows how long it'll be.

We are cultivating the finer flower of a post-European resignation. After all, Minoa had to face it, and the Cyclades have lost all trace of it. I feel very Petronian about it; down with the silver age giants!

love,
larry

10th August 1940

The peasants are lying everywhere on deck eating watermelons; the gutters are running with the juice. A huge crowd bound on a pilgrimage to the Virgin of Tinos. We are just precariously out of harbour, scouting the sky-line for Eyetalian subs. What I really have to tell you is the story of the cocks of Attica; it will frame your portrait of Katsimbalis which I have not yet read but which sounds marvellous from all accounts. It is this. We all went up to the Acropolis the other evening very drunk and exalted by wine and poetry; it was a hot black night and our blood was roaring with cognac. We sat on the steps outside the big gate, passing the bottle, Katsimbalis reciting and Georgakis weeping a little, when all of a sudden he was seized with a kind of fit. Leaping to his feet he yelled out, "Do you want to hear the cocks of Attica, you damned moderns?" His voice had a hysterical edge to it. We didn't answer, and he wasn't waiting for one. He took a little run to the edge of the precipice, like a fairy queen, a heavy black fairy queen, in his black clothes, threw back his head, clapped the crook of his stick into his wounded arm, and sent out the most blood-curdling clarion I have ever heard. Cock a doodle doo. It echoed all over the city—a sort of dark bowl dotted with lights like cherries. It ricocheted from hillock to hillock and wheeled up under the walls of the Parthenon. Under the winged victory this horrible male cockcrow—worse than Emil Jannings. We were so shocked that we were struck dumb. And while we were still looking at each

166

other in the darkness, lo, from the distance silvery clear in the darkness a cock drowsily answered—then another, then another. This drove K. wild. Squaring himself, like a bird about to fly into space, and flapping his coattails, he set up a terrific scream—and the echoes multiplied. He screamed until the veins stood out all over him, looking like a battered and ravaged rooster in profile, flapping on his own dunghill. He screamed himself hysterical and his audience in the valley increased until all over Athens like bugles they were calling and calling, answering him. Finally between laughter and hysteria we had to ask him to stop. The whole night was alive with cockcrows—all Athens, all Attica, all Greece, it seemed, until I almost imagined you being woken at your desk late in New York to hear these terrific silver peals: Katsimbaline cockcrow in Attica.

This was epic—a great moment and purely Katsimbalis. If you could have heard those cocks, the frantic psaltery of the Attic cocks! I dreamt about it for two nights afterwards. Well, we are on our way to Mykonos, resigned now that we have heard the cocks of Attica from the Acropolis. I wish you'd write it—it is part of the mosaic.

Love to you all,
Larry

Institute of English Studies, Kalamata, Greece
Nov. 10

[1940]

Dear Henry:

I hope you will get this some day. At the moment everything is upside down and what with air raids and one thing and another I have hardly time to think. We are submerged in the struggle. Well, the Epirotes have been having a picnic up there as I prophesied. Katsimbalis has ridden off gigantically with the artillery; Tonio is away with the fleet—just had a note from George Seferis. In the meantime I have been trying to go up to Corfu with the Navy or the Air Force with no result. They say they are not operating at all in the sectors which I want to help with; and the Greeks seem not to need help now. Everyone has been in raptures over Greek successes. Meanwhile the air raid siren has entered our lives three or four times a day: a most unpleasant experience. However, we live and learn. We are in good fettle and so grateful to you for helping us out. My mother is sending you back the dough slowly from London.

I see no end to the business. It will go on for years because we are no nearer to the individual solution—and the outer struggle is only a reflection of it. Nothing remains really except one's personal honour and one's love for the killers. We shall see.

Love to anyone over there who might be in need of disinterested love. Ah Lao-tse, we need you here!

Larry

MARCH 1941—NOVEMBER 1942
(Miller in New York and Hollywood)

———◆———

ONLY five letters survive from the three years following Durrell's last from Greece, all of them from
Miller. He is on the move during this time and traveling
light. The letters contain echoes of *The Air-Conditioned
Nightmare*, Miller's odyssey across the United States and
back. Afterward he settles in Beverly Glen, outside Los
Angeles, making a vain attempt to earn a living in Hollywood. Down and out, as he explains in "The Plight of the
Creative Artist in the United States of America," he appeals for food, clothing and money, offering water colors
in exchange. One of his neighbors in Beverly Glen is a
librarian at the nearby University named Lawrence Clark
Powell who offers Miller all the library's resources and
later instigates *The Books in My Life*.

*   *

March 1st, 1941

[Written from New York on this stationery]

Dear Larry and Nancy—

Your letter of November 10th from Kalamata just reached me the other day on my arrival in New York. Where can you be now, I wonder, and will this ever reach you? They say no mail gets through for Greece but I am taking a chance. Maybe the miracle will happen. You see from the above where I just came from. I had to fly back (ten hours) owing to my father's death. I arrived just two hours too late but understand he passed away peacefully in his sleep. Now I am returning to Natchez where I left the car (a 1932 Buick) and will resume the trip. I'm going by train via Pittsburgh, Cleveland, Detroit, Chicago, St. Louis, Kansas City, Memphis, stopping off at all these towns to give them the once over, as we say. With the whole world torn and confused and thinking of nothing but war, war, war, why it's like a journey in Limbo. I am still detached, inwardly. Curse me, if you will, but I can't work up the necessary hatred. So I go on with my own plans and make what I can of my life until the madness is over.

You mentioned that your mother would repay me. Please stop her! I don't want anything back. It was the first time I ever really raised such a sum for anyone in years and years. I couldn't send a drop more, believe me. Nor now either, should I want to. I just get by from town to town by the skin of my teeth. I have more confidence than ever in accomplishing anything I set out to do. It's as though now I had the gods on my side. I feel as if any desire will be met, provided I walk the line. And I'm doing just that. I have no doubt I will go from America to India—perhaps via Mexico—just as easily as I pass from

170

my hotel to the railway station. What more can I tell you?

Do write me if you can. I am eager to know if letters do get through. My love to everyone there, if you're still in Athens. And hereafter write me c/o Russell and Volkening, Inc., 522 5th Ave., New York. Though if you forget, letters or messages to the Gotham Book Mart will always reach me.

I cross the Mississippi soon for the Far West. God, if I could only have you with me now! It's strange how destiny decrees that we each go our own way. But I'm thinking of you always.

Henry

Listen, Larry—whether the U.S. enters the war or not, there will be a world-wide revolution to finish this off. *You* will yet see a wonderful period. Neither England nor Germany will win. We're in for the greatest change the earth has known. Mark my words.

New York City
Dec. 28th, 1941

Dear Larry—

The other day a typewritten excerpt from a book by Fraser (about my skull portrait) came—but no letter with it. I'm sure you addressed the envelope. Yesterday a postcard from Seferis in Pretoria, S.A., saying I could reach you at the British Embassy, Cairo. I take it you never got any letter from me at that crazy address—Luna Park Hotel! Did you ever get *The Colossus*, sent to this latter address? Now I'm having New Directions send you *The Wisdom of the Heart* c/o British Embassy. One day I wrote a letter which a chap named Wayne Harriss promised to air mail for me with a word from himself about his publishing plans. He and an Irish girl (from Isle of Aran) are crazy not only about *The Black Book*

171

but about your poems. So far no tangible results. Have had wonderful praise for you of the poems—likened you to Donne, Blake and others. The young and evil ones seem to know. My friend at Viking Press was very enthusiastic but the firm couldn't see how they would sell more than 500. This, of course, is *America*. American attitude towards everything. They sell you the war in the same fashion. It must pay or no use. Et cetera.

You know, I'm back from the tour. Covered about 25,-000 miles. A year wasted, I'd say. Am bringing the book to a close soon. Now well over 500 pages. But I doubt that it will ever be published. I may put it in the Library of Congress—for the archives. That means handing back the advances I received—about a thousand dollars. Will have to take a job soon—I owe much more, as a result of the trip.

I am still hoping to get to Mexico, India, China, Tibet. But how? Yet, I know I will. I am just cooling my heels. You know, I always have the feeling that I will bump into you and Nancy in India—either in Burma or Nepal. How is Nancy? And dear little Berengaria Penelope? I wonder how it is in Cairo. Interesting, no doubt. Here in New York I have the feeling of being in the "Bardo." Absolutely. All that is needed to complete the picture are the bombs. And they will soon be here, no doubt. Nothing is changed here, on the surface. Plenty of neckties, silk bathrobes, etc. Business as usual. A complete air of unreality.

Listen, Larry, I will write oftener now. I feel you are *there*, in Cairo. Before I was dubious. If you get a chance look up a book called *Cosmic Consciousness* by Bucke. It's for *you*.

Henry

Address till further notice:
c/o Satyr Book Shop, 1620 N. Vine St., Hollywood, Cal.
or *c/o Russell and Volkening, 522 Fifth Avenue, N.Y.C.*

Dear Larry,

I was overjoyed to get your letter of July 4th, the first I have received from you since you left Greece. If you wrote others they must have gone to the bottom. Once I got a queer letter from some young Englishman, giving his reaction to a portrait of me he saw in a book shop window in Paris. It was from Cairo and seemed to have been sent by you, but there was no word from you with it. Recently I had your letter to Fred, forwarded by him. . . . Well, so you are alive! That's marvellous. And Nancy and Berengaria in Palestine! That's incredible. How I envy you both! I wish I could be sent to Palestine or Syria or Timbuctoo—or Cairo. I swear I wouldn't mind the dirt, disease, or anything. It seems so rich to me, that world you are in. Even the crazy alphabet. Even the postage stamps look intriguing.

You see, I am in Hollywood—since three months nearly. Thought I might take a snap job in the movies— in order to get the money to go to Mexico and ultimately to India, etc. But I have made no effort to get myself a job. I loathe the work and the people who run the show. I meet them all socially and it is enough to make you vomit. I am living with a writer named Gilbert Neiman and his wife. That is, I eat with them. I sleep and work next door with the Jordans—from Czechoslovakia. A writer of detective stories, gruesome ones, for which he gets *$700.00 a month!* We live in a canyon about six miles out from Hollywood. Quite isolated. A wonderful climate and rather interesting scenery—mountain, sea and desert. A Lotus Land. The only bugaboo (for them) is the gas rationing. Soon they may have to hoof it to and fro.

Now and then I go to a studio to watch them shoot a film. It's grotesque. Like work done under a microscope. The film advances about a millimetre a day with tremendous clatter and clamour. In an atmosphere which is suffocating. The lights alone drive you nuts. Most of the people involved are technicians. The camera dominates everything. Millions of little screws to turn. Everything mechanical. The acting seems quite secondary. One wonders how the film ever gets produced finally. When I think of writing a script my hair stands on end. I have tried it in collaboration with a couple of fellows—I understand the technique—very simple—but, as Huxley told me in a letter recently (he's living nearby in the desert now) — it's like fitting a jig-saw puzzle together. There is a type of young writer now who seems particularly adapted to this work—the new Soviet workers for whom art is a thing of the past . . . a Pleistocene luxury.

Just this morning I was offered a job as ghost writer to an old actor who is writing five books at once. And getting them accepted too, by some New York publisher. I could have a luxurious place to myself, good food, use of a car, and all that. But I can't see myself writing those books—can you? I am asking a thousand dollars *a week* for my services—in order to hold them off. But I am afraid one day some one will actually offer me such a sum. Any price goes here. Though William Faulkner only gets three hundred a week at Warner Brothers Studios—where I had a sunstroke one day walking through the artificial movie streets of Casablanca. Temperature 120 in the shade.

The war! Everyone is being drafted, shifted about, uprooted. They are talking of raising thirteen million men here shortly. Soon there will be nothing but women and old men left. I hope I shan't be too old—I mean for the women. I read the papers once a fortnight, roughly. Just the headlines. Wonder how many years it will be before one side or the other collapses. And will it be a bright new world, when it's over?

There is a Ramakrishna-Vivekananda Center, a sort of monastery, on the border of Nepal, where I am offered hospitality, if I can ever make it. I know a couple of swamis representing this order. Meanwhile I am working on *The Rosy Crucifixion* (sequel to *Capricorn*). Have 700 pages done and must do about the same amount before I'm finished with Volume 2. I really have no problems any more—except the petty one of food and board. I earn no money. $450.00 last year, for royalties and magazine articles and everything. Handsome, what!

No, Larry me lad, my serenity increases. I don't give a shit what the set-up is. I go my way. My health improves. I seem to be getting younger, instead of older.

I'll write again, now that I know where to reach you and that you're still there to read my letters. I guess you'll be meeting lots of Americans in Cairo. The latest about *Tropic of Cancer* is this: that in Washington Madame Litvinov begged a friend of mine to let her read the book. The *Colossus* is now being translated into modern Greek by a young Greek professor in New Jersey—Homer Economos, of all names! Secker and Warburg are bringing out an English publication this fall. Seems strange to me. Why would they want that book? Well, I never did understand the English. As Houghton says, they're fantastic—and always waiting for a miracle to deliver them. And the miracle always happens! You must read the Julian Grant book—it will bowl you over.

My love to Nancy and blessings on the little one. I must go in to Hollywood now to give an English lesson to a Russian refugee. Cheerio, then, Larry me lad.

Henry

Dear Larry,

It's Fred who suggested I write you via London, to expedite delivery. I'm hoping this may reach you in time to wish you a merry Christmas—you, Nancy and Berengaria the third. I'm pulling up stakes soon, to return to New York. Earned exactly a hundred dollars here where diamonds grow in the street, doing an abstract of Wassermann's *The Maurizius Case*. The studios wouldn't have me, it seems. Unheard of. No screen credits. Too highbrow. And so forth. The only interesting thing that happened to me here was meeting Melpomene, the Greek woman. She is the apotheosis of all Greek womanhood. I hope to see her when I return to New York. It's cold here now, about like Athens was that month of December, when they turned the heat on an hour or two at a time, you remember?

Well, I'm thinking that soon the American troops will be landing in Athens. At this moment things are looking up a bit. The invasion has begun. I suppose Cairo is agog with expectations of one kind and another. At this writing the Germans still hold Bizerte and Tunis. But it's no longer a toe-hold, from all reports. I'm wondering what you will think when you get a glimpse of the Americans en masse. I suppose there's already a bit of rivalry afoot. Coincident with the turn of the tide, Churchill announces that he is not giving the Empire away (sic). That didn't meet with such a warm reception over here. We want the English to give their bloody Empire away, doesn't he know that, the old pfoof?

I just finished reading Céline's *Death on the Installment Plan*. It took me over two years, oddly enough. I gallivanted through the last two hundred pages. Magnificent. Ferocious. Still the best writer alive today, I do think. After they defeat the Axis powers they will have to lick Céline, it seems to me. He's got more dynamite in him than Hitler ever had. It's permanent hatred—for the whole human species. But what merrymaking. He has a bloody corpse, towards the end, that provides more hysterical amusement than a band of comedians. Blood-curdling humor it is. Sometimes it turns your stomach. Do get hold of it, Larry, it will pep you up. You may enjoy it even more than I. The translator was English, and all the slang expressions, some of which are Greek to me, are in British English. That makes it quite droll. Imagine a Frenchman saying "bugger off."

The movies have definitely entered the doldrums. No good pictures being made any more, not for the duration. All flub and foozle, with a $25,000.00 a year ceiling wage for the stars. Tough titty for them. How can they get along on a pittance like that? It's tragic. That's mere chicken feed to them. They need more than the President, more than the Pope at Rome, b'Jasus. I met one recently who was earning $1200.00 a week. A *week*, mind you! All he has left, after paying taxes, alimony, state, federal, poll tax and Christ knows what else, is ninety dollars. How can a man get along on ninety dollars? He never heard of a coolie, I suppose. Nor did he ever see the Hindus sleeping naked in the streets of Bombay. Nor the child prostitutes in Shanghai. To believe our radio gents, we all need Vitamin B. A plain American meal lacks the necessary ingredients for health—that's what they tell you over the air. So buy vitamins—and Cuticura Soap and Electric Razor machines, and well . . . you know what. Yes, that fine, soft, tulle-like toilet paper. It will help win the war. The buying and selling goes on—right till the crack of doom. If people don't revolt at that stuff how will they revolt at anything? The way these bastards

177

talk over the air you'd think the war was just a big football game with a dollar sign on it.

Listen, you gave me a stinking picture of Cairo. Don't tell me there's nothing more to it than that. What about the night life? There must be millions of foreigners there now—I should think it would be exciting. I'd certainly rather be there than here in Hollywood.

Damn it all, I miss Fred. In this bloody country I never get a good belly laugh. I don't find anything to laugh about here. And it's not because of hard times. Christ knows, everything is going along swimmingly. We haven't begun to feel the war yet, not to my eye, at any rate. Fred always used to say war-time is a good time; everybody has plenty of money. At any rate, one spends it freely, in war-time. People spend for fear it will be taken from them, I suppose. So far, everything is still deluxe. Wait till we have to smoke cow-dung or go on a rice diet. Then I'll write you.

Well, the next will be from New York, I guess. Remember that Christmas in Sparta and the woman bringing the eggs back and forth? Who ever thought then that the year 1942 would see you in Cairo and me in Hollywood? And Fred in Scotland. Really, I think Fred got the best break of all, don't you? Must be beautiful country up there. Right in the Highlands he is, the cute little bugger. Always did know how to pick himself a soft spot. Merry Christmas, Larry, and to you, Nancy, and to you Berengaria!

Henry

CHRISTMAS 1943—MAY 1945
(Durrell in Alexandria—Miller in Big Sur)

———————◆●◆———————

As the war begins to near its end, the correspondence begins to revive. Miller and Durrell are so remote from one another they might be on different planets, cut off not only by distance and time (letters take five or six weeks each way) but leading altogether different lives. The first extant Durrell letter after three years suggests this feeling of remoteness—a brief note written on the Christmas and New Year card of the Hellenic Department of Information in Cairo. Durrell has been in Egypt since 1941, working in the British Information Office; his letters from Alexandria are full of the raw material that will metamorphose over the years into *The Alexandria Quartet*. Meanwhile he is trying to write *Prospero's Cell*, editing a little magazine (*Personal Landscape*), and producing two volumes of poetry. He also writes the title piece for *The Happy Rock*, a collection of essays on Henry Miller.

Early in 1944 Miller moves to Big Sur and becomes a Tibetan monk. His open letters to all and sundry begin to have some effect now, he is painting and publishing at a prodigious rate, and with the G.I. invasion of France his *Tropics* become best sellers.

*   *

[Alexandria, Christmas 1943]

Dear Henry—

Wonder where you are and what you are doing. Just been re-reading your Greek book and trying to write one myself. Strange mad times—and how remote—last meeting in Tripoli in the falling rain. I told Faber to send you my book of poems despite your dislike for poetry. Maybe some images will recall Greece to you. I am in Alexandria now and work in a little tower, very smart alec and quaint, but we are all so worm-eaten by the war that I do no work at all. I see Seferis and have recent news of Katsimbalis, who is alive still. Greece is going right under this winter : heartbreaking situation, famine, disease, and internal anarchy—walking murder abroad. Meanwhile salut for *The Air-Conditioned Nightmare*—it is great stuff. For the rest we are dying steadily inside and hoping for it all to end as soon as possible.

Nancy is in Jerusalem with the child. We have split up; just the war I guess. After Greece, Crete, and the Alamein evacuation we got to understand what the word "refugee" means.

Will you write some time—and disregard my bloody humours?

Love,
Larry

Information Office, One Rue Toussoum, Alexandria, Egypt
February 8, '44

Dearest Henry—

It is so good always to have a post card from you or a little book with that characteristic joyful (euphoristic) handwriting. Now today I get the notice of your show; I do hope it was a success, even a financial success—for by now it must be over.

I have been so long barren that I fear to tell you that I am working once more: for fear I shall blow up and fall into an Alexandrian frenzy of apathy. I have finished one book of verse, and am half-way through a book about Greek landscape—Corfu only. It's not a big book or even a book at all, but I feel I must wind up the old spring and tidy the "time past" of the clock if I am to expect any "time future" (*Burnt Norton*) from it.

I occasionally read your frenzied appeals to reason in the avant garde papers—sounding but so remote and so much like the voice of conscience as we reach into the fifth year of this sickening war—which mercifully some of us have escaped partially. Our feelings are those of the periphery, everyone going quietly bad and mad inside. Me too.

There is little to add. The Alexandrian way of death is very Proustian and slow, a decomposition in greys and greens. But the women are splendid—like neglected gardens. Rich, silk-and-olive complexions, slanting black eyes and soft adze-cut lips, and heavenly figures like line-drawings by a sexual Matisse. I am up to my ears in them—if I must be a little literal. But, as my friends remark, "Les femmes, comme les peintres d'Alexandrie ont trop de technique mais peu de tempérament." But one has never had anything lovelier and emptier than an Alexandrian girl. Their very emptiness is a caress. Imagine making love to a vacuum. You must come here for a week after the war. After that you'll be so emptied of worldly goods that you'll be ripe for Tibet and all it means. Meanwhile we are crawling through the ever-narrowing conduit of this bloody war. Do write from time to time. You are like a voice from something very far but completely understood, while here one talks into the air round people, and words fly gently off into space,

sound and fury. Love to Anais and Edgar——where are
they all?

Larry

Now I think of the correct simile for the Alexandrians.
When they make love it's like two people in a dark room
slashing at each other with razors——to make each other
feel——?

Big Sur, California
Easter Sunday

[Open Letter, April 9, 1944]

Dear friends:

I should like to put the ad given below in a few literary
magazines, perhaps for several weeks hand running. I
do not have the money to do this. Perhaps some of you,
in reading the proposed ad, may have a better suggestion,
may know some one who would be willing to lend me the
money required and thus obviate the publicizing of my
predicament. It is immaterial to me how I get the money,
or who furnishes it. Nor do I care what conclusions people draw about my state of impecuniosity. ("Persons
Magnetized by the stars walking on the Music of a Fur-
rowed Landscape." Miro)

To you whom I consider my friends I would like to
explain briefly what my circumstances are. Ever since I
arrived in this country (America) I have made no more
than four or five hundred dollars per annum. This past
year was an exception, due to the fact that I had a mod-
erate success with my water colors. What many of my
friends do not realize is that, foolishly or not, I immediately paid out the monies which suddenly poured in from
the sale of water colors——something like $1,400.00. I had
naively thought it would continue ad infinitum. (I was
an optimist and slightly delirious.) Now I am being abso-

182

lutely honest when I say that all I got out of this sudden influx of wealth was three pairs of woolen socks, a plaid woolen shirt, and some good water color paper. The corduroy trousers which I so much wanted were given to me as a Xmas present by my friends Holve-Barrows. I didn't even get a good meal out of it. Immediately the checks came in I paid off my debts, the more pressing ones, that is. (Ask Dudley who lived with me at the Glen during this period.) I still owe roughly $24,000.00. That is what it has cost me to write as I pleased for the last twenty years.

As I say in the ad, the reason I want this money is because I want to finish two major works I have in hand. They are: 1.) *The Air-Conditioned Nightmare*; 2.) *The Rosy Crucifixion*. If I can get the sum demanded I shall go to Mexico to live. In one year I can finish those books. Once I get to Mexico I have no fear of being able to survive. I trust the Mexicans. I am at home in a foreign land. It is only in my own country that I am out of luck.

It gripes me that in a year when seventeen books of mine are being published, here and in England, I should be in this predicament. It is phenomenal to have that many books published in one year. It is even more phenomenal that the author of those seventeen volumes should be reduced to the ignominious position of a beggar. But that has been my lot always in this country. And that is why I want to flee it as soon as possible.

You call yourselves my friends. You have all at one time or another offered to help me in some way. This is the way you can help me at the moment. As I said, if you know a more direct and immediate way of obtaining results, tell me. All I want is fifty dollars per week for fifty weeks. In that time I shall have accomplished what I set out to do. I cannot guarantee how long it will take me to pay off the loan. Whoever offers it need not trust *me*; arrangements can be made through my agents, Russell &

Volkening, 522 Fifth Ave., N.Y. They receive all monies coming to me anyway. All that needs to be done is for me to sign a paper saying that I will accept no money due me until the lender has been paid off. (Simple, what?) I say in the ad that I will gladly give $3,000.00 for the $2,500.00 I ask for. As a matter of fact I will gladly give $5,000.00, which is double the amount asked for, if that would prove an incentive. Because once I have finished the books in question I do not care whether I write another book or not. Neither do I care how I get along. I can get along quite well if I have nothing on my mind but the business of getting along. Herewith the proposed ad :

> In order to finish two important books I will need $2,500.00 in weekly or monthly installments over a period of fifty weeks. Do not know how long it will take to pay off the loan but will give $3,000.00 for the sum demanded. Arrangements and guaranties can be made through my agents in N.Y. Over a dozen of my books are being published this year here and in England. Will some one take a chance on me?

Henry Miller

Big Sur, California
May 5th, 1944

Dear Larry,

I wrote you a couple of weeks ago on hearing from you. Now yesterday two letters at once, dated Alexandria where I write you henceforth. The other letter was addressed to Cairo—hope you get it.

Anyway, since that last letter I posted good news. Lots of news. First, I've found a patron—for a whole year—who is giving me fifty dollars a week and no strings to it. I am to pay back when, how or if. No interest charges. This as a result of a round robin letter dated Easter Sunday, when I also answered the lovely cable I most unexpectedly received from Osbert Sitwell, Renishaw Hall, Renishaw (near Sheffield) England—bloody England!

When I get copies made of all these open letters I have been writing I will send them on to you. They will appear in book form anyway soon. I am deluged with letters by all and sundry. It's colossal. And many contain little checks or just plain bills (cash), or promises. Some send packages of clothing, paper for writing or painting, tubes of paint, etc. etc. etc. I am like a receiving station.

The show in Hollywood was quite a success. I sold myself about twenty-four paintings before the show started. Got from $30 to $100 apiece. Some hang now in famous collections. At present Caresse Crosby is showing me in Washington, D.C. where she opened a gallery recently.

In short, Larry, there will be 17 books coming out this year here and in England. Every bloody thing I have is being printed. When I finish *The Rosy Crucifixion* I shall be able to take off for a while. By that time maybe the war will be over and I will join you somewhere, you and dear Alf in Scotland, and Edgar, who is now somewhere in England, a sergeant. In short, a year of complete fulfillment and realization. All except love. Blast me, but I have had more ill luck in that direction than I could ever imagine. I am just hors de combat, as it were. All ends disastrously.

So, when you write me about the Alexandrian vacuum with razor blades flashing and all that I am in a paroxysm. Let's get there! Christ, it's dead here. All this business flurry, books published, water-color shows, means nothing to me. I'd give it all up to wander with you through those streets and see those sloe-gin fizz eyes, drown myself in that abattoir of love which you describe so eloquently.

No, Faber have not yet sent me your poems. They will come one day. Everything comes—eventually. Even Christmas. And so will peace come. And then it will be the merry whirl, and we will be planning the next war, bigger, better, more efficient, more ferocious. Listen, I am just finishing a rather long excursus (in the *Nightmare*), called "Murder the Murderer." About 65 to 75 pages long. I think I will send you a carbon of it; you may want to use it in that magazine. It's a marvellous piece—savage humor, wisdom, serenity, optimism-pessimism, satire, vaudeville, charley-horse and everything. Nobody has written about war this way. You'll love it, even if you don't agree. Remember, it will be from *The Air-Conditioned Nightmare*, which is due out before the end of the year.

Well, Larry, I must stop. Mailman is due soon. Mail here only three times a week. He brings food too. We are 35 miles from nearest town—rugged country, very much like Greece in the mountains. Cattle ranges all about. The last of the old pioneer country.

Do give warm greetings to Seferis, if you still see or communicate with him. I do hope Katsimbalis comes through. I think he will.

Henry

British Information Office, One Rue Toussoum,
Alexandria, Egypt

[Spring 1944]

Dear Henry:

Yes, I got the letters. I'm in touch with the embassy, representing them, so they pass them on. Your news sounds marvellous. Of course anything is less than what the world owes you for opening up the world with your own bright eye. Seventeen books sounds an awful lot to me. Let me have any old duplicate proofs that come your way—I haven't read anything of yours since the marvellous Greek book. Here we are sweltering in an atmosphere that demands a toast—great passions, short lives. Everything is worn thin as an eggshell; it's the fifth year now and the nervous breakdown is coming into the open. Old women, ginger dons, nursing sisters begin to behave like bacchantes; they are moving in and out of nursing homes with a steady impetus. Meanwhile we are crippled here by an anemia and an apathy and a censorship which prevents the least trace of the human voice—of any calibre. We exist on a machine-made diet of gun bomb and tank —backed up by the slogan.

The atmosphere in this delta is crackling like a Leyden jar. You see, in normal times all the local inhabitants spend six months in Europe a year, so they are as stale and beaten thin as the poor white collar man. The poetry I exude these days is dark grey and streaky, like bad bacon. But the atmosphere of sex and death is staggering in its intensity. Meanwhile the big shots come and go, seeing nothing, feeling nothing, in a money daydream; there is still butter and whisky and café viennois. A kind of diseased fat spreads over the faces and buttocks of the local populations, who have skimmed the grease off the war effort in contracts and profiteering. No, I don't think you would like it. First this steaming humid flatness—not a hill or mound anywhere—choked to bursting point with bones and the crummy deposits of wiped out cultures. Then this smashed up broken down shabby Neapolitan town, with its Levantine mounds of houses peeling in the sun. A sea flat, dirty brown and waveless rubbing the port. Arabic, Coptic, Greek, Levant French; no music, no art, no real gaiety. A saturated middle European boredom laced with drink and Packards and beach-cabins. NO SUBJECT OF CONVERSATION EXCEPT MONEY. Even love is thought of in money terms. "You are getting on with her? She has ten thousand a year of her own." Six hundred greaseball millionaires sweating in their tarbushes and waiting for the next shot of root-hashish. And the shrieking personal unhappiness and loneliness showing in every face. No, if one could write a single line of anything that had a human smell to it here, one would be a genius. Add to all this a sort of maggot-dance of minor official place-hunting, a Florentine atmosphere of throat-slitting and distrust, and you will have some idea of what anyone with a voice or tongue is up against. I am hoping the war will be over soon so I can quit; I'm glad of this little death for all the material it's put in my way about people and affairs in general. But I'm worn thin with arse-licking and having my grammar corrected by sub-editors from the Bush Times in South America. Here in Alexandria, though, I have my own office and almost no interference; so I can run things in the way I like. You always used to laugh when I said I was an executive man, but I was right. My office hums like a top; and the people working for me LIKE it. The basic principle is that of the old blind pianist in Paris—remember? Edgar's friend Thibaud or some such name. "Anything that needs effort to do is being done from the wrong centres; it is not worth doing." Some time I'll tell you how I applied that to the running of an effortless speed organisation.

I've done about half of a little historical book about Corfu; tried writing in the style of a diary—you know the French anecdotal novel type of things. Poor stuff but I feel I must keep the machine running or I'll die.

No other news; the sloe-eyed people are still here. There's a lovely English wren and a girl with the hips of an acrobat. But it's all really quite meaningless. I want a long rest from this incessant plucking of little people with little minds at the root of one's reason and self-respect.

How about a year in Poros now—baked hard rock and glittering sea; followed by autumn in Athens with Katsimbalis and George (both still alive and all right) ; and then Paris and Edgar and Anne of Dumfries? No more writing but lying about and taking a long myopic and unbiassed view of the universe. Or do you prefer Savings Bonds, Maximum Employment, better plumbing, and a prefabricated spiritual life in tune with the Stock Exchange graphs?

It's so good to know that you're writing. I found *Tropic* the other day and read it again with such yearning for Paris and Villa Seurat; and Betty Ryan and Mr Chu, and Châteauneuf-du-Pape, and Denis Seurat, Nijinsky, *Booster-Delta* and the whole works. Maybe we have it all ahead of us and not behind? Write again soon.

Larry

Since writing the last few lines I have been called to Cairo for a week or so and have just returned, blind with heat and sweat and apathy. Have managed to sell another book of poems for the spring lists next year and am on the last lap of the Corfu book. I have Theodore conveniently staying with me so I am picking his brains diligently. It was intended to be a book of atmospheres, but it is terribly scrappy and ill-starred. If I had a little leisure and energy.

Four years is a long time to spend without ever once encountering a person who has an interest besides making a woman or making money; and I've forgotten almost how to express myself. But I am unjust to a strange, smashing, dark-eyed woman I found here last year, with every response right, every gesture, and the interior style of a real person, but completely at sea here in this morass of venality and money. The only person I have been able to talk to really; we share a kind of refugee life. She sits for hours on the bed and tells me all about the sex life of Arabs, perversions, circumcision, hashish, sweetmeats, removal of the clitoris, cruelty, murder. As a barefoot child of Tunisian Jewish parents (mother Greek from

189

Smyrna, father Jew from Carthage) she has seen the inside of Egypt to the last rotten dung-blown flap of obscenity. She is *Tropic of Capricorn* walking. And like all people with the Tibetan sensibility she felt that she was going mad—because nobody knew what she was talking about. It has been fun re-articulating her experience for her, and curing her panics, and finding her books to show her how great a part of the world of sense and creation is nonsense to Alexandria.

I think if I could get to some Greek island and live in real poverty with somebody like her, I could work like a fiend. I have really grown up now and have plenty to say. I wonder how soon I can get free from the world of sub-men in order to say it.

We are publishing an anthology of our work in Egypt here, a few of us. It's called *Personal Landscape* and Tambimuttu is publishing this autumn, so we will be alongside you once more, firing our pom-poms in support of your great scooping broadsides.

The world has walls of dung really, and the human being a mind like a sponge. The next ten years should see us in full cry over the hills. Simple needs this time. A girl, an olive tree, a typewriter, and a few great friends like you. What do you think?

Larry

British Information Office, 1, Rue Toussoum, Alexandria
May 23, 1944

Dear Henry :

How wonderful to hear from you at length again, the old hard gayness which is like a lost world quality shining over the rim. I have just posted off a little essay on you for an anthology of homage which some American wants to publish—I guess you know all about it.

I am in charge of a goodish-sized office of war-propaganda here, trying to usher in the new washboard world which our demented peoples are trying "to forge in blood and iron." It's tiring work. However, it's an office full of beautiful girls, and Alexandria is, after Hollywood, fuller of beautiful women than any place else. Incomparably more beautiful than Athens or Paris; the mixture Coptic, Jewish, Syrian, Egyptian, Moroccan, Spanish gives you slant dark eyes, olive freckled skin, hawk lips and noses, and a temperament like a bomb. Sexual provender of quality, but the atmosphere is damp, hysterical, sandy, with the wind off the desert fanning everything to mania. Love, hashish and boys is the obvious solution to anyone stuck here for more than a few years. I am sharing a big flat with some nice people, and atop it I have a tower of my own from which the romantics can see Pompey's Pillar, Hadra Prison, and the wet reedy wastes of Lake Mareotis stretching away into the distance and blotting the sky.

This is the world of the desert fathers and the wandering Jews; the country is eaten away like the carious jawbone of a mummy. Alexandria is the only possible point in Egypt to live in because it has a harbour and opens on a flat turpentine sea line—a way of escape.

There is lots of amusing and exciting news I could give you about the Greeks, and about people like Fielding but I'm afraid censorship wouldn't let it pass so I must content myself by asking you if you realise how close you are to Melville biographically? And will you read his biography and send me a copy of *Pierre?* Books here have got a Middle Ages quality owing to their rareness; all the popular editions are out of print of EVERYTHING—I mean the classics like Dostoievsky and Proust and all those wonderful half-crown editions you could buy before the war. So we have a sort of hungry look when anyone gets a new book—even if it's only a detective story. Among recent discoveries is a copy of *Tropic* which has knocked everyone silly here. When they read the Greek book they asked me what I was babbling about when I said Miller was the greatest contemporary writer. He was certainly good etc. etc. Now they begin to see . . .

Apart from that I have got stuck about half-way through a little book about Corfu—a guide to landscape. Hard going. I feel played out.

Wonder what sort of future there is in store. I see a gathering at Constantinople or Baalbec in Syria before we start off to the land of the Book of the Dead. My only consolation now is Lao-tse of which Eliot kindly sent me a copy—funny patient crazy rectangular man that he is. This I have explained in detail to Gipsy who understands every word, but it doesn't prevent her from scratching my face open for infidelities which in this landscape and ambiance are as meaningless as she, I, or Pompey's Pillar are. Feel we've come to the end of a spool, and I am trying to live as little as possible until the new film gets put in the camera.

It's funny the way you get woman after woman; and exactly what it adds up to I don't know, each more superficial than the last Gaby, Simone, Arlette, Dawn, Penelope. But their sex here is interesting; it's madly violent but not WEAK or romantic or obscure, like Anglo-Saxon women, who are always searching for a tintype of their daddies. It is not preconceived but taken heavily and in a kind of war—not limp northern friendship—but fierce and glaring, vulture and eagle work with beak and claws.

Well, the last few days we've driven out through Bourgh El Arab, and slipped down through the battlefields to a long beach where the real Mediterranean comes up in great green coasters and sky is smothered down to violet, all lambent and turning your body in water to a wonderful rose. The sea citron-green. cold and pure with sandy floor. For the first time in four years I felt I was in Greece. Bathing naked. At our back the dunes running away to the deserted crusader fort, nibbled battlements misty and like a mirage. Thousands of empty rounds of ammunition, dirty bandages, twisted wreck of enemy tanks, lumber. Strange atmosphere this deserted battle-field with the sea inking in the edges of the sky and the old fortress glowing like a jewel. On the road an occasional Bedouin with his camel. And palms like old camel-flesh trees clicking stiffly in the wind. Stranger transition to Cavafy's Alexandria, and a letter from George Seferis on my desk saying he is feeling happier and happier now that he has dropped propaganda.

There is not much else to tell you that can be conveniently written. Forgive the mad haste of this. I must see what the world-fronts are saying on the radio. Gipsy is coming for a drink at one. Life is long, art short, as Goethe did not say.

Wonder when it will all end? Do write again soon, won't you?

Larry

Big Sur, California
July 6th, 1944

Dear Larry:

Just got your charming descriptive letter of May 23rd, and was delighted to see from the photo enclosed that you look like your old self—perhaps two or three weeks older, but no more. As for Gypsy, I could swear I've seen her before—maybe in Athens, maybe in New York, maybe on the rue de la Tombe-Issoire.

A number of things will come to you in next few weeks and months—a whole slew of things. Incidentally, if you had an outlet for them there in Alexandria or Cairo, or anywhere, I could send you typescripts of a number of things, especially completed fragments from the *Nightmare*, all of varying texture, length, quality and attitude. It's a crazy book. I've got 500 pages solidly done, about 20 chapters, ending Part One with the excursus. Go on to Part Two now, which will be a farrago of nonsense, misinformation, fantasy—gaga, in short. Wish I had begun the book that way. Wish I had written it in Paris. There is a long preface, 25 to 35 pages (am rewriting), also a document in itself. An abridged version was published in Reginald Moore's anthology: *Modern Reading*, I believe. About 15 chapters of the book have been published in magazines thus far, hardly any of them bringing me any money. Laughlin (New Directions) has agreed to publish it if Doubleday reject it, which they will, of course. I am urging them to reject every letter I write.

In your letter you speak, as do the English in England, of a scarcity of books, good books. How wonderful! Here everything is plentiful, including milk and butter, honey and oregano. I'll send you books from time to time, and magazines too.

Yes, I'll have one of the book shops send you *Pierre* by Melville. Is this what you mean by his biography? I read it in Paris, at instigation of Benno, the painter. No, I don't realize the similarities, except in the delays and buffets I'm subjected to, but that's classic. Anyway, with this year's production I shall have nothing to complain of any more on that score. If only the *Tropics* were allowed to circulate—God, I'd be on easy street. Every one of the Paris books is now being reprinted in America, for discreet circulation, of course. The only book not contracted for— and I haven't even tried yet—is *The Rosy Crucifixion*. This revives the mantic and the obscene, and how! And will be devilishly long. But readable. Yes, that I can promise—very readable.

I must send you a lot of things: copies of *View*, of *Dyn* (Amerindian number), *Clowns and Angels* by Wallace Fowlie, Fechner's *Life After Death*, and so on. But I would do without all the books if I could be with you in Alexandria. More soon.

Henry

British Information Office, One Rue Toussoum,
Alexandria, Egypt
August 22, 1944

Dear Henry:

It's wonderful really to be able to correspond at such a short remove—under a month each way. I had the illusion that it was impossible, an illusion perfectly matching my burnt-out state. Thank you for the essay. IT IS TERRIFIC. I haven't read anything of yours for so long that the impact of it came with something of the pristine clearness I first felt when I opened *Tropic* and heard those first gruff symphonic rumblings—as of a great orchestra tuning up in darkness. Incidentally in England they are beginning to wake up to you—not to mention Egypt. I have given several talks on your books, chiefly to Jewish ATS here in Alexandria. Tremendous black-eyed big-bottomed girls, and all taking notes at terrific speed. They study literature as if it were more interesting than sex.

Now the war seems to have taken a definite turn and we hope that it will be over in a month or so. I am written down for Greece. I terribly need to recover my sanity a bit—disoriented and bruised a bit still, and haven't seen anything but sand and palms for two years. I did not know before what Gaul meant to the exiled Roman poet or Siberia to the Russian. Now I know. Your heart shrivels in its case for lack of moisture. It has rained once since I've been in Egypt—for half an hour. A dirty brown exhausted rain which was tepid and unrefreshing. One could not continue to live here without practising a sort of death—hashish or boys or food. Yet it has the kind of fat deathly beauty of a caterpillar. The connection, by the way, is the one you mentioned in the Greek book, at Corinth. Fat red and sensuous—it was an Alexandrian atmosphere we were smelling that mad Christmas in Corinth. I have learned so much here that I'm bursting to start writing again. I have a wonderful idea for a novel on Alexandria, a nexus for all news of Greece, side by side with a sort of spiritual butcher's shop with girls on slabs. But I can't make the big effort for a while until I am free, so I think I'll do a short anthropological study of the English tabus—like one would plot out the depth and shape of an anti-tank ditch before moving forward in force.

I can't judge from your writing what sort of impression you have had of the war; it is detached and ex cathedra beyond anything I could achieve for several months after it. But I think the issues you've stated in this essay are the biggest and wisest things written. In everything you do you are the great man of your age—even in your absurd begging letters. But what is so exciting, Henry, is that the structure of your prose has changed, to judge by this essay. It has become limpid and crystalline in structure without losing any of its fluency at all. The stream of images—often too cloying in their strength—has been incorporated into the formal *line* of the theme; no more digressions, but real *cadenzas*. I am dying to see some major book by you at this stage. It should blister and crackle and vomit without any sign of effort; you seem to know your own strength now and don't have to try—wonderful feeling.

Seferis has just returned from London after a short trip and I hope to see him here this evening; we shall have a real talk over some wine and I'll show him all these carbons and things you have been sending. It is curious that he is practically in the same state as I am—sort of exhaustion. In fact, though he is my best friend in Egypt, we almost never meet. It's as if meeting people who have real human demands to make of one is too tiring—or perhaps too guilt-making since we are both involved in this web of idiocy and panic—and I don't see what sort of political future waits for Greece. It only affects me in as much as I hope to live there and recover from this wave of world neurosis.

What about you? You must I feel come back and see that landscape once more. Spend a quiet year going round and tasting it all. Then I think we could get in touch with Mulk Raj Anand and ask him to give us the names of friends so that we could move off slowly towards Tibet. It's more than ever clear that Tibet is winning the war— this war and the next half dozen.

News of Katsimbalis: he is thin but talkative as ever. Gives public readings of his pet poets every week. Soon we shall be seeing them all. And you too, I hope—very soon.

Love and admiration,
Larry

Big Sur
Feb. 18th, '45

Dear Larry,

I've been looking through your recent letters and pulling out all the queries you raise. There's so little time to write a real letter any more, what with the fan mail, the water colors, and the unfinished books. First let me tell

you of a letter I received from a soldier in Paris recently
—one of many similar ones—in which he speaks of seeing
all the Obelisk books in the Paris book store windows—
rue de Rivoli and rue de Castiglione particularly. Your
Black Book was there and two of Anaïs'. The exchange is
low and the soldiers are buying them up like mad, he says.
I had a letter from Kahane's son, Maurice, some months
ago, too, saying he had continued business all through the
war, was I writing any more books for him, and could he
do my books in French now? He changed his name during the war to M. Girodias, and the name of the firm is
now Les Editions du Chêne—16 Place Vendôme, as before. The Germans did not destroy the books, nor any of
my private possessions I left with him. I think you might
get in touch with him—maybe there are some royalties
due us. And maybe too you could get *The Black Book*
published in French. At any rate, it's good to know there
are copies to be had. In England they tell me the censors
don't bother seizing importations now—too busy with
military censorship. So you could pass the word along to
your friends who want to own copies. I'm going to give
him *The Rosy Crucifixion* to publish, when I finish it—
which won't be for a long time.

You know, the English take about everything I send
them. It's amazing. I've burst out there in the magazines
and anthologies like a sun flower. I think that's where
I'm going to get my real royalties. The three books Laughlin printed here have all come to a second edition now, the
Colossus too. How many copies of the *Cancer* were printed
nobody knows—probably ten thousand or more. Now
soon the *Capricorn* comes out, privately printed—also
Aller Retour New York. Imagine that since returning to
America I have never seen a copy of the latter for sale
anywhere. Not one copy!

I'm very curious to see your *Prospero's Cell*. I remember your talking about the idea when we were in Corfu. And do send me some of your water colors, yes! I wonder how you paint now. I'm painting more than ever, and quite seriously. Last year I made over three hundred, all of which I disposed of. I've had a half dozen shows in different cities.

Just had word yesterday from my publisher, Bern Porter, that *The Happy Rock* has at last gone to press, and that your piece is the first in the book. Also from Patience Ross that she likes yours best and hopes to find an editor for it soon in one of the English magazines.

In Washington, when there, I made eight records for the Library of Congress—for the archives, at their request. I read from *Capricorn* and *Black Spring*. Quite an experience.

I see that in an old issue of *Horizon* Alex Comfort speaks highly of your poems, in a blurb. I only lately read something of his, an anarchistic diatribe, which I enjoyed hugely. Is he a friend of yours? And whatever became of Dylan Thomas? And your brother Leslie, and your sister?

Going to bed now. End of a quiet Sunday at Big Sur. My Polish wife, Lepska, has just been telling me stories of Poland. Every day here we take a sun bath. It's like spring now. Amazing climate and gorgeous scenery. Something like Scotland, I imagine. It's one of the few regions in America you would like. I must describe it to you some day. One of the features of it are the vultures. The other is the fogs. And the third is the lupine which is like purple velvet over the mountainsides. There are also four crazy horses which I meet on my walks through the hills. They seem glued to the spot. And two of them are always in heat. I have a wonderful cabin, you know, dirt cheap—ten dollars a month. I have a young wife (21), a baby on the way probably, food in the larder, wine à discrétion, hot sulphur baths down the road, books galore, a phonograph coming, a radio also coming, good kerosene lamps, a wood stove, an open fireplace, a shower, and plenty of sun, and of course the Pacific Ocean, which is always empty. Alors, what more? This is the first good break I've had since I'm living in America. I open the door in the morning, look towards the sun rising over the mountains, and bless the whole world, birds, flowers and beasts included. After I have moved my bowels I take the hound for a walk. Then a stint of writing, then lunch, then a siesta, then water colors, then correspondence, then a book, then a fuck, then a nap, then dinner, and so to bed early and up early and all's well except when I visit the dentist now and then. So write soon again, and cheerio!

Henry

British Information Office, One Rue Toussoum,
Alexandria, Egypt

[Spring 1945]

Dearest Henry:

I have just received from Tambimuttu his anthology, which has your poem in it. I like it very much. It's strange to see you handling a new form with the same assurance and pleasure as a water-colour. I am marking time here, waiting to go to Rhodes as public information officer, looking forward to it very much indeed. Supposed to be more beautiful than Corfu in an Aegean way—hard white water and rock and trees. I'm aiming to try and take a long rent on a tiny little house in a cove by the sea and settle in to work for a year or so.

And now comes your long exciting letter with all the news and the *Creative Artist* pamphlet. Yes, I got *Murder the Murderer* last week. I've read it twice and have handed it to Etiemble for translation and inclusion in his *Valeurs*, a new journal coming out this month, I think. He is a great fan. Myself, I didn't like *Murder the Murderer* as much as some of the other things in the book—which have absolutely no parallel in literature and which mark you off as being several stages above your position in the *Tropics*. O Prospero, what are you doing with another wife? Is she beautiful? It's great news about Kahane. I have drafted about twenty pages of the new version of the Book of the Dead—it's about incest and Alexandria, inseparable ideas here, but will take me a year or so to do and with little hope of English publication. Tambimuttu is dickering for *The Black Book* in England. Next year would be a good time perhaps. I have some new poems, really good this time, called *Cities, Plains, and People* just coming, followed by *Prospero*, followed by *The Dark Labyrinth*, which is a queer cosmological tale about seven modern European tourists who get lost in the labyrinth in Crete where the minotaur has begun to make a comeback. It is really an extended morality, but written artlessly in the style of a detective story. Guilt, Superstition, The Good Life, all appear as ordinary people; a soldier on leave, a medium, an elderly married couple (Trueman), a young unfledged pair, a missionary. I have deliberately chosen that most exasperating of forms, the situation novel, in which to write it. I wonder what you'd think of it. I knocked it off in a month in order to hold my depression at bay. I've been down low, very low; Gipsy has been a life preserver. Hoping to take her along to Rhodes with me. Would you like me to get you a little villa?

Now, something vastly more interesting. I have unearthed some facts about a cabalistic group, direct descendants of the Orphics, who throughout European history have been quietly at work on a morphology of experience which is pure Pythagoras. There are about six or seven in the Mediterranean area. They teach nothing;

they assert nothing; they do not even correspond; they are pre-Christian adepts. I am going along to see Mr. Baltazian one of these days to find out all about the circle and the square. He is a small banker here. What they have to say is interesting: the pure symbol, which is non-formulable in the rational sense. You have to grow the extra-sensory awareness of the symbol and accommodate it in your experience—not express it. It is not esoteric—it just doesn't make sense unless you are it. I'm using all this stuff for my Book of the Dead, which I suppose we'll have to do in Paris once again. It is a calculus of pure aesthetic forms, a game like a heavenly chess; it brings out the meaning of the Tarot and all kindred morphologies. Maybe I shall appreciate enough to become one of them and fall into "the silence of the present" in my old age. Ah, but the purity of the symbol—I am just beginning to see it as the extension of the field of concepts—it is something so rare and so pure that one is dizzy. I think I have mastered the first two thought-forms, whose "contemptible" representation are the circle and the square. It is very exciting. It is as if everything to date had taken place on the minus side of the equation—with the intention of producing One-ness.

THE MINUS SIDE	THE PLUS SIDE: PURE FORMS

THE ONE

	I II III IV
All human searching for perfection as strain or disease, all concepts from Tao to Descartes, from Plato to Whitehead aim at one thing: the establishment of a non-conscious, continual	You enter a field or laboratory of the consciousness which is not dangerous because it is based in repose. It does not strain you because having passed through the impurities of

STATE or stasis: a point of cooperation with time. In order to nourish conceptual apparatus, moralities, forms, you imply a deficit in the self. Alors all this WORK or STRIVING—even Yoga—aims at finding Rest or relaxation in time. It aims at the ONE.

WHAT HAPPENS AFTER THAT IN THE FIELD OF PURE REPOSE?

the ONENESS OF EVERYTHING, you are included in Time. NOW FORMS EMERGE. Because "contemptible" numbers are the only way to label them, you can say 1st State, 2nd State, 3rd State, like an etching. This is what I have called THE HERALDIC UNIVERSE. You cannot define these forms except by ideogram: this is "non-assertive" form.

THE HERALDIC UNIVERSE

Needless to say I have not yet passed through the ONE from the minus side. If I had I wouldn't be able to conceptualise it all this way or label it THE HERALDIC UNIVERSE as I do. But it is like a giant game of chess with the heavens; it is another version of THE REAL.

Now what does art do, dear brother Henry? Art makes sudden raids on the inarticulate—across the border from minus to plus. And so you find in the form of sculpture, or the shape of a poem, a preserving Heraldic structure sometimes which puzzles both maker and enjoyer. Art is bad because it uses the will to do this. Hence the strain and pain of the contemporary artist. Rimbaud, etc.

But this cell, this cabal, has been quietly working away for over a thousand years at pure apprehension. Meanwhile the rest of the world, artists, saints, everyone has been aspiring to the One. These people, then, are the magicians of the new age. We are learning the inner silence. It is not, as some say, that we have potentialities which are stunted or undeveloped; there are new functions which we grow . . . But enough of this.

Glad you like the little essay; wish I could have done better. A slightly more tightened form is probably going to *Horizon* in England.

All good wishes for the new adventure. I shall be after writing you an epithalamion and all one of these fine afternoons.

love,
larry

Big Sur, California
May 28, 1945

Dear Larry:

Got your last Heraldic Universe letter the other day, with water colors on back and front, and the Cabalistic plan of the Ancients. Also, immediately thereafter came the Groddeck book and your Poems from Faber. Everything looks exciting. Have only dipped into things. More of this later . . .

Meanwhile another letter from Girodias (young Kahane). Says he is thinking of bringing out new editions of all my books (10,000 each) in English, and wants rights for French translations. Things are booming there. Monies impossible to send until international agreement is settled. His accounts are in a mess—due to the occupation, etc. Meanwhile letters, inquiries, from other foreign publishers. There will be a flock of these. Have you an agent in London? Better tell him to get busy for you. I think you could be translated now into a half dozen languages at least. And what's about Arabic? Wouldn't you like to see *The Black Book* in Arabic? I would!

About Rhodes . . . are you serious? A villa? Do I want it? Sure. But how to get there these days? No visas, no passports for a year or more. What news from Jerusalem? Are we selling there? We once had a market there,

204

do you remember? Now we must open Saudi Arabia and Afghanistan.

I'm writing Katsimbalis and Seferiades of course—instanter. I'm writing everyone wherever peace has been restored. I seem to be communicating with the whole world. Peace! It's wonderful! Best to Gipsy. Send more photos of her and of yourself. More about the squalor of Alexandria, the fleshpots, etc. Had a card from Fred, from the Dôme, Paris, on V-Day, where he went to celebrate. Says everything was just the same, lovely as ever. Can you beat it?

Henry

———◆———

WITH the European war ended, Durrell is liberated
from his Egyptian prison and free at last to return
to Greece—to Rhodes this time where he edits three newspapers in three different languages and leads the life
described in *Reflections on a Marine Venus*. Here he finds
real peace. "Like a little limbo, twelve lovely islands in
a sea of political unrest." But he is all too painfully aware
of horror and starvation on the mainland.

This is a productive period for Durrell. Faber and Faber
publish *Prospero's Cell* and a volume of poems, *Cities,
Plains, and People*; Tambimuttu publishes *Personal Landscape* ("the Egyptian anthology") and *Cefalu*; Durrell
himself prints a few elegant private items on his own
press.

In Big Sur Miller is equally productive, indeed an international publishing enterprise, with every letter full of
new schemes. He engages George Leite, editor of *Circle*,
to bring out an American edition of *The Black Book*
(which never materializes—the book is not to appear in
America until 1960, after several publishers have under-
taken and abandoned its publication) and urges Durrell
to get in touch with his Italian publisher, among others:
"Wire him! Flood him! and send him photos of yourself.
With one of your inimitable wizardrous letters giving
landscape, fauna and flora."

Life in Big Sur is anything but peace and solitude now.

207

Miller is constantly besieged by pilgrims. Several major changes take place in his life : he becomes a father, a landowner, and suddenly, a rich man—though only temporarily, until the devaluation of the franc.

*   *

Henry,

I have just got back after ten days in Rhodes which is lovely rather in a Corfiot way, with Turkish mountains backing the skyline and the sea hushed and blue. The Italians have a great reputation as restorers and so on, but really they are super perverters of scenery. This tiny island is a mass of little nooks, artfully cornered off with walls and gardens and splashed madly with purple bougainvillea—a little too conscious. Meanwhile the imposing waterfront lacks a single taverna or fruit stall. Dull-faced public buildings, each on a huge scale, face the sky in a mock-medieval manner. Theatres too big to hold anything at all, modern cinemas and law-courts on a Roman scale. Here a superstructure of Italian officials live a heavily upholstered life in steam-heated apartments converted from medieval buildings. Charming, charming, you repeat, but what a white elephant for a poor state to inherit. The poor Greek patters about in clogs or bare feet and wonders what the hell it is all about. Why, the lavatories actually work and the phone. There is a decorative order and prettiness which must drive him crazy. Of course all this will last about a week after the Greeks get in. Then the pig-sties and confusion will begin.

I am not sure I'm going yet, so when you write please do so to the above address. Our Egyptian anthology is out and I've asked Tambimuttu to send you on a copy; also Groddeck has been sent. Hope you enjoy him, particularly his refusal to write professionally and his Heraclitean adaptation of Freud which makes organic sense of the discoveries as a system, instead of a mechanistic attachment to Victorian physics. Ach, I can hardly express myself any more. I've got a book brewing but it will take time. Somehow I must escape from this nightmare of working for a living. But it feels like the stubborn end of an epoch, and the new world refuses to get born. I'm sick to death of uniforms and idiocy.

More soon,

Larry

Public Information Officer, MOI, BMA, Rhodes, Dodecanese
[Fall 1945]

Not exactly Governor of these twelve islands, but damn near. I have just been up to Leros, Cos (a lovely Epidaurus kind of island), and Simi. Am living in quite a barrack of a hotel on the sea-front getting ready to enjoy my first Greek winter for six years; can't tell you what a feeling of a cloud lifting to get out of Egypt. I face everything equably now, even the burden of producing a couple of hundred quid to get the divorce cleared off. I've been working like a beaver.

Prospero is out and a copy is coming to you. It will bring back many old memories, I hope, with its portraits. Theodore and Spiro, etc. Too bad you never met the great Zarian or old Dr. Palatioano, a fine mythological old man on whom I modelled the count. He had the skull of his mistress on a velvet square before him on the writing desk; liked holding it up to the light and talking to it.

Now, my dear Henry, I am sitting in this charming medieval building with the hum of linotypes. My office is very lovely, built round a medieval courtyard and draped in bougainvillea. The Italian daily has been set up, the front page matrix of the Greek is finished, and the weekly Turkish is being censored. Gipsy with her seven languages is busy upon them now, looking charming black and smooth.

Ah Henry, Europe is so far upside down that it will take a few years to settle. I reckon we have five years before the atom war. Can't we all meet and create a little of the warmth and fury of the Villa Seurat days: a glass of wine and pleasant soft furry murder of typewriters going; Anaïs in her cloak and pointed ears; the letter to Nijinsky; Fred and Madame Kalf; Betty Ryan and Reichel. It is all fixed now inside like a kind of formal tapestry—you with the skylight open, typing in your hat, and little Joe unwrapping the cheese with delicate fingers murmuring "Ja Ja das ist gudt." And do you remember Mr Chu? And the chiropodist whose legs you cut off before throwing her in the Seine in No. 2 of *The Booster*. And Valaïda Snow? Have you a set of *Boosters?* And Herbert Read in the black muffin of a hat giving his young son an ice at the Deux Magots, and how you insisted on paying Chez Henriette to the acutely British discomfort of same? And how furious you were when you tried to sell *Booster* No. 1 to some bastard in a bar and he was insulting about it? And those long icy walks by the Seine with Anaïs in her cloak through the garish sulphurous ruins of the Great Exhibition into the Latin quarter to find the little street where Dante wrapped his feet in straw and where you found only the suicide Max? And those strange evenings on La Belle Aurore with Moricand the astrologer? And walking in the Louvre like mad angels? And the sudden scream that Soutine gave one night? Had he discovered another painting? And Fred writing letters to himself in that little dog-leg room, starving to death. And Edgar talking talking talking talking, his noble pure face caught up in a tic of anguish like a curtain pulled back. It was a complete finished little epoch. I remember the particular smell of the *Tropic* typescript, and the early novel you showed me. And lovely black little Teresa Epstein at the Closerie des Lilas. Hell, what are we going to put up against all that now that the war is over? I think Athens is a convenient mythopoeic centre, with Paris coming up all the time. Do you plan to return to Europe now you are a father? By the way, boy or girl? You will make a charming crazy father. Now of course that you've got a basic salary and are a free man you could I suppose travel without panic and pain. I've just lost the tiny private income I had.

Yesterday we went out in the big German office car, Romilly Summers, Eve and I, and walked right into the landscape carrying our food. Romilly is another old Greekite and adores the *Colossus*. We sat under a tree and drank red wine and talked about friends past and present and watched the blue whipping sea bursting against Turkey in great muffled blows, and the sinking crusts of islands northward. We talked about Xan Fielding, who was a secret service agent in Crete for two years, and nearly died countless deaths. His last escape: in Gestapo prison in France, due to die at six A.M. A Polish girl, his accomplice, managed to get on to the R.A.F. which BOMBED THE FRONT DOOR OF THE PRISON FROM LOW LEVEL AND KNOCKED THE WHOLE PLACE DOWN ABOUT HIS EARS, and he escaped. Ambushed in Crete many times on the end of a tommy gun. Finally his friend Paddy Leigh Fermor walked off with the German general in charge of Crete—fantastic piece of cloak and dagger like a bad novel. He writes from Kalimpong, Tibet, asking for news of you. I've given him your address. They were going to drop him in Tokio if the war hadn't ended. We talked of Seferis and Katsimbalis and the others. And we drank swingeing great draughts of wine and ate our bully and bread, and heard the slow clonk of sheep-bells and the wind in the olives. Something in this landscape talks to one —a sculptural utterance. Hush. Maillol is dead.

Well, Henry, that's all for now. Drop us a line when

the wind blows our way. When shall we be meeting
again? Soon I hope, in Greece or Paris, Tibet or Damas-
cus. It's all one. I belong equally everywhere now. Am
happy.

love,
larry

Big Sur, Calif.
Dec. 17th

[1945]

Dear Larry,

I just realize how close Christmas is and what a slim
chance this has of reaching you in time. For weeks I have
been carrying an envelope around addressed to you but
never a chance to write. Have been back and forth to San
Francisco several times. The baby was finally born, a
month late, at Berkeley—Valentin Lepska Miller. She's
a little beauty, an angel, and I'm madly in love with her.
Gives no trouble at all. Sleeps perpetually and hardly ever
cries. A real back-to-the-womber. Now in a few days we
move to another cabin. A dump by comparison, originally
a convict's shack. Like one of those photos you will see in
the *Nightmare* when you get your copy. I take it Porter
sent you a *Happy Rock*. Three more books coming out
shortly. A flood of books this year. This Paris thing looms
big, but I can't seem to connect with the money—no fault
of Girodias, however. If it comes to the worst, I'll invest
that money in a house and land in southern France. And
another later in Greece. I'll build here in the spring. One
must have a number of homes these days in case one is
bombed out. Nowhere does one hear of hope or optimism.
The whole thing is a shambles and a fiasco. It is getting to
be precisely as Spengler predicted, with Germany the
cancerous core.

213

Your last letter with the Paris retrospect knocked me for a loop. I intended to answer immediately. Fred is now en route for Germany, working for our UNRRA, I believe. I sent you a few books the other day—wonder if they'll ever reach you. Do let me know, because I can send lots more.

Those post-cards from Rhodes excite me enormously. You must indeed be happy now. And how does Gipsy like the change of scene? I wonder when in hell we will be able to travel. Still no hope. And the news of conditions abroad is appalling. No infant could survive the change of scene and diet.

It's glorious to hear that you are on the last lap of the labyrinth book. You seem to have a bagful up your sleeve. I haven't done a stitch of real writing in eight weeks. But with the move we now make everything is set for work. I have a little studio near the house, made from a horse shed—like one of Van Gogh's habitations. Am delighted with it. Made of driftwood and corrugated iron. Am going to start fishing soon from the back porch. Will send you photos shortly of the interiors of both places.

Have just been reading Krishnamurti—*Ten Talks*. Will try to get you a copy, think it will interest you. Expect to visit him very soon. He is about 150 miles away.

In the next few days I'll make you your Christmas present—a water color which I have long promised you. You will see if I have made any improvement. Probably not.

To think that I have over 3,000 pounds waiting for me in Paris and can't touch it—what irony! When I pay the mail man today for food, kerosene, laundry, etc., I will have left exactly six dollars and some cents. But I never worry about the money problem. It always comes when I need it. I could write a wonderful luminous essay on Desire. Desire versus Craving.

Merry Xmas! And to you too, Tiny Tim!

Henry

HENRY

HAPPY NEW YEAR FOR YOU THREE. Your latest letter
is written while waiting for the baby. By now the little
titan will be born. What is it, boy or girl? Do you enjoy
it, the nappies and the sun treatment and the fuss? I think
you will. I did after the first week. As good as having a
new book out. Books grow in the same way and shed teeth
and walk and sing.

Talking of books I've just been reading the last you
sent me—*Saturday* or *Sunday After the War*. Terrific
stuff. I've been adding to my notes on you and am publishing the "Happy Rock" essay in England—twice as
long as the original. I am not putting in any more personal material, never fear, just criticism and comparison.
You and Freud emerge as the great giants of this epoch.
It is very hard to write about a great man you know easily
and fluently, to give the feeling of a man who is producing the work of a genius. The tendency is to pay an exaggerated attention to the way he talks, smokes and walks,
as if they were any different from the way a hundred other
people behaved. Or else to exclaim with wonder that the
man is just a simple guy after all, like you and me—the
way the press treat the king.

I've just come back from PATMOS where Gipsy and I
spent Christmas with Father Porphirios. A little white
island, crowned by the battlemented monastery with its
white walls and strange turrets—like something built by
Genghis Khan. Shattering whiteness and play of light.
Like stepping into the silver of a mirror, or into the heart
of a crystal. From the reception room you look out and
everywhere islands in a glittering sea, like loaves of dark
bread. While we were sitting talking to the Abbot and

eating the fine lunch he had prepared for us the sky slowly darkened, swelled, became bitumen grey and then black with clouds, the sea like a lake of pitch. It was like a chapter from the Apocalypse. Then the rain broke green from rents in the cloud, breaking open pencils of light which played on the darkness like the beam of searchlights in close focus. Strange moving pencils of green rain racing across the sea like fingers. And thunder struck out of the silence, like a huge metal gong, and the Abbot had his voice cut off—as though his tongue had been pulled out by the roots. A marvellous mysterious haunted island. You must visit it. You approach it along a dark waterway of broken rocks like teeth and fur, like the white breast of a sail, you see the sugar loaf mountain with its white crown. Can't tell you what an impression the visit made on us. Beyond words. Wonderful library of ancient MSS scrolled and illuminated with dragons and horned heads.

HURRAH, JUST GOT YOUR LETTER. SO IT'S A GIRL!!! WHOOPEEE! Many many congratulations to you Henry. I see the glorious future opening like a peacock's studded tail. I guess you earned it with every breath you've drawn. I must design the child a porringer at the local pottery.

This job is going to fold up on us in a little while and heaven only knows what the future may bring. I just signed contracts for the labyrinth book in USA and England. Finishing the fucking thing at top speed. What a life! My total takings will go down the hungry throats of the lawyers. Never mind. I feel the big happiness advancing with cat-like tread upon me—the superlative silent murdering panther in its spotted coat, crouching to spring. Skoal!

larry

Dear Larry,

Had no chance to write you last few weeks due to moving. Address still the same, however. Only now I am at the ocean, right over it, writing you from a little hut which is my studio, the first real isolated studio I ever knew. It's marvelous. Nothing but sky, ocean and cliffs and mountains. Waves pounding under my feet—like dynamite.

What I think of today is this . . . Bern Porter is now publishing a book I wrote to Emil Schnellock in a printer's dummy, by facsimile process, called *The Waters Reglitterized*. It's a wonderful process and the book will probably sell for $3.00 instead of $25.00 as we once thought. I thought of the one I wrote to you, and one to Seferis. Wonder if they are still existent, and if you would care to let me get them reproduced in the same way? Anything I put out now sells. Maybe you have something of your own you would like done this way— you have a beautiful hand and beautiful illuminations in margin.

I was showing your postcards the other day to Angelino Ravagli who now lives with Frieda Lawrence. They are spending the winter here at Big Sur, took over a sort of medieval castle by the sea with some other friends of ours. Frieda is a wonderful person. We get on famously. She said to me once, "If only Lawrence had known you when alive. You would have been the very friend he was looking for." (I wonder.)

I am expecting any day now to get a two-acre piece of land from a neighbor at a cheap price—magnificent site on a high hill, overlooking everyone. Couldn't ask for a better home site. If I succeed, I will start building this

217

spring. Then if you want to come to America, we can put you up. I will try to build a guest house too. But think long before you decide to come to America. The novelty will wear off soon. Creature comforts you can have, but nothing else. You will dry up here in no time. I feel that Europe or Africa or China or India—any of these is better than America with her creature comforts. But if you want to make a visit merely, fine, any time. How good I am as sponsor I don't know. I think one has to have money in the bank for that. But we could think up some people who have when you are ready for it.

Will write oftener now, I hope. Am all set in my new quarters, and have a secretary for the fan mail correspondence! The letters have weighed me down. I am swamped. Alors, cheerio! Happy days are coming. I am deep in Rimbaud.

Henry

Am now exchanging water colors for wonderful art books and music records. What luck! Am getting everything the heart desires. How is little Gerald? Does he continue to write? And your sister Margaret?

MOI, BMA, Rhodes, MEF

[February 1946]

Henry my dear:

I have just spent a week in Athens and am still bewildered by the warmth of my reception there, both from those I knew, and from all those unlikely people whose existence I had forgotten: the Institute porter, a girl student, the kiosk man from whom I bought the paper and a pack of cigarettes every day, Andrew in whose little bar we drank so often. For the first day I was in a whirlwind of embraces and tears and kisses. And most wonderful of all, most mysterious, was that Athens was under deep snow: purple and bistre shadows under the Acropolis, steamy breath of oxen and men. I walked beside the Colossus in a daze listening to his great voice filling in the span of years that had separated us with stories of all they had passed through. Neither Katsimbalis nor Seferis have changed—though the world has changed a good deal round them. Athens is unbelievably sad, crowded, ill-housed, with money practically worthless and prices soaring; and yet in some singular way what they have gone through has made them gentle and friendly and sympathetic to each other as they have never been before. Even in George, behind the tremendous effervescence, you feel a repose and resignation—as of someone who has faced death in his imagination for a long time, so that it has detached him from the ordinary life—which is only after all the joy of expectation. Yet the stories are more wonderful than ever. When I next write I will tell you the story of Palamas' funeral—at which George suddenly shouted insults at the German embassy representative who was laying a wreath on the tomb, and began to sing the national anthem, then forbidden under pain of death. "Like a man in a nightmare . . . yes . . . ten thousand people . . . no one would sing . . . my voice broke on the top notes . . . eyes bulged . . . finished the first verse alone amidst a terrified silence of the crowd . . . I was trembling all over . . . Aspasia trying to shut me up . . . Seferis' sister pulling my arm . . . I felt as if I had gone mad, quite mad . . . Terrific hush in the crowd and everywhere people whispering, 'By God, it's Katsimbalis . . . it's Katsimbalis . . . ' I started the second verse alone . . . not a voice raised to help me . . . German looking round angrily . . . felt like a drowning man in the middle of that huge crowd . . . Then over opposite me saw a fat Corfiot friend of mine . . . fat man but a big rich voice . . . He joined in and we finished the second verse together. . . . Then suddenly as if you had thrown a switch the roar of the crowd took it up and we sang it with tears running down our faces. . . ." Of course after this demonstration George was in danger of being shot and was terrified for some time. His description of hiding here and there is very funny. And of course there are other wonderful stories. But I feel that in some peculiar way Athens is very sad and exhausted at the moment. Write to George Katsimbalis, care of the British Council, Kiphissia Road, Athens, and to Seferiades, Political Adviser to the Regent, The Regency, Kiphissia Road, Athens. Send them books, any and every kind. And if you have a few pounds from time to time send it to George to use at his own discretion to help Greek poets: many of them are starving, Sekilianos among them. I saw the little captain Antoniou too—he has been through it, though he is as silent and smiling as ever. I'm afraid you will have to give Athens a year or two to settle down politically etc. before you can think of going there. But keep in touch and don't be worried if they don't write; they are working sixteen hours a day and meet only rarely. But the intellectual hunger is terrific.

I see your reputation is riding higher and higher these days; glory in your well-deserved security, your studio, infant and secretary; hope the new books follow through. You have a tendency to splay rather these days, which is perhaps the influence of the US. But the *Sunday* book is a big gun; the sound follows the flash. I would like to see the latest two big books. Are they finished? No time for more. Must work.

Love to you three,
Larry

[1946]

Dear Larry—

If I don't write you this minute I never will. Have been putting it off for weeks because I had so much to tell you. So much to answer. Your letters are marvelous, the only decent messages I get. But my nose is kept to the grindstone receiving unwelcome visitors, answering stupid bores. You'd think I was the Dalai Lama! I can find no rest, no peace. No hide-out. They track me down like sleuths. All wanting advice or encouragement—sometimes just to touch me. I feel as though I were on exhibition. I ought to be in a cage on permanent view. This is the result of writing in the gnomic aorist (first person historical singular). It's become such a problem that I am growing desperate.

So you still look to America with loving eyes. Well then, come and see it. I'll give you six months to get a bellyful of it. Perhaps less. Perhaps six weeks. Here you will see how meaningless is the full larder, the full wardrobe. You have never seen the desert—wait till you see America.

On the other hand I realize how terrible it must be to live without. Sans tout, no doubt. Frightful. When you say Katsimbalis and Seferis are locked in gloom, that means things are truly unbearable. But I'm afraid it will get more and more that way. No visibility yet. More catastrophes.

I've been getting all your books and brochures. Seems like you must have your own private press there. *Cities, Plains, and People* came too. Book fell open right on page about H.M. and Rimbaud! It's a beautiful volume. So was the Parthenon one. And then those wonderful photos from Patmos—and you and K. strolling down the open street. K. looked so trim—as if the war had done him good. I must write him and Seferis too—but when? I can get nothing done these days.

I am still sending you books. Hope you get them. And an occasional MS. Did you ever get *Quest?* or the MS (2 parts) on Rimbaud? Use anything you like. *The Black Book* is at the printers still. Due out very soon though. Is George Leite going to publish anything else of yours here? Is Girodias (Paris) doing the translation of *B.B.* or any other of yours? He should, by God. But the censorship is strict there now—for the French versions, at least. He had to cut five pages of *Capricorn* at last moment or face the police. No more houses of prostitution in Paris. This is all the work of the Leftists, I feel. *Purity. Castration. Work. Paradise.* A.D. 9,560,434,009 or until the next atomic bomb.

By the way, I am doing a book with a Palestinian painter, Bezalel Schatz—an art work. Won't be finished for six months.

Groddeck—yes, I promise. Soon! I have always a dozen or more books stacked up to read—for duty's sake, by request, etc. Maddening. Now and then I sneak one over and read something for my own pleasure—like a convict. One of these was Ramuz' *The End of All Men* (*Présence de la Mort*). Glorious. Trying to get a copy for you.

Girodias came across with a partial sum of 300,000 francs. Not bad. Made $2,000. Gone the day I got it. Buying land, me boy. Hope to build an anchorage here. Then get out and travel—by rocket plane only. We now have a plane which flies from Los Angeles to Paris in 12 hours. $240 for a passage. Cheap, I'll say. China in about 18 hours, I believe. About same price. Like this I'll be seeing India and Tibet after all. And coming home for breakfast, be Jasus!

222

My warm greetings to Gipsy. So glad you were able to smuggle her out. Have you seen the ghost of John the Revelator? What do you know—of interest—about J.C.'s life between the Resurrection and the Ascension?

I hope to write again soon. Am with you always. Cheerio!

Henry

MOI, BMA, Rhodes, Dodecanese Islands
May 20, 1946

Dear Henry:

Things are slowly getting into focus—but with a deathly slowness. We live in an atmosphere of privation, spiritual as well as physical; and from all over Asia and Europe the famine reports are pouring in. It's hard to feel anything until you've seen the effects of the war. It's lucky you have been spared them. Athens would make you weep: smashed currency, labour shortage, dearth of raw materials, hunger, syphilis, and the ruin of the common man. Only the rich still glitter. Sorry to harp on these things but they are all one has to think about—unless you think that existentialism provides more than an intellectual fillip on an empty tummy. One learns too. I have learned a great deal about the way society is put together, the dependence of the money in the bank on the tin of beans in the window, of the relations between price and quantity. It is interesting really to plunge into the economics of the world—like examining the entrails of a favourite whore that has been cut in half by rocket-fire. A world dies like a human being. The look in its eye is the same. You catch fragments of it behind Katsimbalis' stories, Seferiades' despair, and the screams of the mad patients in the hospital across the way. It is possibly good for one as an artist. I feel terribly strong, and *light* and prepared to help on all fronts at once. For it's false that the work of art doesn't have an effect on every corner of the body politic. It even brings down the price of bread, or at least offers the staff of life as a substitute.

Apropos the existentialists—there is, it seems to me, one terrible metaphysical flaw in the whole Sartre thesis. The lack of CRISIS. The only justification for the art of *stasis* which is XXth century art is in the precipitation of crisis. The crisis in the drama precipitates the crisis in the audience—and thus the cathartic principle of change of stance—the reborn self. This is missing in these boys, I think.

I am not very much at home among ideas after so long an absence, but I think this is a valid criticism. Bless you, in your high spirits, you won't care whether it is or it isn't. Incidentally, you may be glad to know that your book about Katsimbalis saved his life. He was starving when a friend of mine called Southam found him a job on the British Council because of the book. Now he has become the established raconteur of Athens and is much petted and admired by people who would have lacked the wit to see how wonderful he was if they had seen him only, but who treasure him through your eyes, as it were. The book is unpopular because you panned the English in it. My God, if they had a clue as to what I was preparing behind my facade of polite irony, they would be sending me to Mexico. I have done a little bit of the Book of the Dead, from the beginning this time. I am using Alexandria as a locale, and it comes out bold and strong in bright colours. I'm itching to have a few months free to devote to it. It aches me. As for style, I have developed a newish kind of prose—not surrealistic but gnomic. It is lucid and yet enigmatic—I think nearer to me as a person than I have got yet. (Christ, you will say disapprovingly, the conscious artist.) But I have had such a terrible gruelling in journalism that I developed a kind of horror of inessentials and am looking for a diamond-bright lucidity which will be QUOTABLE and MEMORABLE, not because of marvellous metaphors and bright lights, but because the thread of the EXPERIENCE shines through, as when you turn a tapestry round. It is something that you try after but in a very diffuse way; you carry about twenty tons too much supercargo. In *Murder the Murderer* there were whole passages which I would have cut. Where you really hit the jackpot is in the *Rosy Crucifixion* bits in *Saturdays After the War*. That is the greatest prose of the century, I think. And it's the strangest thing about the American genius—in this it resembles the Elizabethans more than we do—that it descends from over-exuberance to mannerism and cheapness very easily. If one isn't careful the man becomes a gramophone like Saroyan or Hemingway. And in the greatest Americans, Melville, Miller, Whitman et alia, one needs a mental blue pencil to run over the detours and excrescences. I think it's time, by the way, you published the first edition of *Tropic*, the big typescript I read once. It would be a revelation. A great book in a different way.

My dear Henry, ripeness is all. In a few months the clouds will have lifted and we'll be meeting again over the wine and grapes to get to grips again. Bless you, keep firing away; however it comes, it's like an electric massage for a dead world. A fountain running wine.

love,

larry

BMA, Rhodes, Dodecanese, MEF

[May–June 1946]

Dear Henry,

Have found a little house—half the size of Villa Seurat —in the Turkish cemetery here; lovely spreading tree under which we have our meals; near the sea too but hidden in foliage. Here I hope to rest off and gradually pull the strings together. Dimarras and his wife are here for a holiday; extraordinary how the sufferings of the occupation have refined people. Everyone's nerves are weak, and their hair greying, but there is a kind of fragile tenderness and love between people that there wasn't before; friends cling to each other's hands when they talk, and husbands and wives keep little protective holds on each other's elbows or sleeves—like people who have been too long in dread of losing one another. Everyone still has a stupefied shocked look—you see the rows of corpses round Bukarest Street if you look into their eyes. Katsimbalis' description of the dying lining the roads in the snowdrifts crying "I'm hungry; I'm hungry" is terrifying. I'm afraid Greece faces a famine as bad as '41 next year unless someone helps out. Ach! This preoccupation with food. You must be sick of it. So am I. Dear Henry, keep writing like a furnace and do a few extra lines here and there for me, and the rest of us who won't be able to get back to our typewriters for about another year and a half, or perhaps two years. I send you some spring pictures of Eve and me at Monolithos—the great stone hump in the west of the island where the crusader boys built a fine fort but had to walk miles for water. We were wise. We took our own—and very little got into the wine.

Love,
Larry

Big Sur
7/26/46

Dear Larry—

If I don't pen a little word this minute I'll never write you. I've been meaning to for weeks, ever since I got your good messages (always the wizard!) and those photos and posters showing Gipsy in her most alluring guise. What a beauty! I like the one in the restaurant—so natural, so sincere. How I wish I were sitting there with you. (The decor gave me the impression of eating in a maison close.)

It's an infernal activity here, where one really ought to sit and meditate. A continual va-et-vient. New day, new faces, new problems. Never a decent interval of peace and solitude.

But I am getting more and more determined to take a short trip around the world—by plane—which will permit me to visit you at Rhodes, see Fred in Frankfort, gaze wistfully at the Villa Seurat, listen to the storytellers in Dublin, kiss the Blarney Stone, meet the critics in Oslo, Stockholm and Copenhagen, and so on. The new home, half paid for now, we will occupy before winter comes, I do believe. From this vantage point in the clouds I hope to dash forth now and then and get a view of the great world dying in ruins. I will soon have finished with everything but *The Rosy Crucifixion*. When I look at the list of titles I feel I deserve a vacation. Fortunately I write so that death can interrupt at any moment. The biographers will do the rest.

The baby is a girl, didn't I say? Little Valentin—very gay and healthy, and full of vital energy. Just beginning to walk and talk—8 months old. I hope she will always remember Big Sur. Such a great place to be born in. (If I sound Irish it's because I've been rereading Synge and others. How I love, after 25 years, *The Playboy of the Western World*.)

Well, this is more of a scratch than I thought I'd be able to write. I'm going to write Tom Hopkinson, London (*Picture Post?*), to see if he would finance a quick trip around the world. Connolly says I can fly to Shannon in one hop. I suppose 12 hours or so. Christ, we can fly to China in a day now. *Why aren't we flying?* I could be with you in three days—if ever I found the means to do it. It makes one's scalp itch. How I would love to see Patmos through John's eyes. (I think Lawrence was cock-eyed about the "Patmossers"—*Apocalypse*.)

If you feel old I must then be hoary with age. No doubt we all look much different. These seven years were no ordinary seven years.

You know, the more one thinks about the fucking stink bombs they're inventing, the jollier it all seems. If Augustine revelled in the destruction of Rome, how we will revel when the whole works is blown up! Then it *will* be an adventure to find one another. We may have to learn to swim like dolphins, fly like eagles, roost like the hens, *etc*. (The "et cetera" is important, as I said somewhere once before.)

All my love to you both. Keep it harmonious this time. You ought to be well mated.

Henry

MOI, BMA, Rhodes, Dodecanese, MEF

Sept. 25, '46

Dear Henry and Lepska :

Just got your long letter—realise from it that being a public figure isn't all jam. You will have to take a rest from your admirers. Still it's better than being unknown, I guess—though I wonder whether *The Booster* days were not FREER and HAPPIER all round.

Things have been marvellous here. One is only wondering how long it's going to last. Have moved into Villa Cleobolus at last : two rooms, studio and bedroom, bathroom and kitchen. It is smothered in trees which curve over it, and as you enter the gate the gloom of dense oleander branches envelops you. I can't tell you what wonderful peace and quiet it is, having a house of your

228

own after so many years living from suitcases in hotels, or sharing flats with awful people. We have breakfast under a sycamore tree off pottery which we cast and painted ourselves at the local pottery. Life at times begins to get its old prismatic hue.

I am casting about in my mind for the form for a verse play about Sappho—dealing with the problem of action and non-action: taking war as simply one of the types of destructive action since the EGO was let loose on the world . . . The great "I will" . . .

I don't know what is to become of us. My job ends with the handing over of these islands; there will be a British Council here but I don't think they'll give it to me. One says glibly "starve"! It's hard to starve.

Meanwhile I am slowly like an earthworm scribbling out bits from the next BIG book. I'm completely in the dark. I've got a mass of confused colouring and some wonderful people to play with. Need a little detachment from these vulgar cares. By the way, there's a piece of yours I want to read and can't find anywhere: "The Alcoholic Veteran with the Washboard Cranium." If you have an old carbon do send it over.

Meanwhile we are all screwed down here waiting for the atom bomb. . . . How long do you give it? The results at Nagasaki, as published in the British white paper, were fascinating. Complete sterility the most interesting. Now read Groddeck's chapters on all human creations symbolising unconscious desires. We are able to set a positive term to the life of the human race. It's a great relief. I was afraid they were going on like this forever.

I'm hoping to go to Athens with Eve next month and show her round; but to judge by the present disorders it will be wiser to stay here.

Love to you both. . . . Stay in USA another few years. . . . You don't know what it's like. . . . You can't. . . . I didn't until I left Egypt, which must be rather like the US is, fat, well-off, selfish, self-seeking, etc.

Larry

Dear Larry,

This time I answer on the nose—otherwise it's never. First, notice the enclosed letters. I am taking care of Spiro's son—food, money, clothes. Moricand turned up in Switzerland. Desperate, of course. But alive. And Reichel writes now and then. Now I no longer have any old clothes, nothing but what I absolutely need. How can the war-torn world be salvaged? It's beyond me. The little all of us who have can give is a drop in the bucket. It makes one despair.

Girodias, after sending me about 4,000 dollars, now says he owes me ten thousand more. Which I will get peu à peu, of course. I've got the house and land almost paid off—will be in the clear in a month or so. That's something. This place will have to be my Tibet, pro tem. It's got everything but—the essential. I have to supply that.

Since *Cities and Plains* no books of yours have come. Do send them, no matter how bad. How can you be bad, even if you write a bad book? *The Black Book* is still at the printers, I believe, but due out any day now. Hope Leite sent you the latest *Circle*, with your work "up front," as Saroyan puts it. I am going to send you a heap of books in a day or two—have been putting them aside for you. Suppose you still read voraciously, no? I get books flung at me from all sides and of course never read them. The ones I want take me years to get. I seem only to want what is unavailable.

These photos you send always get me. I do a riff, or

take a riff, when I see them. And your Eve (Gipsy, I suppose) is such a wonderful looking person. How lucky you are!

Capricorn is now in the 45,000th copy! Girodias, Gallimard and Denoël will all be brought to trial in a few months for publishing French versions of the *Tropics* and *Black Spring*. A real shindig! Meanwhile the books are selling like wild fire. I have over 200 clippings from French reviews and literary weeklies. A tremendous furore. They now talk about "Le Cas Miller," as they talked once of the Dreyfus affair or the Baudelaire or the Zola cases.

I must confess I've never written Katsimbalis or Seferis. I don't know why. I don't know where to begin, I suppose, so much has happened, and what can I say that will lift them out of their despair? If only I could help them! But how? Everybody is asking me to sign affidavits, to help them get to America. I'm signing my head off, knowing all the while that after a few months of America they will want to be back in Europe, no matter how terrible the conditions.

Salut and blessings on you both,

Henry

I finally sold a water color to the Museum of Modern Art in San Francisco. Alors, I am hanging now! I think I have made great progress there.

MOI, BMA, Rhodes, Dodecanese

[Fall 1946]

Henry:

I am inundated with them—books! You must be paying a fortune in postage. I only hope that you are not buying the books too—that they are review copies. I have just sent off a new book of poems; there's one in it I dedicated to you—a congenial theme, "Elegy on the Closing of the French Brothels." Coming out soon I hope in England. By the way, my first editions of *Cancer*, *Spring* and *Capricorn* have just arrived safely from Athens. I can't tell you with what emotion I riffled through them—little stubby red binding I had done in Corfu. With the dedications—Anaïs' fine hand and one of your rootin' tootin' blow-me-down dedications. I have just started and read you all the way through again. I think it's time someone did a serious critical essay on your prose; it has some very curious elements—quite new to prose, I think. For example the amount of double talk and non sequitur you indulge in is really incredible; it's the perfect packing for the image.

By the way, Theodore's book is out. It's called *Climax in Crete* and is a diary of the Cretan campaign where he was caught with his pants down; and it's really a marvellous mirror of his quaint temperament. Botany and parachutists go hand in hand. At the most critical moments, when all seems lost, the camp about to be rushed, bullets flying, he breaks off to observe, "I noticed with surprise a remarkable specimen of the flora tinctulitis growing by the road and took a specimen to press in my album. Flora tinctulosis, better known as verbena gladiola, is a low-growing mucilaginous musk-ox with little affinity to the flora of Crete . . . etc. etc." While I am on the subject of Crete, we have just had Xan Fielding through on his way to England—a lovely week. He was living in Crete for three years as a spy, you know—disguised as a shepherd. His adventures are really hair-raising. With him came a wonderful mad Irishman called Leigh Fermor who was also in Crete and who captured the German general commanding there, took to the mountains with him, and dodged the German army for 18 days before he was able to get the general to Egypt on a submarine! Really fantastic adventures. The two of them reading Dostoievski in caves! Being ambushed etc. etc. and reciting poetry all day long. Leigh Fermor is quite the most enchanting maniac I've ever met. Speaks five languages really well. We sat up in my churchyard till three every morning reading aloud. Can't tell you what a wonderful time I had talking books—first time for years. Xan is very keen on your work, and remembers vividly a meeting in Athens. Together we printed a little booklet of his poems here on the army press and this he is sending you from London.

Have you any objection if I turn the "Happy Rock" into a full length essay on your work for England—fifteen thousand words? And I don't mean a reportage about you—in order to praise the shit out of myself for knowing you—but something that would slug the English critics where they need it?

Send me a picture of the baby.

Love to you both,

Larry

The egoismus cult is very bad for young men. You should know, you've had a wicked effect yourself on the young in England. They think if they splash about in the bath it's interesting because it's THEM. Little do they realise what practice and technique and elision goes into making your free-and-easy effect. May I say that the first draft of *Tropic* was some 600 pages long and that had it been published as it stood it would have been a very near miss as compared to the bullseye you put out? In the essay I mean? I think I'm the only person who has read "Clipped Wings," the whole first draft of *Tropic*, and all Anais' diary.

Love,
Larry

233

Dear Larry,

Certainly you should go ahead and expand that article on me. Do you realize that you could write a fat book now —and *get paid for it?* True, no one of consequence has gone into the books themselves at length. Most stuff is sensational, newsy, chatty, gossipy, scandalous, etc. Which I loathe. They could get all the dope about me from my books, which as I allus says, are "autobiographical," but they seem to disbelieve.

I'm sitting in the new studio this morning and it's raining like hell here. It's an old garage, transformed. The house, one large room with a little annex for the baby, is quite simple and beautiful, almost Japanese in its austerity. I have 2½ acres, not five, as I once thought. And it's mostly hillside—but no matter. I bought the view— sea, wind, air, sky, stars, not land. Have enough to grow all the vegetables for twenty people—and by God, maybe we will begin doing that soon. This next war, which everyone expects, will see the demolition of all the big cities, all the arteries. We may have to be self-sustaining.

I asked *Town and Country* to send you the February issue with a text from the latest tome—*Remember to Remember*, Vol. 2 of the *Nightmare*, due out in April or May in book form. In it are three black-and-white drawings I made at their request, for which they paid me an extra $300. That means $550 in all. Several times I've suggested you try them—with prose perhaps—something of the Mediterranean world, Rhodes, the Apocalyptics, the nature morte, etc. You know—like your letters.

Céline is in Copenhagen, in prison there, I believe, and has lost 70 pounds. The French want to try him, and execute him, I suppose, but the Danes are trying to preserve his life. He says, "How could I be called a Fascist or collaborator? I despise the whole lot of you, no matter on which side."

Well, according to Man Ray, the existentialists and the surrealists are now about to join in battle. They are both ausgespielt, in my opinion. Two cadavers fighting a foolish fray, what! What the world wants, I find, is— coffee, sugar, grease and warm clothing. The ideological warfare is over. Russia and America are dividing the world between them.

Well, my love to Gipsy Eva, yourself, Cefalu, Patmos, that whole beautiful desperate world, which I would love so much to see. God be with you, and if it grows too desperate for you, why come over, but at your own risk. I don't recommend it. Except to fatten up.

Sending a recent photo (sans lunettes) by separate mail—"surface" mail, as they call it. Gave me a jolt to hear that word—means definitely we are in a new age. Cheerio!

Henry

The baby is now walking. She's adorable. Jabbers away in her own tongue—has the gift of gab, I see. Cyril Connolly paid me a flying visit recently. I suppose we'll read about it in *Horizon*. What he really came for, I think, was to see the last of the lost race of otters, which are off this coast. But he saw none—and showed his disappointment keenly.

FEBRUARY 1947—DECEMBER 1948

(Durrell in Argentina—Miller in Big Sur)

———◆———

THE correspondence is at low ebb in these postwar years: Miller is too harassed most of the time to write more than short telegraphic notes; Durrell is depressed—homesick for the Mediterranean and oppressed by the New World. He scarcely mentions his job with the British Council, or his lectures, which will emerge some years later as *A Key to Modern Poetry*. Chiefly he is turning over in his mind a critical study of Miller which he is never to write, probably for much the same reason that led Miller to abandon his book on D. H. Lawrence. Durrell also plots *The Henry Miller Reader* (the "Omnibus" referred to in these letters), which is not to appear till 1959. There is much talk of reunion, but that too must wait another decade. Meanwhile Durrell meets Perlès in the Highlands, and Miller spends his French royalties bringing Conrad Moricand, the astrologer friend from Villa Seurat days, to Big Sur, with the disastrous results chronicled in *A Devil in Paradise*.

Two comments here are noteworthy for the correspondence. Durrell, returning to Bournemouth for the first time in eight years, is surprised and delighted to find Miller's prewar letters in Alan Thomas' loft. About the same time Larry Powell, already a Durrell fan, becomes custodian of the Miller archives, including Durrell's letters. So Miller's remark is prophetic: "I have a feeling there will be reverberations from all this."

*   *

Henry:

In great haste. This week leaving for Egypt en route for England! Owing to a balls-up the job I wanted here hasn't materialised and I am attempting a transfer from the Foreign Office to the British Council. The idea is to get sent to Italy or France, but it is possible that I shall fall between two stools and get stuck in England. In that case I am going to make a bid for it and strike out for USA with Yve. Might even get over to see you. It would be fun! I'll let you know the moment I am certain. Meanwhile address me c/o Faber and Faber. Got married yesterday so at least am free to move. Money restrictions are killing them in England. Only allowed to take 75 pounds out of the country.

I find that journalism—even literary journalism—doesn't pay except in the USA. For England the best thing is books and more books. I am doing one on Rhodes. How didn't you get *Prospero?* I signed a voucher for it. Anyway I have sent Faber a telegram to send you one.

Too distracted to write more. Will write you from England.

Larry

52 St. Alban's Avenue, Bournemouth, England

[June 1947]

Dear Henry:

Just this minute laid down the phone and here comes your card. It was little Joe telephoning from Scotland, asking me to come on up. We shall meet next week. I shall take the night train up to Inverness. God knows HOW he lives right in the heart of Scotland like that. It'll be wonderful to see him again—how I wish you were going to be there.

What a meeting it would be. But listen, next week I go up for an interview with the British Council. It looks as though they are going to send me to SOUTH AMERICA. I don't know where as yet but will certainly let you know pronto. Perhaps we could meet in RIO? Could you make that? Wouldn't it be wonderful? Jesus, I'd love to see you again.

Henry, I've mapped out the book on you, scribbled out little sections. It looks good, balanced and lucid as well as full of fireworks. But there's one thing missing from the picture. I haven't seen any of *The Rosy Crucifixion* volumes except the extracts published in the two collections by New Directions. Are they available in typescript? Could you send me a flimsy—promise to return it. The essay on you is chiefly on the *Tropics*—that is your direct line of development. The Greek book, Rimbaud, the essays, *Hamlet*, are all peripheral really, though they give one clues and kicks in the pants, and some are terrific, notably "The Alcoholic Veteran" and "Reunion in Brooklyn," which are masterpieces of the first order. But your prose, to judge by the excerpt from *Rosy Crucifixion*, has undergone a radical transformation, has got rarefied and beaten out thin like gold, and unless I see a tidy chunk of this part of the saga I am in the position of someone trying to write about Proust who has seen only three of the seven volumes.

Apart from that one small thing needs to be done before I begin the book on you: I must walk through Paris again, along the Seine, the Rue Saint Jacques; I must revisit Villa Seurat and Zeyer's and the Closerie des Lilas, just once to recall it all and feel the current of Parisian life, which fed you, flowing again over the bridges.

Then another thing: could you give me permission to

quote from your work and letters in writing? Not for me but for the publisher who will do the book. They demand all these kinds of safeguards against future complaints. I promise you that you shall see the book in MS and delete anything you don't like, as well as comment.

I have been out of a job for a couple of months and using the time to try and make a little money from translations and various hack work. I send you a little essay from Rhodes which mentions you, and which seems to have been received here with some admiration and not a little irritation by the people I flicked over the rump.

England is really very pleasant, the easiest country in Europe to live in despite our groans. The Socialists have done a wonderful job on food distribution and price control. Though one is limited in everything, prices are lower than anywhere in Europe, and the distribution is equitable and just. People are hard up, but the old tag about the greatest benefit of the greatest number applies here more than anywhere else in the world. I am really very impressed and delighted. And civil liberties haven't suffered as in dictator countries. England and France are the hope of the future, I think—but haven't seen France yet.

Kahane was in London for a day but I missed him. I saw Eliot—gentle, sweet, now older, more grey and worn-looking, but very gentle and tired. He gives off a radiance now I didn't notice before—always felt he was like a senior civil servant. Dylan Thomas I missed—he is in Italy.

By the way, Gerald—you remember my youngest brother—has turned out a zoologist as he wanted and is leaving for Nigeria in September to collect wild animals and snakes for the English zoos. Margaret (who is married to an airman) sends her love. At present I am sharing mother's house with her until I know for certain what my plans are.

Curtis Brown told me that his New York office wrote saying that George Leite was broke and couldn't raise the funds to do *The Black Book*, so they have contracted with New Directions instead. I am sorry. I knew of course that he'd overshot the contract mark by about a year, but I thought he'd make it. However, if New Directions will do without loss to themselves so much the better. By the way, a correspondent from New York congratulates me on the production of "Zero" and "Asylum" by Circle—does he mean book form, or in the magazine? Have you seen a book around with the stories? If so I'd be glad of a copy. Haven't heard from Leite for several months, though I wrote him from here.

Reynal and Hitchcock are bringing out all my stuff in the States including poems, so at last I am fixed up. On principle and from long experience I avoid little presses and solo enthusiasts—and I'm always telling you to. They don't produce any *money* for one. And after one has had the fun of writing something, the next best thing is spend the money it brings on your girl.

Now Henry, don't feel obliged to write me : the occasional post card if you feel like it : I know how it is to be pestered to death by people : keep going on the big jobs and let us all go to hell.

Do you remember Spiro? Here is a picture of him cooking an eel with red sauce for Gerald, then aged about 12. The old car in the background. Just after this was taken the car was nearly carried away by the sea and we had to stand up to our waists in water and dig it out.

Love,
Larry

[1947]

Dear Larry :

A hasty scrawl in answer to yours from Bournemouth about article on me. I don't want to ship you the MS of *Rosy Crucifixion* for the reason that as it stands it is in the first writing, with not a correction and I may delete whole pages or sections when I get down to it. You are wrong, I think, to judge from excerpts you saw : there is every sort of style and treatment in the 750 pages I have written, and a good bit is diffuse, opaque, rambling, hugger-mugger. When it comes to the autobiographical narrative I really don't change much. Also wrong of you, I think, to consider *Rimbaud*, *Hamlet*, etc. as "peripheral." It's all one. If one lived long enough the whole man would come through in the work—ideas, sensations, experience, philosophy, aesthetic, and everything. Those *Tropics* warped the readers' minds. "Cannibalistic" I notice was used somewhere. Only the Anglo-Saxon would use such a word where frankness is concerned. Certainly you may quote from books and letters, but I do want to see the passages and approve, of course. You must also get permissions from the publishers for quotations from books, but that's almost automatic. I'll try to remember to send you a story of 30 pages I wrote expressly for the book Léger is to illustrate—about a clown named Auguste. Called *The Smile at the Foot of the Ladder*. Just had letter from Léger begging me to write something different, something in the vein of *Black Spring* or the *Tropics*. This is really different from anything I wrote. But doesn't indicate a new trend. All these "new trends and directions" which the critics discern with each new work—all this sort of apperception is false.

I'm writing Leite to send you *Zero and Asylum*—yes, beautifully done—amazed he didn't send you them.

I can't leave this place yet—too many entanglements of all kinds. It's all I can do to get to town (Monterey, 45 miles distant) when I have to. Always without a sou. And pressed on all sides. And now have to raise passage for Moricand to come here—he has his visa to travel. I do no work, nothing . . . just sit and plot how to beg or borrow. Frightful. Been going on for months—was never worse off, not even in those bad days in Paris.

Best to Gerald, Margaret and everyone. And more soon. This on the wing. Writing Joey tomorrow. Are you still in Scotland, I wonder? Alors, what by the clock?

Henry

52 St. Alban's Avenue, Bournemouth, England
July 9

[1947]

Henry:

For the first time in two months of business and travelling I've got a little spell of rest to tidy up my papers and write you a line. Seems that I shall be heading for Buenos Aires in August some time; rather looking forward to it. Propose to visit Paris for a month or so first, taking little Joe if I can. We have just parted after spending a week together in the wild highlands of Scotland, on the shores of a marvellous loch. We had our picture taken by the village photographer specially for you and sent it off, pronto.

Meanwhile I forgot to mention that the evening before we flew from Athens we had a little meeting, Katsimbalis, Ghika, and Seferis with Rex Warner, to listen to the marvellous reading on the disc you sent me. It was so strange in that quiet book-lined room to hear your burring voice reading out those long ghostly sequences from *Cancer;* I remembered Paris and Corfu. Sef and Katsimbalis had tears in their eyes. Finally when it got time to say goodbye I gave them the disc and they thanked me as if I had given them a portion of you, a hand or an arm, or a voice. I think of Seferis sitting there alone now listening to it and shaking his head with that sad smile as he repeats: "Ah Miller, Miller, what a fellow."

The next big thrill was seeing little Joe standing in the market place at Inverness, with his wrists up like a praying dormouse, bubbling and glugging like a child. It was a marvellous reunion. We set off for a sixty mile trip across the razor scarps of the Cairngorms or whatever the range is called to Ullapool in a crazy little car through a bleak bare countryside full of polished lakes and great trees. Needless to say, we broke down near a place called Garve and were stranded. However we finally made the Picks' house and found a terrific supper. A lovely bungalow by the water's edge in a bay not unlike Koloura in Corfu; great bare mountains all round and a still lagoon; some islands on the horizon. Sunlight—almost Greek in its bareness of line. All the trip I was remembering that other crazy trip we made to Sparta—through the great cloud that covered the mountain. Remember the green flashes of the Eurotas shining up through the cloud as we slithered down the mountainside?

Joe has changed—not in looks. And Henry, what an amazing change. He has become self-supporting, absolutely reliable, responsible, calm, unpanicky. A hundred times greater than the Fred we knew. Also (he says it is old age and is rather worried about it) he has learned what his physique is, how to handle it, how to take things calmly and easily, with frequent naps. He has become almost a little saint. "On the Path," he says sardonically. When we got to London we made a crazy disc for you which perhaps you will have received by now—just to let you hear our voices, though God knows it sounded quite crazy on the playback. Meanwhile Fred is much exercised about some money you have in France and is worried that you might lose it in the devaluation; hence our cable from Ullapool.

Joe aims to hang on here until his British passport comes through. Meanwhile he is okay for dough and is writing a book about the *Booster* episode in Paris, panning us all. I hope in South America to do the Book of the Dead. I have about 200 pages of material and a mass of notes. By God, it'll knock their eye out. I'm glad I've held off a while; every day increases my control and technique in the actual medium. I calculate that I can now write with fifty per cent less waste of energy and concentration than I could five years ago. Joe says that next year we must both come over and visit you in your Japanese grand lodge. But I'm wondering whether I couldn't fly up from Buenos Aires for a week or so and see you before.

All the best to Lepska and the babe,

Larry

I've found a whole bale of your letters in an old trunk which I thought lost. Marvellous reading. Have spent the whole morning re-reading them.

Big Sur
July 24th—6:00 A.M.

[1947]

Dear Larry,

What with the bombardment of cables, photos, postcards, and finally that incomparable disc (just played it last night), I couldn't sleep all night. Was up at daybreak 4:45 A.M. this morning, and out over the hills surveying the broad Pacific. Wish I could afford a cable to send you all my blessings. It was so wonderful to hear your voices, as though you were in the next room. (I never realized how foreign Fred's English accent was till now. Living with him I never noticed it. And that bloody French he threw in—*extraordinaire!*) Sure, you know I would have come a-running if I could. But it seems each one of us is being made to play his own part, go his own way, just at this moment. But the time for reunion is soon, I feel it— and even Edgar will be with us, then, and perhaps Reichel too. And of course Moricand. I just heard from him too yesterday, telling me all about that malevolent Pluto. He says this coming month of August will see some sort of diabolical conjunction, very similar to the set-up in August 1914 and September 1939. He can't be hinting at another war, can he? Maybe just a "crise" or a "craque"! Anyhow, and this will comfort Fred—it's his idea too— when it gets bad for the world (as it will next year, he promises), it will go good with me. And probably with you, and surely with Fred, who lives the miraculous life of the cockroach and the bedbug combined.

Now a word about the paintings. If I had those paintings here I could sell them. I am to have a show next month in Hollywood, at the Coronet Theatre, where our silk screen book will be exhibited. John Houseman (who started the Mercury Players with Orson Welles) is sponsoring it. But you'd have to work fast to get me them in time. On the other hand, if something can be done in Merrie England, fine! Breton wrote me some months ago that he was sending someone over to get them in order to exhibit them in Paris. But I suppose nothing came of it. There were, I thought, something like forty—right? Breton has about three or four, I think, for his show. Above all, see Breton—42 rue Fontaine, Paris (9). He has a copy of the silk screen book *Into the Night Life*, which you must see.

Well . . . so you may be going to South America! Or to Paris? Either way fine, I'd say. And if you can't, come to Big Sur. When I heard your voices I couldn't believe it was eight years since we last met. I remember vividly how I parted from you—in the rain up there in the mountains. Or how I parted with Katsimbalis. Partings, partings. Enough of them. More reunions, I say.

Cheerio and Toodle-oo!

Henry

c/o British Council, Lavalle 190, Buenos Ayres

[November–December 1947]

Dear Henry:

This is just to let you know we've arrived and that the address is O.K. This is a perfectly fantastic country, but then so is the whole continent. The interesting thing is the queer lightness of the spiritual atmosphere: one feels buoyant, irresponsible, like a hydrogen balloon. One realizes too that the personal sort of European man is out of place here: one cannot suffer from angst here, only cafard. So much is explained here about the American struggle, the struggle not to get de-personalized. Because this is a communal continent; the individual soul has no dimensions. In architecture, in art, religion, it is all community —skyscrapers, jitterbugging, hyperboles—it is all of a piece. I understand now why the American artist has no sense of form—because his soul is continually being siphoned off into the communal soda water fountain, and his struggle is to concretize it enough to suffer. In other words everybody is happy in a mathematical sort of way, and the huge skyscrapers of Rio when the jungle swallows them will be not unlike the fantastic Inca remains, the temples and altars they keep finding. The fury, the destructive fury which you inveigh against so much comes from the European soul trying to gain a slippery footing in this oxygenated air and getting panicky because nothing, nothing has any value here : break it, break it. All this is quite understandable the moment you hit Rio. But what sort of white ant's dream is the art of this continent? The Maya, the Inca, you can see the sort of thing which is possible; the rest is European panic, European guilt. But there is something quite new and strange about the atmosphere here. It is a spiritual vacuum flask. I am not sure Tao is not like that. Maybe the Indians can tell us? Have they said anything yet? Have they spoken? Human faces, clouds, the Andes, the pampas—it is all somehow unqualifiable in European terms . . . damn it, I'd better stop before I write a book about it.

I left Joe in rather a bad state of mind : his book had just been turned down, and he was rather worried as he is living on his writing. If you can send food parcels, coffee tea sugar chocolate etc., send him one. Also if you have a carbon of your projected *Black Book* introduction send it on because I am thinking of doing an English edition here later this year. We leave for Cordova tomorrow night for a two-month spell in the hills. Mails will be forwarded.

Love to you three,
Larry

Big Sur
12/19/47

Dear Larry—

Just got your first letter from under the Equator. Have written Nancy Leite to send you copy of my preface to *B.B.*, have none here. Will keep after it.

Am just reading Joey's MS now and laughing my head off. Didn't know it was turned down in England—too bad. Still some hopes here however. There are some wonderful sections in it.

I hope this reaches you during the holidays. A Merry Christmas to you and Eve! Expecting Moricand any day now. Maybe next spring you all and Joey and Edgar will get here for a reunion. If not, I may go to Paris. Waiting to see what this winter will do to Europe. Things couldn't be worse apparently. Nearing page 1,000 now of *Rosy Crucifixion*. And going strong. More soon. Cordova-in-the-hills sounds wonderful. Like your article on Rhodes and all the lost Colossi. What a traveller you are!

Henry

Had a strange warm letter from Somerset Maugham.

Big Sur
3/18/48

Dear Larry—

Do you see any chance down there to use my friend Moricand in some humble post—reader, translator, secretary or what? He can't adapt himself here—too rough for him, no comforts, and no possibility of work or even of getting his books published in translation. Everyone is now looking to South America as a refuge. Next war seems more and more imminent. I could arrange his passage by boat. He has a Swiss passport, speaks French and only a little English, but reads it quite well. Also a little German. Has a friend in Brittany trying to get him a post in Argentina in October—all hazardous, of course. Meanwhile he's a burden to us. Lepska is having another child in a few months. Place too small, etc. This is just a chance —one never knows.

Things seem frightful in Europe, worse than ever. And here not very good either. Another war and we will be finished too. I'm planting vegetables and fruit trees. Maybe I'll get cows, chickens and rabbits too—or peacocks!

More soon. Think of you always. Send picture postcards—of the future.

Henry

The British Council, Lavalle 190, Buenos Ayres

[March 1948]

Dear Henry:

Just a brief note to hope you are managing to keep on working despite the world situation which looks more like war every day. By the time we get back to Europe it will be about as interesting as the deserts in Texas. I think a very short war—say six months—could account for all the major cities of Europe—which means, of course, that Man is tired of city life as such. What sort of civilisation can follow? I don't know, but the answer lies with the USA, strange and hideous as such a thing may sound to you. Wyndham Lewis is writing a book called *America and Cosmic Man* which sounds interesting: sounds heretical to you perhaps, but then everyone loathes his own country and countrymen if he is any sort of artist—and this doesn't mean to say that I disagree with what you have written in the *Nightmare* book—au contraire. But I am thinking of the future. The other day I sent you off a plan for a Miller anthology—hope the idea appeals to you. It is better than nothing and you are publishing in such a fragmentary way that your great genius is not as widely accepted as it might be. You are considered a superlative "performer" merely. We have settled into a flat in Cordova—very dull town. Would you consent to visit Argentina as a travelling lecturer if I could get you invited? Three or four lectures only? It would be such fun to see you again. I haven't *talked* to a real person for so long I feel my speech organs are in a state of atrophy almost. What a noble beautiful monument to our life in Paris *Remember to Remember* is—one of your finest works. I've read it so often that I know it almost by heart. It's a gem! And how well I remember Joe coming out with that phrase! How we laughed! I have a new book of poems coming out and have done a real translation of *Pope Joan*.

Love to Lepska and the kid,

Larry

Argentina

[March 1948]

Henry:

Apropos Moricand, I was afraid that you would find it rather cramping. Glad to hear there's a second kid on the way. Not much of a world to get born into though . . . six months before the next war it looks like. Argentina for Moricand? I think it would be a disaster. Argentina is exactly like USA in 1890, full of tough go-getting tycoons fighting over the undeveloped riches. The weak are driven to the wall. The only menial jobs might be a job on an estancia, but you need physique and energy, and if M. speaks no English it would be a great handicap. Argentines know only Spanish and English. Surely there are a hundred astrological societies in and around Hollywood that would look after him. Theosophical Society? Why doesn't he try and become Paris correspondent of *The Astrologer?* You see, from the impression I had of him he is quite helpless—as a baby. And his only subjects astrology and literature, which as you know don't pay. It's an awful fix to be in. I do wish you calculated a bit before saddling yourself with learned but helpless people. What about French lessons? I'm afraid he would find B.A. worse. Climatically an inferno and morally the final circle of hell. Everyone with any sensibility is trying to get out of this place, including me. I think I would rather risk the atom bomb than stay on. It's so dead . . .

> Love,
> Larry

9/9/48

[Big Sur]

Dear Larry—

Just a word to let you know we have a son now, named Tony, born 8:35 A.M. August 28th at Carmel (hospital). Both home now and everyone happy. Father will now begin to recuperate. I left off my own work about 4 weeks ago—in middle of a sentence. Was going full blast.

Just heard from Joey—London. Says he's O.K.—had some little worries. He looks splendid—from photo enclosed. I'm getting thinner and thinner. Weigh 129 lbs. now.

Anyway, there has been much confusion here and more than the usual quota of visitors. Hence my inability to write or even try to.

I hope you and Eva are O.K. Joey says you'll be back in England soon again. I hope next spring to try going abroad—with the troupe.

> Henry

c/o The British Council

[Argentina, September–October 1948]

Henry—

Congratulations on the boy-child! Bravo Lepska! How lucky you are to be settled enough to enjoy children. We are on the move again. I've resigned my post here and propose to reach London by Christmas—probably an atomic Christmas! What fun if we could meet. But I shall be on the bread-line, I guess. There are so few jobs going and I can't earn enough by writing. We propose to make a bid for Greece. Rather starve in Athens than anywhere else. The climate is so magnificent, one feels so well. Here it's awful.

A few days ago I sent you and Laughlin a sort of ground-plan for the Omnibus after doing a thorough re-reading. Think it should make a fine book. Like all great men you have nothing to fear from selection, and like all American geniuses you have no sense of form whatsoever, so that helps. I've been studying your changing prose style. Your American as against your European style. It has gained vastly in power and flight, but you have lost a great deal of the critical control over it. Maybe the USA undermines values in a subtle way. I thought, for example, that quite half of "Murder the Murderer" could have been blue-pencilled out. It seemed repetitive and platitudinous. Could have been cleaned up a bit. Also the later portraiture. Compare "Rattner" to "Reichel"—the latter so compact, the former so loose and wandering. But the best of the new style is far and away greater and wilder than the old. "Rimbaud," "Balzac" and "Remember to Remember" are terriffic—as the two late stories ("Reunion in Brooklyn" and "The Washboard Veteran") are. The difference is perhaps in the use of the blue pencil. These observations may sound a bit impertinent, Henry, but I'm thinking of the books to come. To get the best out of your new powers it seems necessary to frame and trim them up like a water colour or else the book becomes a Bergsonian rampage and its positive qualities get lost because they are not contrasted. The clear hard limestone-formation of the thought gets muddled. Looking forward eagerly to see what new work you are doing. Hope to have the Omnibus ready for inspection by

253

January or February. It's a great honour for me—I couldn't have had a nicer compliment paid me by Laughlin. Will you come to England if you go abroad? Or shall we meet in Greece? I know just the island to spend next summer in—Patmos. Bare as a sculpture, a few orchards, a white stream, blue sea, and the Apocalypse—

Love,
Larry

Big Sur
11/8/48

Dear Larry—

Feel you ought to know what a devoted friend and admirer you have in Lawrence Clark Powell, an old friend of mine who is head librarian at U.C.L.A. He was here to see me Saturday and tried to get me to make a talking record about you. I was at a low ebb and totally unprepared—made a dismal stab at it. Finally read your poem "Alexandria."

This fellow really and truly appreciates you. He's mad about you. Collecting everything by and about you he can lay hands on. I have a feeling there will be reverberations from all this.

And he's not the typical librarian. He's a musician and writer himself. He's sincere and loyal. He knows what he's doing.

Why I tell you all this I don't know, except that it is good to know sometimes where and in whom you have a staunch friend and supporter.

I send this to England, assuming you will be there very soon. And then off to Greece, what? Lucky man!

Writing soon again. Up to the ears in work now. Same old story—only it gets worse with time. And Laughlin writes that my books hardly sell at all now. Q.E.D. However, there is still Europe.

Cheerio!
Henry

Santos, Brazil

[December 1948]

Loading in a tropical port which might well illustrate Rimbaud—the later phase. Silence, haze, huge mountains. All this is very different from what we've just left —Rio built like a great dazzling pipe-organ, the pipes the Organ Mountains, the town with skyscrapers running up beside sugar-loaf ant-hill formation mountains. The main street is one of those empty-ended streets that bisect a Chirico painting. Think you would like Rio. Sitting in cafés drinking the milk from green coconuts through a straw.

Myself I am sitting on deck reading Laforgue's *Hamlet* which couldn't be more appropriate to what we all feel in our shrinking European souls at this vastness and luxuriance. Brazil is bigger than Europe, wilder than Africa, and weirder than Baffin Land.

Larry

JANUARY 1949—FALL 1952
(Durrell in Yugoslavia—Miller in Big Sur)

———◆———

DURRELL returns from South America and after six unsettled months in England goes to Yugoslavia with the Foreign Office, there to spend the next two and a half years as Press Attaché amidst the raw materials of his cloak-and-dagger thriller, *White Eagles Over Serbia*, and his diplomatic sketches, *Esprit de Corps* and *Stiff Upper Lip*. None of this appears in his letters, though as always he writes evocatively of his surroundings, political as well as scenic.

The most dramatic moment in the correspondence occurs at this juncture. Durrell reads Miller's latest book, finds it inexcusably bad, and says so—too bluntly, Perlès feels. But Miller's magnanimity is equal to Durrell's candor. What might have been a crisis proves a climax. And in the process both write some of the most illuminating criticism of Miller's works.

Both hope constantly for a reunion. Several times Miller announces plans for Europe, but each time they fall through. In August 1951, Durrell visits England (where his daughter has been born—"Don't name her after a battleship!" Miller warns), hoping Miller will be there, but again false alarm. There are several lulls in the correspondence when both are swamped, Durrell by politics, Miller by visitors, letters and domestic cares. Presumably they keep in touch by postcard during the intervals.

*   *

[1949]

Dearest Henry—

Sorry for my long neglect. I haven't been awfully well this past six months—bad nerves—due to Latin America as much as anything, I think. Felt too fed up to answer letters or think even. I'm resting up at home for a month or two. It's hard, you know, to reconcile the conflicting claims of jobs and writing. Perhaps one shouldn't try—but I don't like starving and I feel under obligation to be an ordinary human being too, paying for a wife and child etc. . . . Consequently these periods of gloom and exhaustion.

England is wonderful after Argentina—the damp particularly and the cold. I resigned from my last job and am trying for another soon which might take me to the Mediterranean. I have yet to see a country as fine as Greece and we are still aimed in that direction. I haven't got beyond the ground plan of your Omnibus book. At the moment I am simply loafing about waiting for this frightful melancholia to pass. I'm planning a long essay on you for *Horizon.* People are reading you a great deal, you know. England is fatuous and apathetic as usual—the sweaty Christians are out in force—publishers demand a strong pietistic note. As if we weren't *religious* writers!

I don't feel any older, only much wiser and a bit exhausted with things. Waiting for the spring.

Larry

2/18/49

[Big Sur]

Dear Larry—

Wrote you a tremendous letter (in my head) two days ago at the sulphur baths here. Felt something was wrong

—and with Joey too. No word in ages from him. Take a
good rest. Don't worry about literature. I often think the
Consular Service must be the ideal solution for a writer.
But evidently it doesn't pay enough to keep two wives and
a kid. Writing books and articles to make money is what
eventually destroys one, I believe. Do anything else, if
you can, rather than that. Nothing is going to sell well
any more, as I see it. It will take twenty, maybe fifty years,
to get a new and better (?) world order. Get some fun
out of life and reconcile yourself to receiving no due reward for your labors.

I get tired, very tired, of pushing editors and publishers
around. Make a hundred suggestions, but no action. Fi-
nancially, things are at their worst now. I am bartering
for the necessities of life. But go right on working. Made
the sixth and final revision of Volume I, *R. C.* Waiting to
see how I will get paid before mailing to Girodias. Hope
to get you either a carbon copy of it or proofs—if not too
late. In the middle of Volume II now. I enjoy every bit
of it. Write with a smile, even when it's horrible or tragic.
That's progress, I think.

Will get a real letter off very soon now. So much to tell
you. Think of you constantly.

Cheerio,
Henry

Bournemouth
Feb. 25

[1949]

Henry:

Thanks for your good letter—it comes apropos . . .
I've just put Joey on the London train after spending a
marvellous weekend with him here. We walked by the sea
and talked a great deal about Villa Seurat and you. He is

very happy, working night shifts on international tele-communications, talking to Amsterdam, Vienna, Copenhagen and Moscow. He works in with 6000 French-speaking girls—a lending library, he says. But working this way he has had to cut down on friends, and more particularly on correspondents, hence his long silence. He sleeps all day, and does his writing at the switchboard during the night. He's now British, you know, and seems awfully pleased about it. Although he's become a sort of little saint, very steady and sensible and radiant. No more worrying about money, writing, contacts . . . He's rewriting his novel now and expects to spend a couple of years or even a couple of decades on it. Sounds good to me. I enclose a little essay I did for *Horizon* on you. Joey thinks it okay for England. It's to brush up interest in you here. It has flagged rather. The books published are so full of fragments that people have no idea of what you really are. Connolly asked me to try and make up an essay on you. At the moment no job, no money. But that I can stand well enough as soon as I get over this period of blank gloom, which I hope is due to end soon. Joe thinks that you should move to France now where you'd be received with open arms by the French. . . . Why don't you? Come alone and prospect, get a house, scout an income and then send for the family. My daughter is eight and lovely now. See quite a bit of her these days.

Love to you all,
Larry

Big Sur
3/14/49

Dear Larry,

Just reread your long critical essay for *Horizon*. Superb piece of writing. Merlin, you say somewhere. Mais, c'est vous! If any one can seduce, drug, exalt the English, it is you. I wonder what the response will be. . . . Wondering if this copy is for me to keep or to be returned with suggestions? Holding it temporarily, till I hear from you. Meanwhile a few observations which may or may not be of interest to you.

To begin with, I feel you might have taken advantage of the occasion to belabor your compatriots for not having published the autobiographical books. Whose fault is it but theirs if they are reading only fragments of my work? Had you thought of that, cher ami? Toynbee (the nephew) in reviewing a recent work bemoans the lack of the virulent *Tropics* material, but would he lift a finger (as did the French writers en masse recently) to fight the government? More of their bloody hypocrisy, you see. Just as here in America. You almost kowtow to the bastards. I see your point—you want to win them over. O.K., but you should rub it in, too. Never miss the chance, Larry me lad.

Freud . . . You've made these statements about my absorption of him and the influence several times. True, I've read him well, but as for "influence," I'd rather say that of Rank and Jung, if any. Bergson belongs to my "youth" (tailor shop days) . How much he influenced me is imponderable. The great influences were Nietzsche, Spengler, yes, Emerson, Herbert Spencer (!) , Thoreau, Whitman—and Elie Faure. You can't stress the last named enough. More and more he stands out like a giant, to me.

And about "the artist" . . . It's not that I put the sage or saint above the artist. It's rather that I want to see established the "artist of life." The Christ *resurrected* would be such, for example. Milarepa was another.

This ties up with the progression, as you put it, from Bergson-Spengler to Chinese-Hindus. I think I've passed that too now. The key-word is Reality (few have put it better than Gutkind in *The Absolute Collective*). The nearest philosophy to my heart and temperament is Zen, as you probably know. I find individuals here and there, all over the world, who belong to no cult, creed or metaphysic, who are expressing what I mean, each in his own way. As near as I can put my finger on it, it always comes back to reality here and now, nothing else, nothing before or beyond.

"Poor literary sense" . . . It seems to me you have an ambivalent attitude here. You make a good defense of my "formlessness," etc. Yes. But then you make these concessions to the dead-heads. Picasso said once, "Must one always turn out a *masterpiece?*" Where does creation lie —in the thing done or in the effect? What and how a man does, acts, thinks, talks, every day is what counts, no? If you have this criterion of "literature" you nullify the other important points you make. You are talking of something altogether "illusory." The makers of literature are not the masters of art. Great books are—literature isn't.

"No *characters*"??? Perhaps. But I think with *The Rosy Crucifixion* you might speak differently. Certainly they are not characters in the novelistic sense, but they are full-drawn, ample, rounded. Some of them have already made their debut in the earlier works. I keep a list of them on my wall, so as not to forget—i.e., who they really were, their real names. Quite a collection of them now.

Lastly, you may not like *R.C.* at all. In some ways it is a reversion to pre-*Tropic* writing. Much more conversation, direct and indirect. Many episodes, dreams, fantasies, throwbacks of all sorts. But a steady forward progression, chronologically, because I am following my notes (written in 1927!). *Capricorn*, as you know, took about two and a half pages of these notes, only. This first volume was written in New York, in about six months—first half of 1942. Hence all the bloody revision. Though no drastic changes. But I've labored to make the expression more perfect—more effective. One day you will see the revised script. It's a beauty. Anyway, in writing Vol. 2— half done now—I began to get real joy out of the writing. Laughed and chuckled a great deal. *And*, there is a perceptible change from Vol. 1 to 2. Inevitable after 6 or 7 years. Good too, I feel. When I finish Vol. 3 I intend to do the little book, *Draco and the Ecliptic*, like putting a cap on a milk bottle, to seal it hermetically. Haven't the least idea what it will be like—just know it must be done—and masterfully. Then I am off into the blue. . . . Joy through work hereafter. No more compulsion. I will be emptied. Maybe I'll just whistle, like a peanut stand. But I want to try sheer nonsense.

So glad to hear of your daughter. Eight now. I wish I could meet her. Send me a photo of her as she is today if you can. . . . Don't think I'm not trying to get over. It becomes more and more probable every day. (I must see Ireland—and Edinburgh.) My ideal trip would be to these three cities by plane—no in-between stops: Timbuctoo, Mecca, Lhasa. I dream of it often.

Hope you don't take my observations as carping criticism. I think you did a superb job of it. Too damned good for *Horizon*. Ask Connolly to lend you the issue in which Herman Hesse wrote about himself—it will please you enormously. Toot a loo!

Henry

P.S.   Penguin Books, England, have contracted for the *Colossus*—first of 1950.

P.P.S.   Are there still copies of *The Black Book* available in Paris?

The British Embassy, Belgrade, Yugoslavia

[July 1949]

Dear Henry—

A brief line to tell you that we have arrived and that conditions here are far from pleasant, though much better than Latin America. The diplomatic circle is completely ostracised by the people, who will not meet you and dare not even be seen talking to you. Consequently the life we lead is a chain-gang existence. Communism is something so much more horrible than you can imagine : systematic moral and spiritual corruption by every means at hand. "The perversion of truth in the interests of expediency." But when you see it at close quarters it makes your hair stand up on end. And the smug cooperation of the intellectuals is also terrifying! They are paid to shut up—and they have. The terrible *deadness* of everything is fantastic! It really is a menace, an intellectual disease. How to combat it is another problem. At any rate England and the USA are havens of tremendous calm compared to this place—and the only hope for the future, if any. Sounds odd perhaps, but it's true. This brief line is just to tell you to use the diplomatic bag in writing me. It's safe and quicker.

> Yours with love,
> Larry

British Legation, Belgrade
Sept. 5, 1949

Dear Henry :

Just a brief line : frightfully busy. Received *Sexus* from Paris and am mid-way through Volume II. I must confess I'm bitterly disappointed in it, despite the fact that it contains some of your very best writing to date. But my dear

Henry, the moral vulgarity of so much of it is *artistically* painful. These silly, meaningless scenes which have no raison d'être, no humour, just childish explosions of obscenity—what a pity, what a terrible pity for a major artist not to have critical sense enough to husband his forces, to keep his talent aimed at the target. What on earth possessed you to leave so much twaddle in? I understand that with your great sweeping flights you occasionally have to plough through an unrewarding tract of prose. But the strange thing is that the book gives very little feeling of real passion. The best parts burn with a new cold luminous ardour—mysticism; and you have interlarded this with chunks of puerile narrative. You won't mind my saying this, because you know that I consider you one of the greatest living masters. But really, this book needs taking apart and regluing. The obscenity in it is really unworthy of you. It is just plain silly to murder the good parts of the book with this silly kind of vituperation written so badly. The anecdote on page 24 of volume I is the kind of thing I mean. It's just painful—nothing else, and contributes nothing to what you are trying to do. I'm fearfully depressed to have to sound impertinent to a genius I admire so much but Henry, Henry, Henry . . . ten minutes' thought would have saved the book. As it is it gives the air of being written by Jekyll and Hyde, and the Hyde is not really monstrous and frightening, but just painfully disgusting. . . . You will probably blow me out of the water for writing this, but I think it's better to be candid about it. All the wild resonance of *Cancer* and *Black Spring* has gone, and you have failed to develop what is really new in your prose, and what should set a crown on your work. The new mystical outlines are all there; but they are lost, lost, damn it, in this shower of lavatory filth which no longer seems tonic and bracing, but just excrementitious and sad.

One winces and averts the face. What on earth has made you slip back on a simple matter of *taste*—artistic taste?

No time for more, we are in the middle of a lively crisis and much work on hand. It's a joy to read you nevertheless, you bastard, even though I'm angry because I think you've failed yourself on this one.

Love,
Larry

.CDU114 15 PD INTL=CD BEOGRAD VIA RCA 10 1305=
LC MILLER BIGSUR=
     =CALIF=

1949 SEP 10 AM 6 45

SEXUS DISGRACEFULLY BAD WILL COMPLETELY RUIN REPUTATION UNLESS WITHDRAWN REVISED LARRY=

SEXUS=

Big Sur
Sept. 28th, 1949

Dear Larry,

Today I got another letter from you about *Sexus* together with your carbon to Girodias, which was really "the works." I know you'd feel better if I did get angry with you, but I can't. I laugh and shake my head bewilderedly, that's all. Naturally I can't take an objective, detached view of my work. If I could perhaps I could see what you're driving at. To judge one's own work is impossible. Maybe you are right—maybe I'm finished. But I don't feel that way, not even if the whole world condemns the book.

The other day I finished Book 2, which I am now cor-

266

recting. About the same length as the first. Not much sex in it at all. But it will probably have other faults in your eyes. What I want to tell you is this—I said it before and I repeat it solemnly: I am writing exactly what I want to write and the way I want to do it. Perhaps it's twaddle, perhaps not. The fact that I put in everything under the sun may be, as you think, because I have lost all sense of values. Again, it may not. I am trying to reproduce in words a block of my life which to me has the utmost significance—every bit of it. Not because I am infatuated with my own ego. You should be able to perceive that only a man without ego could write thus about himself. (Or else I am really crazy. In which case, pray for me.) Since 1927 I have carried inside me the material of this book. Do you suppose it's possible that I could have a miscarriage after such a period of gestation? Perhaps it's a monster I'm giving birth to. But really, I don't care. The paramount thing is for me to get it out of my system—and in doing so to reveal what I was and am. I made a herculean effort to represent myself for what I then was. The only artistry I endeavored to employ was the capturing of that other self, those other days. I've been as sincere as I possibly could, maybe too sincere, because it certainly is not a lovely picture I made of myself. In justice, however, I think you, you particularly, should be able to read between the lines, to reconcile truth seeker with artist, liar, playboy and what not.

It was not my idea to bring these volumes out separately. I had wanted to hold them until I had reached the very last page. But Girodias implored and I gave in. I keep telling you to wait until you have read to the end. Not that I think there will come a change of style which will appeal to you, but simply that everything will then fall into place. Even trivial things take on a different light when viewed from the proper perspective. "Life's traces,"

wrote Goethe, speaking of *Wilhelm Meister*, I think. I
read that in my teens, that phrase, and it sank deep. I want
this book to contain "life's traces." Whether it is in good
taste, moral or immoral, literature or document, a creation or a fiasco doesn't matter.

I am trying to give you my honest thoughts, not to
coerce you into changing your mind. One of the hardest
things to accept is the divorce of a loyal admirer. You are
more than that to me, of course. But aren't you trying to
protect what you have always hoped I would be? Those
defects you always spoke of blushingly, now they have
come to a head, apparently. Soon I shall be just "a bundle
of defects." That's classic. Inevitable, did I persist in
going my own sweet way, which I have, you see.

Did I ever tell you, by the way, that *Sexus* was written
from the end of 1941 (after the *Nightmare* trip) to the
middle of 1942? I read it over since about four times,
making revisions each time. The last time I read it over—
correcting proofs—I was dazzled by it. In short, it seemed
better to me each time I read it. If proof were needed to
show how far gone I am, there you are! Of course, I ought
to implement the foregoing by explaining that each time
I read those incidents of my life I relived them, and quite
presumably (as authors will) read into them all that I
might have left out in cold print. On the other hand, it's
usual to feel a growing disgust with a work on each re-
reading. Especially when it comes to the proofreading.
Faute de mieux, that was my sole criterion.

Book 2 was written these last two to three years, and
under rather harrowing circumstances. Yet I like it even
more than Book 1. And as I make ready to tackle Book 3
I have a feeling of regret that I am coming to the end of
this priceless material. My autobiographical life will then
be done for. What's to follow God alone knows. Maybe

I shall retire—defeated. But Larry, I can never go back on what I've written. If it was not good, it was true; if it was not artistic, it was sincere; if it was in bad taste, it was on the side of life. If I were a braggart and an egotist I might have written more gloriously. There is a poverty and sterility I tried to capture which few men have known. Far better to have been a gallows-bird! But I had only this one life to record. That passion you sense to be lacking has been put into the minus side. That life of "senseless activity," which the sages have ever condemned as death —that was what I set out to record. But as I say towards the end of Book 2, I suffered out of ignorance, and thus was highly instructed. Perhaps in the summing up, my life will be seen to be a huge pyramid erected over a minus sign. Still, nevertheless, a pyramid. Perhaps better understood when placed upside down.

Thinking of your "defection"—if I may use that word without harshness, because I feel none towards you—I am suddenly reminded of a curious fact about myself, that when I like a writer profoundly I can read anything he writes and enjoy it—and I mean literally "anything." In a recent work Cendrars writes that he is the sort of reader who when he takes to an author not only reads him all the way through, and in the original language, but reads everything that was ever written about him. That I can't do. But again, what I am trying to say is—and this is undoubtedly my unconscious "plaidoir"—what one looks for is the man, and the man is always there if you will examine the fibre of his creation. . . . But men deteriorate sometimes. Yes, Larry, they do. When I come to realize that I am deteriorating I shall hide away and never be heard from again. I promise.

But you should be here, we should be talking face to face. Then we could meet heart to heart. Anyway, it's not arrogance or conceit that dictates this response. I don't have those thoughts about myself, my relation to others, to the world, which you impute to me. I have no thoughts about myself. I know what I am. It doesn't make me proud. I am . . . you are . . . he is. What does it amount to? That we are all one and the same. The important thing is that God is. And that we know ourselves to be part of HIM.

The "considered opinion" about this letter is that you are to feel at liberty to baste hell out of me to all and sundry. I will understand that you are doing it out of love for me. I would be a fool if I thought otherwise.

You know, when I laugh or weep over my own words, as I do on re-reading the *R.C.*, I think sometimes that I hear the whole world laughing and weeping. As a veteran, though perhaps still a "sentimentalist," you must admit it is not so easy for me to do this. But if I am laughing and weeping alone—ah, then there's something wrong! "Quick, Watson, the needle!"

So far I have heard about the book only from you and two other readers. Haven't received a copy of it yet. Maybe somebody else wrote it and signed my name to it. (!!!)

Ever yours,

Henry

OAO94
O.CDU410 08 PD INTL FR=CD BEOGRAD VIA RCA 29 1950=
HENRY MILLER=
   BIGSUR CALIF=
DEEPEST APOLOGIES UNJUST CRITICISM WRITING NOTHING SAID QUALIFIED ADMIRATION YOUR GENIUS HOPING FRIENDSHIP UNAFFECTED=
   DURRELL=

[Big Sur]

Dear Larry—

I had just mailed you a long letter when your cable arrived. You will see that I did not get angry. How could I? It is your privilege to attack me if you feel I have written a bad book. I understand too that it must be rankling—especially coming on the heels of your *Horizon* panegyric, about which I am still getting enthusiastic letters. Why don't you ask Connolly to give you space again and blast hell out of me? Barkis is willin'! In these matters friendship can only be asserted and maintained by the strictest probity. I have long ceased to defend myself against criticism or judgments. The work has to stand by itself. This doesn't mean that I am immune to criticism. Any good effects therefrom will have to be revealed in subsequent works. Argument and dispute is time wasted. I am not "the master."

"Fratres Semper" (see Book 2). A vous toujours.

Henry

Belgrade

[October 1949]

Dear Henry:

I knew you would be wounded and of course it upset me bitterly to write to you. I shouldn't have done it really —little Joe is right. I enclose his letter, every word of which I heartily agree with. But knowing how robust you are and how much yourself, I felt I could take the risk of telling you how deeply horrified and disappointed I was by the book. But you say it is just the book you want, the way you want. And that is enough for me. Who knows really? You see far into the mists of the future and are

271

probably a better judge than I of what will be what. But if I had seen the book in MS I would have pleaded with you not to publish. I think you know I love you more than any man I have ever met; I owe you a lot. I felt I also owed you a truth or two about my feelings; it was no use pretending that I liked the new work. What I did not realise until I got Joe's letter was that my own criticism was ill-tempered, waspish and liable to injure an old friend. Perhaps it was due to the fact that I found myself in a frightful dilemma. After the *Horizon* article I accepted three invitations to review your new book in three good papers. I tried to think what the hell to do. The book I thought really frightfully bad. Was I to do the usual murmuring trick that critics do? You wouldn't like me to do that. Yet you wouldn't want me to do what fashionable critics do, i.e. praise something because a friend had written it. I drew a deep breath and decided to come out in the open with it. I didn't realise that the tone might wound you—little Joe is right, I should have written differently. I was so god-damned hopping mad with you, however, and so god-damned anxious to try and boost English interest in you that I nearly died of blood pressure. I took my annoyance out on you and I'm deeply deeply sorry. And if you were a lesser sized man you would punish me by breaking contact. I did a review (I did eight reviews in all, in fact) for *Horizon*. It is what I feel; it is terribly unkind.

Meanwhile from another angle the *Herald Tribune* was running a banner blurb for the book quoting me, and in this service we are supposed not to get our name in the papers; all published stuff has to pass the filter. The essay was O.K. But if *Sexus* had been the sort of book I hoped for I would have skipped that; as it was I felt so bad about it that I asked Kahane to take my name off the blurb. If it

had been *Tropic* (which in some ways is much fiercer),
nothing would have budged me. But Henry, I simply
couldn't defend *Sexus* to myself, let alone anyone else. It
was a ghastly dilemma. Believe me, if I wounded you it
was not in any spirit of wanton idle silly malice. You stand
as high as ever you did for me. No one can take away what
you are and what you say. But where I disagree with Joe is
here: he thinks that you should be lulled and indulged.
I DON'T THINK YOU ARE WRITTEN OUT. I THINK YOU ARE
AT THE EDGE OF THE MOST FERTILE PERIOD OF YOUR
LIFE. A PERIOD WHEN THE SCALE OF THE MAJOR WORK
MAY TIRE YOU, BUT WHERE THE LUCIDITY IS BRIGHTER
AND SHARPER THAN IT EVER WAS. When I read the good
20 pages of *Sexus* in an anthology I thought it purer and
greater than anything yet. But buried in the body of
the book nobody will ever find it. I also knew that in
USA you would not find friend or critic worth facing
you on the issue. What a wilderness of cross-purposes.
How sorry I am. I know that criticism doesn't really teach;
but what is one to do in a case like this? Now I get your letter and I'm heartily sorry for my smallness. Please forgive
me, and let's forget the whole business if you still care to.
How I wish I could talk to you for a moment, could reach
across the gulf. I know that you would see that in my heart
I revere and honour you as a great genius of the XXth
century. The rest doesn't matter really. But I must be true
to the real you which I didn't feel was fairly represented in
Sexus. Forgive my bloodiness and believe that really, far
from being your bitterest critic, I am still 100 per cent for
you and with you. Forgive me, will you?

love,
larry

Dear Henry :

Just a brief flash—I'm madly busy at the moment, as you can probably guess. I hope you got my great packet of apologies and embarrassments. Furthermore I hope you swallowed your most justifiable rage and accepted some of them. Meanwhile I have been reading you in Sarajevo, reading you again. I know what's wrong with the book now—its subject matter is no longer of any interest to you fundamentally; so you deal with it in a conscientious enough way but without the mad poignance etc. of your other books.

Sarajevo is a strange place—a narrow gorge full of rushing waters; granite red mountains and the town perched up a cliff in a series of coloured bubbles of minaret and mosque; veiled women. Narrow streets full of mountaineers and mules. Wild crying of eagles in the air above it and all around a petrified ocean of rock with roads bulging round mountains, coiling and recoiling on themselves. I had a poem for the road which wouldn't get any further than

> Ideal because their coils were apt
> To these long sad self-communings
> Among alien peoples . . .

So I threw it in a gorge and took the flat road over the plain to this dreary white city on its dirty rivers. Life is an awful bore. Looks like plenty of trouble by the spring.

love,
larry

Dear Larry and dear Fred—

I wrote you, Larry, a longish letter about ten days ago, assuring you that I was not offended and urging you to get permission from Connolly to blast hell out of me about *Sexus*. Now comes your letter with Joey's marginalia and his letter. I want you boys to stop worrying about me. You don't suppose that after all I've been through I would fold up because a dear friend happened not to like what I wrote, do you? I see you are concerned about my eventual, or immediate, sterility. Joey looks forward to my going gaga soon. Hold your horses, lads! True, I am approaching the grave, but I don't feel finished yet. J'ai encore quelque chose à dire. . . .

I wish, Joey, you were here sometimes to help me with my French. I'm now correcting Roger Cornaz' translation of my Rimbaud opuscule. I know what is wrong with his phrases but I can't tell him how to say it, in French.

Only the other day I received a copy of *Sexus* for myself. Haven't had a chance to re-read it yet. Busy revising Book 2 (*Plexus*).

I think the one word which sticks in my crop, after all the jeremiads launched at me, is "vulgarity." Such as it is, it is deliberate. And I begin to wonder if this ingredient will not also have to be reappraised, as was "obscenity" previously. Always remember that "I am just a Brooklyn boy." Recently I tried to re-read my great favorite, Petronius, the father of the novel. Couldn't stick it. But there are analogies and reverberations there to *Sexus*, I do believe. Sometimes I think that you, Larry, never really knew what it was to live in our modern age of asphalt and chemicals. To grow up in the street, to speak the language of the voyou.

275

More and more, as I think of your words, Larry, I smile to myself, especially when you refer to the inane or inept or trifling conversational passages, some of them quite long too. I was rather proud of myself for having caught these so well. It is as if I took a few steps backward—towards an outmoded realism—but not really. I don't know how to explain what it is which, to my mind, saves this work from being "realistic" in the crude, vulgar sense. But I am sure of it. Perhaps you have to examine more closely the work of certain painters who, though masters, were able to deal with "trifles." I think that the "trifle" was very important in my life—if you get what I mean.

Still planning to come over with the family next spring. Soon even the small nations will have their atom bombs. Why worry?

Good cheer to you both, and no more apologies. Dying to read the blast. You know, I've always said what I need is a good enemy. In this case "a friendly enemy." (Ennemi-frère, as the French say.)

Henry

British Legation, Belgrade
Oct. 27

[1949]

Dear Henry:

Just a brief line on the eve of leaving for Salonika by jeep where we hope to spend a week. I am on duty but it will be pure pleasure to get out of this filthy echoing rambling town, full of sodden Serbs, and strike out for the Macedonian hills again. Our crisis grows steadily uglier like a screw tightening, a little bit every day. Nobody can see the outcome, and the funny thing is that people loathe the Tito regime so much that they are completely apathetic about the outcome. Many would like to see the Russians come just in order to watch the block knocked off these communist gauleiters with their neat little theories. Of course they realise with their rational faculty that the Soviet would be much worse. But they are simply desperate with the present police conditions. In this context I can assure you, having had a close look at communism, that the USA, witch-hunting and all, is taking a far more sensible line than anyone else. We are still rotten with woolly liberal socialism and industrial guilt and are playing into the hands of these swine with every word we utter. There is simply no issue for us along Marxist-Leninist lines; it means the destruction of every value we stand for—as writers I mean. I know that our own culture was rotten, but compared to this it is flourishing in its decay, it is hopeful. This is sheer death. I am sending George Katsimbalis a telegram to ask if he can meet us in Salonika—it would be fun to see him again and talk over old times. You have immortalised him so successfully in the Greek book that he is now a famous Raimuesque character in Athens, and everyone calls on him just to say they have really met him. More news when I get back—if there is any that is not in the headlines.

I've sent Joey *Sexus* in the diplomatic bag : I hope to Christ it gets through all right to him. I'm curious to see what he makes of it, whether he is as enraged as I was. Forgive my stupidity, cher maître.

Love to you all from your devoted

Larry Durrell

[January 1950]

Dearest Henry and Lepska—

A belated line from a snow-bound capital. We've been on the move again, hence my silence. This time we went north, through Croatia and Slovenia to Trieste, a strange treaty port encircled by communists on the edge of the sea. Here at least we could see shops with something in them and people who did not look whey-faced with starvation and fear. Cafés to sit in and smiling faces. But the town for all its Italian population had a curious sedateness, a lack of southern brio. I discovered why—60,000 Slovenes and 6000 Croats. The character of these Middle Europeans is dull, self-pitying and Slav—like the Poles; heavy as gun metal—far far from the Mediterranean lightness and sensuality. It was good however to see Trieste and understand why Stendhal reacted against it so strongly. After Italy he tasted the first harsh notes of central European landscape and character—it smells of the great Hungarian plain and the steppes beyond. Like a wise man he turned back to the warmth. I wish I had the same luck or good sense, or both. I have been reading a deal of Stendhal these days, more and more convinced that in his two big novels he has demonstrated a rationale for fiction which is the one most germane to the writers of the next fifty years. The power of creating a 3-dimensional character in a single phrase, then letting the action develop the character without further interruption. As an autobiographer too he is delightful—struggling with a sensibility too charged with femininity and a shy pudicity —anticipating Freud, by the way, in a remark which follows a phrase describing the death of his mother, "Là commence la vie morale!"

We are way below zero with heavy snow and ice. I won't begin to tell you what the Slavs are suffering—no coal, not a scrap of warmth or decent clothing for any but communist officials. And the government frantically depressing the standard of living in order to buy capital equipment which is broken as soon as they try to use it. What a madhouse communism is. And how grateful we are to the USA for taking it seriously. Europe is a sheepfold full of bleating woolly socialists who simply *cannot* see that socialism prepares the ground for these fanatics. I wish you could come here and see it for yourself.

Needless to say this fetid atmosphere is not conducive to thinking or writing; and this political set-up gives me an awful lot of work to do. Nobody can tell how it will end, but there is a brief détente while the snow and ice hold out. I don't know how the Russians see things at all, but this protestant movement is having an effect in surrounding countries as it is in England. It offers the psychological chance for socialists who have begun to doubt to get off the band wagon and still save face. But what an unhappy country this is! Thank God we held Greece. I'm afraid, though I hate to admit it, that Churchill's view of things was the right one. But if *I* had to come to a communist country to understand that you can well imagine how muddled everyone is who has not seen this in action. Let's hope the old boy gets back into office—though we always let the mess become irretrievable before we invite him to clear it up for us. What a world. Are you writing anything?

Love to you all from a snow-bound
Larry and Eve

[Big Sur]

Dear Larry—

Always put off writing you because I seem only to send you notes. So difficult to find time to write a letter. I have been working feverishly since January 17th on a new book—about books, my experience with them. Fascinating! Have done 165 pages thus far. Now halting for breath and revising. God knows where or when it will end. But what a subject! Suggested to me by Larry Powell, the librarian. (Bless his name!) When I finish I'll tackle Book 3 (*Nexus*). Paris police seized French version (unexpurgated) of *Sexus*. Girodias put out also an expurgated one for the public, both without my knowledge or consent (sic). More fat for the fire. No tears.

Don't worry about imminent war. If you knew this government's plans and projects (as I don't, but surmise), you'd rest easy. Do you know what? "We" are not worrying about Russia so much as about invaders from other planets. In 50 years "we" (our "spacemen"!!!) expect to reach the planet of a distant star Wulf No. 65231, to have a girdle of space ramps outside gravitational field, et cetera. *Seriously*. Something's afoot—very, very mysterious. I think myself that the inhabitants of other planets are worrying about damage we may do, unwittingly, with our new bombs and other diabolical inventions. Laugh, if you will! Communism will be knocked out not by an opposing ideology but by force of circumstance. Our inventions will upset the present order of permanent conflict. Not superior views, better government, more humanity. You'll see. Rest in peace! Working for the political hounds you lose perspective. Change the "frog" perspective for the "bird's." The age is so far ahead of its seeming problems. There's a knocking at the door. No one hears it. Too busy bickering, worrying, straightening things out.

I've made wonderful discoveries about my early reading—the deeper meaning of books for boys. You'll see when I finish. Discovering more about myself as I write of books. Childhood is *the* great period. Am trying to re-read some very old ones. Just reread *She* (Rider Haggard). Have a look at it some time. May surprise you.

Wish you could get free of "work." You need to be on your own. Is it so impossible? You'll always be working for some one, if you think it's "necessary." Take a good think some day. Map out your life as you'd like to live it. Then jump! You are a "protected" individual. Life will take care of you, never fear. Because you *give* life.

Henry

British Legation, Belgrade

[Spring 1950]

Dear Henry:

Just a line between trips to tell you that everything is okay, by which I mean everything is as hellish as ever here; and I'm afraid my letters must have the same lack of variety as the letters from a prison, for that is what this is—on a scale impossible to understand until you've been here. Unluckily too, the climate of this dust-blown capital is awful too, though the rest of the country is really beautiful. The people are like moles, frightened to death, shifty, uneasy. Meanwhile American and British left-wingers arrive in this centre of barbarism comparable only to the darkest of the dark ages to inform these stinking communists how decadent we are and how we are about to collapse. Hitler was baby play compared to this.

Little Joe is at me for daring to criticise the Master. Goddammit, the master isn't made of putty. He is suffering from post-war exhaustion and doesn't realise you've climbed right up beyond us into an effortless period of pure play, where angustia is quiet. Reminds me I saw a picture of little Picasso at seventy—looking like a thirteen-year-old tomboy. He must be absurdly proud of his good figure as he won't be pictured unless he's in a bathing costume. I was reminded of that peculiar lightness and youthfulness of you in walking or swimming—eternal children. Eliot just sent me his *Cocktail Party*, which is really a little masterpiece; effortless and wry and beautifully put together, with every symbol working overtime, including the cocktail party and all it stands for in this age. To be profound *playfully* is new for him: he's become a Chinaman. And I can't tell you how sweet as a human being—vastly unlike the grave and composed man you met in our flat in 1938. His gentleness and humour and lovability have come to the fore. I'm sending you the proofs of a new essay (in the real sense) : it's a play called *Sappho or the Tenth Muse*, which is due out in April. Wonder what you will think of it. A bit turgid but there are good things in it. Planning to spend June in Ischia with Zarian, wonder if there is any chance of you coming to Europe then? Love to you all.

Larry

Belgrade

[July 1950]

Dear Henry :

Just got back to this hellhole from Ischia where we had a delightful month with old Zarian—who incidentally suggests that you should spend a year in Ischia with him discussing the fundamental problems of life, art, sex, death. . . . On arriving back I'm up to my waist in papers. Tomorrow I leave by car and cross the mountains to Sarajevo and Dubrovnik, and thence north along the coast to Split and inland to Zagreb—a tiring journey through an impoverished if magnificent landscape. Back here all being well in 8 days, I hope, and will write you another letter on arrival. So much to tell you but literally no time. Situation is as ever blackish with few patches of light about. God knows how long it will be before the whole bag of tricks goes up. I'm anxious not to get captured by the Russians either and spend the rest of my life in a salt mine. I guess I've got enough material about men and affairs to furnish a dozen big novels. Next step is to buy a small house with the acre of land. Believe me, I know that every word of your letter is true, but our money set-up prevents me at the moment from buying a place anywhere but England. I haven't adopted this profession for love but because it's a useful means of getting into position to buy a house in a country I like; a Greek or Italian posting would decide the matter pronto for me. I'm unlike you: I plan things as carefully as possible, trying to curb my Irish impulses as much as possible. I am trying to find the owner of a house on Ischia who wants to sell for pounds. If I buy then we shall cut the traces and see what fortune has in store for a writer pure and simple.

No, the discs never arrived. Did you address them properly? Perhaps they violated some customs regulations, but it is odd that the Foreign Office did not notify me of the arrival of anything from the States. If you send me a set of anything like that, that might seem dutiable to the idiots in the customs, please mark the package COMPLIMENTARY FREE SAMPLE, and it might get through. Books seem to arrive okay. As for the Yugoslav slippers . . . my dear Henry, you are crazy. You cannot have the faintest idea what a communist country is like. It is quite impossible. I remember that I could never quite understand what it was all about until I struck one.

I won't try and tell you. Your old shoes would fetch twelve dollars here on any street. There are no new ones of any kind to be had. You can sell needles at a dollar apiece. A ten-cent pocket comb at the moment fetches four dollars. . . . No, but you won't understand even now. BUT IF YOU CAME HERE FOR A WEEK, you'd realise that even a great war would be justified to prevent THIS, and liberate the millions under the yoke of this tyranny, this moral prison. That is why my heart leaps when I see that the USA has really tumbled to communism and has bounded into Korea. Hurrah! While our milk-and-water liberal cryptos are havering, and while the European artist is disgracing himself irretrievably by his support for something 100 times worse than Caligula, at least the god-damned old Yankees have woken up with a start to what this really means. . . . But you will disapprove. You should see this place.

Much love to you both and the kids,

Larry

Big Sur, California
9/2/50

Dear Larry—

The carpet slippers from Slovenia just came—and just fit. A great surprise! Thank you! Lepska bought last pair obtainable for herself recently, for 98 cents. Just had good letter from an old literary favorite of mine, a Croatian, Prof. Janko Lavrin of the University, Nottingham. Hear frequently now from John Cowper Powys, living in Wales. Dylan Thomas was here a month or two ago. Much fatter—very soft, tender, lovable—and wiser. Just finishing Vol. I of my new book about books, for Laughlin to publish next spring. It will run to several volumes. Then I go back to *R.C.* to write Book 3. Girodias hasn't

called for script of Book 2 (*Plexus*) yet. Brought out a
new, one-volume, paper edition—cheaper—of *Sexus*.

Hear from Fred you have a new book out. Good!

George Dibbern, author of *Quest*, first world citizen,
won 10,000 pounds in a lottery and bought an island off
Tasmania. All my friends welcome, he says. Remember,
in case you need a quick refuge. Address—Kettering,
Tasmania.

Everyone loath to believe war will spread. See only
suicide for all concerned. But nobody *knows* anything.
All goes forward, as usual, with secrecy and complacency.

At last I see what your job is, your office. Hoop-la!
You'll be "pro-consul" next.

Love to you both meanwhile,

Henry

11/4/50

[Big Sur]

Dear Larry—

Sappho came at last. Superb work! Enjoyed it thoroughly and marveled at your steel-like grip of subject
matter. Phaon and Pittakos splendid portraitures. Your
language always under command. How could you do it,
living the life you have these past few years? I see now
the poet is unscathed. The dramatist in you most promising. You keep reminding me, in this, of Shakespeare. I
must say that, in spite of yourself, you put the case for
Pittakos, tyrant, victim of life's will, most convincingly.
Phaon, talking to Sappho of his island life, touches the
heights. I'll write you more soon, on a second reading.
Sappho in a new guise, most enchanting and very much
you. (With a tincture of Eliot's gray foreboding wisdom.) But somehow Shakespeare comes out in this—the
flavor of him, his essence, his magic of language. Yet it's

Greek, and of no time, or all time. "We" are not deceived by tyrant-and-mob business. What wots here is the poet, his fate. It's secure. There are passages on the role and effect (of poet) which are revelatory and personal. It's very alive, your play, and the drama itself thrilling. I'd like to see another book in another medium on just Sappho and Phaon. In them you have terrific symbolism to play with. But this is all sketchy, too rapid, unthinking. I'll write again soon. Just wanted you to know quick. I feel somehow that this work will launch you. Don't cut as suggested in back of book—cut down on some of the sometimes too florid, vague, too beautiful (precious) speeches. But it's your poetic utterance I like and the poetic feeling. Do more plays, yes! Hallelujah!

Henry

Have you gotten in touch with Larry Powell—American Express, London? He's dying to see you, I believe. He's one of your keenest, staunchest admirers.

P.S.   Got a wonderful walking stick from John Cowper Powys. He's a darlint of a man.

Belgrade

[September 1951]

Henry dear,

It was a great disappointment to miss you in England. We had both so much looked forward to seeing you. It seems such an age since we said goodbye in Sparta in the mist, and it doesn't look as if we are going to meet in Tibet, does it? We got back here yesterday after a boiling trip in the Simplon Orient with our new baby Sappho, who is charming and very dark like Eve, and shows signs of being good-tempered and pretty. We saw something of little Joe and his wife (who is lovely and very charming) in England and were hoping for a grand reunion, spe-

286

cially as George Seferis is at present in London and very keen to see you again after so long.

There is also a young man who proposes to edit a book of your letters. I felt rather strongly about this, perhaps Joe wrote you. Your reputation is very low in England and it is time somebody did a serious study of your work. I see no purpose in letting somebody who seems not to want to do any of the work climb on to your shoulder into the public view. I very much fear another disastrous *Happy Rock* will be the outcome. I'm only anxious about your sales—I know where you stand as a writer. If I were your publisher I would try and get a serious book written about you and then to press forward with an anthology of your best work on the lines of the ground-plan I sent Laughlin two years ago. Meanwhile I would persuade you *not* to appear in any more little mags free of charge but to demand good prices for your work and only print it in well-founded quarterlies. I think within three years you would shed the reputation for hopeless irresponsibility and take on the mantle of the greatest American writer of the day—which of course you really are.

O dear! I wonder if you see what I mean? At any rate, before sending the letters of yours which I possess I thought I would tell you what I feel about this project. It is no good. Though perhaps I am wrong about it. Let me have a brief line telling me what you think.

I feel that a visit to Europe is essential to you for your work this year. I think the feeling of a vacuum (critical) around you and the lack of competition at your level is bad for your work. In Europe you would feel surrounded by a fruitful medium which would be like a compass-bearing for future books. And with you one always feels that some perfectly astonishing work is just around the corner. I don't feel that you've passed meridian, but that your greatest work lies ahead of you, when the personae of your books can be gathered up and rewoven at a higher symbolic level. I foresee a sort of prose *Faust*. Ah! if you could only lie fallow for a year, not writing, not thinking, by the Mediterranean, it would come, this book full of the innocence, amorality and ripeness of old age. Have you read Petronius? Your books are still middle-aged books. You are now moving into old age with all the ripeness of practice and the terrific equipment of a prose-gift unique in this age. To rehash the subject matter of *Cancer* à la Vol. 1 of *The Rosy Crucifixion* is *not you*. It represents a fixation about an attitude to life which you can no longer support and act from, but even here the traces of the other book are clear. I wish we could drown the project in good wine on some Greek island, and walk among the Delian statues to talk you into your new-old self. The fulcrum is repose.

But *come to Europe*—poor ravaged Europe. You will still find the conversations, the spirits and the food you need for this next step. Eliot sends his greetings to you. And we send our homage and our love.

Larry

Big Sur
10/22/51

Dear Larry—

Haven't been able to write you because I've just been through another crisis—Lepska has decamped. I am to keep the children. Have Val with me now and Tony as soon as I find a woman to help me keep house. As for that book, I leave it to the gods. I do appreciate, though, your concern about it. What does it really matter, however? I am irresponsible, yes, in a healthy way. I can't take measures to preserve my reputation. Me and my reputation will always be separate things.

I'm delighted the girl is called Sappho, and not named after some new British man-of-war!

You know, perhaps when things straighten out here, I may come over with the two kids. I long to see Europe again and you and all the old true friends. I pray every day now that Providence will send me the woman I need for my children—that is all I ask. Otherwise I am safe, sound, hearty, even growing merry again now that the storm is over. But it was an ordeal. Ça travaille dedans. Like Ramakrishna, I must now wear skirts as well as pants. Ça fait du bien. Greetings to Eve, to Seferis too. All will be well.

Henry

Sunday 4/27/52

[Big Sur]

Dear Larry—

Just a word to tell you things have altered radically for me—for the better. In the first place, I've found an "Eve." She's been here since ten days now, and it was a thorough go from the first. Every day I congratulate myself on my great good fortune. I tell you, I feel like a new man—and about 30 years younger! Moreover, I look it. It's just unbelievable what a change she has wrought in me. It's like living on velour, to be with her. And so capable she is, so gracious, tender, full of understanding. Strange thing is that she is the sister of my friend Schatz's wife. I'll send you a photo of her one day. To compare with your Eve. She's Scotch-Irish-French with a drop of Jewish blood in her, a fine leaven. I haven't lost my temper once, nor been grouchy or irritated or depressed. The children will be here with us for the summer. Then I hope we (Eve and I) can take off for Europe, for a few months' visit at least. So, wherever you are, rejoice for your miserable friend who was for many months in the throes of despair. Soon you should be receiving my *Rimbaud*, *Plexus*, and *The World of Sex*—all in French. *Alraune* (my *Scenario*) was given a tremendous and successful broadcast from Paris recently.

Henry

You should also have by now *My Life with Books* from the British publisher, Peter Owen.

Belgrade

[May 1952]

My dear Henry—

I am so happy for you! It is wonderful to feel the sudden lift and curve of happiness come through even in your handwriting. And if you come to Europe can you make Athens? Listen, we leave on the 1st of June by car for Salonika and Athens. We have complete camping equipment to make us independent and the idea is to find a small fishing village about 40 miles from Athens and to settle down for 6 weeks' leave there. We've got our tiny daughter Sappho-Jane with us who must be baptised in the Mediterranean and I want to find a peasant house with a kitchen so that the routine of her feeding and sleeping is easy to fix and doesn't cost Eve too much effort. Myself, I only want a couple of days in Athens to hunt for a possible job, but if there was any chance of seeing you and carrying you both off to my hideout I would, of course, jump at it. Cable me, will you, if there is any chance of us being in Greece at the same time. Failing that, I am planning to spend August camped by the Lake of Bled in northern Yugoslavia. Very beautiful place. Where will you be then?

Best love to you both and Hurrah!

Larry

[Fall 1952]

Dear Henry—

A thousand thanks for the *Books* book which has just arrived and is full of marvellous things. I'm midway in it, and it brings back so many memories to hear your tone of voice again. Last week in Trieste I happened upon a pile of *Cancers* and *Capricorns* in a book shop. The new edition with Anais' preface. Riffling them through I suddenly remembered you standing at the table talking in Villa Seurat, the sun shining, a bottle of Volnay on the table, Betty cooking and Joe repeating "Ja Ja Ja." Such a pang for those good Paris days with *The Booster!* Wonder when we'll meet again. How good it would be to hear your voice.

By the way, I'm quitting the service in December and we are setting off to Cyprus, I think. No money. No prospects. A tent. A small car. I feel twenty years younger. Heaven knows how we'll keep alive, but I'm so excited I can hardly wait to begin starving.

Love to you both,
Larry

291

MARCH 1953—FEBRUARY 1957

(Durrell in Cyprus—Miller in Big Sur and Europe)

———◆———

D URRELL'S next letter comes from Cyprus the following March. Eve has had a breakdown and is back
in England recuperating. This is a very lonely, anxious
and painful time for Durrell, burdened with all sorts of
worries. He is forced to take a job schoolteaching. But if
he is to be a writer, it is now or never. (At about the same
age Miller crossed his Rubicon—to Paris.) So despite
tragedy, turmoil and fatigue, Durrell concentrates his
energies on the book he has been carrying around all these
years. To add to his problems, the political situation on
Cyprus, which at first seems comic opera, develops ago-
nizingly into the story told in *Bitter Lemons*. Altogether
Durrell's sojourn on Cyprus is a most difficult period, but
by the end of it he has finished *Justine*.

For Miller this is a time of reunions. In 1953 he returns to Europe and is warmly received everywhere; his
tour of Europe is a triumphal progress. "Reunion in Barcelona" tells of his exuberant meeting with Perlès after
fifteen years. The following year Perlès goes to Big Sur
to write *My Friend Henry Miller*. Miller himself is at
this time writing *Big Sur and the Oranges of Hieronymus Bosch*. Katsimbalis also turns up at Big Sur, and
Seferis visits Durrell on Cyprus. But Miller and Durrell
are not fated to meet yet; meanwhile their correspondence
is rather sparse and sporadic.

*   *

[1953]

Dearest Henry—

Wonderful to hear from you. I was a bit shocked when I wrote Fred because we had planned this move months ahead and worked it out to the nearest penny. I was to have a whole golden year off to work. We were going to buy a small house etc. etc.—and this comes right on top of my resigning and burning all the bridges behind me. Nevertheless I have stuck to the main plan. I've bought a small Turkish house on a hillside in a village near here; it will be fixed by the end of May. It should be very nice. But of course keeping two establishments and living here is eating into the capital we'd saved for the house.

What a pity you can't come and camp with me for a while. Cyprus is comparatively cheap and I reckon that by about early June I could find you a corner in the house. Think about it, will you? I'm aiming to settle here. It's a big coarse-grained island with lovely spots in it. People nice. Good roads and you can buy anything, English or American. Palm trees. It's a piece of Asia Minor washed out to sea—not Greece. It's Middle East—taste of Turkey and Egypt.

I'm trying to write a book about Alexandria at night, but I'm dead beat usually after handling the baby. She's such an angel. No, I haven't forgotten how to laugh, but there hasn't been a fit subject for the last few months. Eve has been frightfully ill, and now I'm engaged in a desperate gamble, spending capital, waiting for some baby solution which will enable me to work.

I've been watching the tremendous and deserved accolade the French Press have been giving you. Your reputation is at meridian. Hurrah! Think about a visit—you should see where Aphrodite was born and her baths. Pick up Katsimbalis at Piraeus and bring him along.

Love,

Larry

Toledo, Spain
5/5/53

Dear Larry—

We've been motoring through Spain last 3 weeks and a bit fagged out now. Returning to Montpellier, France, next week, via Andorra and will probably rest a week there and decide what next. Money low now. Below par. And the heat in Andalusia just floored us. I can imagine now what it's like in Cyprus and Jerusalem. Pretty certain we will not be able to make either place—for several reasons.

We met Fred and Anne in Barcelona and had 2 full days with them. Fred was just as always, even more so. Hasn't aged or changed a bit. Remarkable. We laughed from the time we met—which was by accident at the American Express. Haven't laughed that way in many a year. And naturally we spoke of you. How much more we would have laughed had you been with us.

This trip to Europe—hectic—has given me confidence in my ability to come over again and perhaps frequently. Now I am so used to Europe I shall miss it once back in America. But I feel a need to return soon and establish my own rhythm. Traveling does not permit of work, at least for me. I go blank, my mind goes to sleep. Spain is a remarkable country. I don't think I'd want to live here, but it is certainly worth knowing. The landscape, always wonderful, often reminded me of Greece. But in no country have I ever been stared at so much! They have the curiosity of primitives. Andalusia is all it's reputed to be.

The impress of the Moors is tremendous—and always good. Seeing the Alhambra, the Alcazar, the Mezquita (Mosque), I feel I have seen three of the seven wonders of the world. Catholic Spain is dark, morose, sinister, brutal.

Well, Larry, I'll write again from France or Italy. Have only a few weeks left. I pray that things go better for you. What a pity you chose to live so far away! But you are right in choosing the Mediterranean world. Curiously, traveling through Spain, I had a strong sensation about Atlantis. Felt we were traveling, at times, over this sunken continent.

Eve sends you her love. Feels she knows you from all Fred and I have said about you.

Keep your pecker up!

Cheerio!
Henry

8/15/53

[Big Sur]

Dear Larry—

We're home almost two weeks now but scarcely adjusted to our New World, which I find is even emptier and more poisonous than ever. I keep wondering how you are getting along. How fares the infant? We (Eve and I) are exhausted by nightfall just looking after our two healthy youngsters—5 and 8 years old.

It was a great misfortune not to get to Cyprus. We really wanted to. But it was just too much this trip. If World War III doesn't break out in a few weeks (as I firmly expect), we plan to leave next September ('54) for Jerusalem and from there come to see you in Cyprus or wherever you are. I read with heartache of the quakes in Ithaca, Zante, Cephalonia. Hope it has not reached your island. If only, in all these cosmic disturbances, there were now and then a bit of old Atlantis brought up from the depths. Traveling through Spain I thought constantly of Atlantis. Andalusia seemed to me to belong to some other world, not just the Moorish world. Mostly it was the way the mountains ran that gave me the feeling. The Pyrenees end Europe.

We saw Joey in Wells, did I tell you? It was more than good to be with him. He's improved and grown younger and wiser. And what a clown—still! How we laughed! Here nobody can make me laugh. We'll have to get back to the Old World soon and remain there. But not England, eh? England is really weird—no other word for it. Yet you can't hate or despise the English. I had a glimpse of Wales—much better. Saw old John Cowper Powys at Corwen. What a joyous old codger! A lively mage.

Well, blessings, me lad. More soon.

Henry

Bellapaix, Cyprus
Nov. 20

[1953]

Dear Henry—

How good to hear from you again and thank you for sending papers, etc. Reading matter always welcome, even though there is no time to read. My job is unbelievably arduous, but I think when I have no house problems I shall manage to do it and also live. At present I'm up at 4:30, bathe and dress, check the car and write the odd letter (this for example, by candlelight). I motor to Kyrenia and thence into Nicosia where I begin work at 7. It is really thrilling—the dark dawns, tip-toeing down the village street with the first yellow flush rising behind the gaunt stone spars of the ruined Abbey of Bellapaix.

My mother is keeping the house and child going while I work. All my waking hours I am writing in my head, but as yet I have not fixed up my little study so I have nowhere to write. But 30 hours' teaching is too much. Nevertheless I am in good heart and if once the house is finished I have any energy left, I shall be able to make *Justine* a worthy successor to *The Black Book*. I'm keeping my fingers crossed of course. Mary Mollo has sent me *Plexus* from Paris, but owing to some fault in the makeup, Vol. I and Vol. II (with different covers) have identical contents. I've told her to notify Kahane about this. The island is very beautiful now in the first snows. Opposite us, over the sea, the Atlas Mountains are snow-tipped.

Night before last there was a bang on the front door and a shout and Seferiades walked in. You can imagine how warmly we embraced each other. He had not altered by a day, still the graceful and lovely humour—man and poet. He had never been to Cyprus before and is ravished by it. The mixture of temples and Crusader forts—Stratford and Knossos—is indeed quite strange. My village is built round a Lusignan ruined abbey like Christchurch Cathedral. Gothic windows and olive-trees!

Owning one's own house is a wonderful thing. I want Sapphy to have a peaceful village childhood here before she kicks off into the world. The beauty of the Mediterranean—one can't have enough of it. I insist on dying somewhere along this holy and pre-Christian shore.

Best love to you both,
Larry

[December 1953]

Dear Henry—

A brief line to thank you for the two great parcels of books which arrived, followed rapidly by two more. It was wonderfully generous of you, and it's good to have something to read in this fragmented life. I'm pushing my book about Alexandria along literally sentence by sentence. I'm dog-tired by the time I get home in the evening, but every waking moment is possessed by it so that by the weekend when I type out my scribbles I usually have about 1500 words. I feel like one of those machines for distilled water—it is coming drop by drop, running contrary to physical fatigue etc. This is really writing one's way upstream with a vengeance! Never mind—I remember your struggles and blush to think of my own.

I'm writing this at 4:50 A.M. A faint lilac dawn breaking accompanied by bright moonlight—weird. Nightingales singing intoxicated by the first rains. Everything damp. In a little while I take the car and sneak down the dark road towards a dawn coming up from Asia Minor like *Paradise Lost*.

Love,
Larry

Bellapaix, Cyprus
Jan. 5

[1954]

Dear Henry—

A letter for New Year to wish you all good things for the coming year and to hope that we shall see you this year. My little house is more or less finished now except for details and we have successfully put up one guest for

Christmas. It was so lovely too to see Seferis again after so many years, as gentle and as humorous as ever. I teach, you know, at the Greek Gymnasium and he was brought down as a distinguished poet and given an ovation, so I was able to be present as a master. He made a touching address to the boys full of thoughtful things very gently said. His hair is going white and his voice has tiny crackles at the edges, of old age—though otherwise he does not seem a day over fifty. He has promised to come back incognito this summer specially to meet up with you. How are your plans shaping? Don't try to do too much; stop off in places for a few months at a time and laze about. I think you will like Cyprus in spite of it being so unGreek—it has the lazy moist sensuality of the Eastern Levant, of Egypt and Syria—the mindless sensuality which made the Sybarites. It is dunned out, autumnal, sleep-impregnated. It would not have suited me as a young man but now in my old age (42!) I think it is a good enough place to settle for a few years to let Sappho get a good grip on life and learn two or three barbaric languages. Of course I have to work pretty hard at present which is a bore as it makes me too tired to get on with my novel—which I think and pray is going to be good— better than anything since *The Black Book* anyway. My youngest brother Gerry has scored a tremendous success with his first book and is making a deal of money. He collects wild animals for zoos and writes up his adventures afterwards. The one pays for the other; how marvellous to have one's career fixed at 25 or so and to be able to pay one's way. The perpetual nibbling of money-worry is the worst of curses when one has children or can't bear squalor; and the lack makes it so hard to see and enjoy one's friends properly.

Zarian is supposed to be coming over soon to start a giant international paper in French and English. He

300

would amuse you. Cyprus is becoming quite a literary centre and hordes of artists and writers are moving in and trying to settle here. There's a little Italian boat which goes from here to Rhodes, Smyrna, Piraeus, Kalamata, Venice—which would please you as a trip. Write a line when you have time and tell me what you *are writing*. Can you send me your essay on Rimbaud? I'm just reading his letters; he worked here—of course you know—and built the Governor's house on Mt. Troodos. There is no mystery about the man. How hard and sane and un-selfpitying his letters are. I'd never seen them before.

Love,
Larry

Information Department, Government of Cyprus,
Nicosia, Cyprus

[Fall 1955]

My dear Henry—

How wonderful to get a long letter from you after so long and at such a time. We are in the middle of a very nasty little revolution here with bombs and murders on the Palestine pattern so that daily life is sharp as a bite into a sour apple. It is so long since I've written that I can't remember at which point in my crowded and disorderly life to take up this correspondence. Eve and my daughter are in England. My little Turkish house I've had to lock up, but there is a deserted mosque (The Seven Sleepers) on the sea-coast where I go for the weekend to cool my mind. The sea-line is bare, barren, stark—not unlike some of the pictures of Big Sur—a savage, lime-green sea, and the little white mosque built sheer upon it. One's loneliness increases gradually—I suppose it to be the only real capital I have. I'm deep in Zen Buddhist treatises these days—Suzuki! What a marvellous speechless religion. Now that travel is dangerous and life getting more enclosed I treasure the sea and the mosque as people treasure jewels of price. I have nearly finishd my *second* novel. You'll remember when I did *The Black Book* I planned 3 *real* novels : youth, maturity and old age. Well, in the midst of all this noise and slaughter I'm half-way through a book called *Justine* which is about Eve's Alexandria before the war. I believe it is very good. We'll have to wait and see. I think probably I shall go and live in the mosque for a while. It is on a barren spit of land by the sea. There is an old shy Hodja in charge who never stirs out of his room. Seven tombs of unknown Turkish soldiers sleep a stony sleep under green awnings. Happiness is really within reach—only this job is killing me. I shall have to leave it soon and starve my novel out of my system. Henry, do send me a few of your books. I'm out of date on your new work. Didn't care for *Sexus*, but I still hear the surf-thunder of your prose in memory as the biggest experience of my inner man. Is Joey with you still?

Love,
Larry

1/5/56

[Big Sur]

Dear Larry—

Just got your last message about Eve and the child. Know how you must feel. It's all a frightful ordeal. However, I can tell you this—I know it—you will soon find that you are better off. A man—you especially—can live with himself and thrive. It will give you strength, courage, purpose, peace of mind. Take your time about finding another mate. Let her find you! Don't get frantic.

Have no doubt Cyprus will gain her independence or

alliance with Greece. All the down-trodden are coming into their own soon, it's inevitable. And there won't be any atom bomb wars either.

Mailing you more books. Tell me what you lack or want. Now, I feel, you will do a great stint of writing. Everyone loves that *Sappho* play.

We are having incessant rains here. Floods, wash-outs, etc. Joey has been back in London since last May. Just got his book, *My Friend Henry Miller*. Did he send you a copy? If not, let me know.

All the best, dear Larry. And don't stick your head in the powder keg. We need you!

Henry

P.S.   My girl, Val, just wrote her first composition for me. She's just beginning to realize that her father is a writer. Curious, what?

Public Relations, P.I.O., Nicosia, Cyprus

[Summer 1956]

Dear Henry—

I am just reading—with what nostalgia I cannot tell you—little Joe's account of you which was sent to me from England last week, presumably by little Joe himself. I am rationing myself in order to spin it out, so wonderful is it to read about Paris in this curfew-ridden town. My goodness, how alive and free one felt in those days! What has happened to the world since then? I have just finished a book about Alexandria called *Justine*—the first *serious* book since *The Black Book*, much clearer and better organised, I think. I will send you a set of galleys when they come in. It's a sort of prose poem to one of the great capitals of the heart, the Capital of Memory, and it carries a series of sharp cartoons of the women of Alexandria, certainly the loveliest and most world-weary women in the world. I had fallen into a bad patch of distress and apathy after Eve left for England in the middle of August with the child, which I miss, and by a stroke of luck a lovely young Alexandrian tumbled into my arms and gave me enough spark to settle down and demolish the book. She is French, Claude, a writer with something oddly her own. Night after night we've been working on our books, typewriters at each end of the dining-room table, sitting up over a scale map of Alexandria before a log fire tracing and re-tracing the streets with our fingers, recapturing much that I had lost, the brothels and the parks, the dawns over Lake Mareotis etc. Outside the dull desultory noise of occasional bombs going off, or a few pistol shots, or a call from the operations people to say that there's been another ambush in the mountains. A very queer and thrilling period, sad, weighed down with futility and disgust, but marvellous to be able to live in one's book while everything is going up inchmeal around one and the curfews settle on the dead towns. Must write about it one day. Wish we could meet. I may be in England in August.

Best love to you,
Larry

9 August

[Cyprus, 1956]

Dear Henry—

Am leaving Cyprus on the 26th for London where I'll spend a fortnight and thence over to France where Claude hopes to borrow a place to live. We have enough money to last us 3 months in which we'll finish our current books. After that what? I don't know. For the first time in my life I shall be prospectless and dead broke—and doubtless on the streets quite literally. Will you write me c/o Faber and Faber, 24 Russell Square, London. I'll write you from France.

All the best,
Larry

Stone Cottage, Milkwell near Donhead St. Andrew,
Shaftesbury, Dorset

[October 1956]

My dear Henry:

My plans went suddenly awry and dammit, here I am for a few months in the heart of the Hardy country, where the people talk in the identical tiresome moralising way they do in Hardy. The accommodation Claude found just outside Paris fell through at the last minute. Meanwhile I have promised Faber the MS of the blasted Cyprus book by Christmas and so I was forced to try and set up a temporary headquarters until the mist lifted a bit. Fortunately Diana Ladas rented me this tiny cottage where at present Claude and I are installed, both working like maniacs on our books. Saph goes to the village school, her accent daily getting broader and broader, but seems to enjoy it. I had a card from Joe giving me his address but as yet have not had a chance to see him. He's in Reuter, he says. I loved his book about us all. And incidentally your study of Moricand is devastatingly good. I remember him so vividly, the heavy personal odour of the baby powder and the lotions, and I can't see a late portrait of Wilde—scented and curled hair, high collar, pearl pin and polished cuffs like cerements—without thinking of Moricand. Only the other day I was going through some papers in a friend's loft and stumbled across my horoscope by him. I am sending you my selected poems which have just come out. And my young brother has just scored a big success with a crazy book about Corfu which I've asked him to send you. He's off on another expedition next month. A best seller now, but only interested in animals.

In a little while I'll be sending you the first volume of *Justine*, a novel about Alexandria which I hope and pray will make you smile and perhaps just faintly cheer. Second volume follows as soon as I have this Cyprus book off my hands, pray God by Christmas. By then of course we'll all be starving and have to find a job, perhaps in France. But meanwhile we are living warmly and economically and working all day, from around eight when all the housework is done and the child off to school. Our only recreation is to visit the local pub where the accent is so fantastic as to be better than the movies. Have no radio, no television, and not even daily newspapers. In fact the best holiday I've had in years. I don't know what's happening in Cyprus—maybe they've burnt my house down by now. Cyprus is so tragic it doesn't bear talking about. Clearly we can't go on being a great power if our political grasp of things is so elementary. Russia can do it because she shoots to kill. But we can neither shoot nor think it seems. Never mind. I'm well out of that lot.

Meanwhile October is all sunshine and green grass and smoke from cottage chimneys. Nothing has changed. The Englishman still laughs without removing his pipe; his wife wears a hat and carries a lap dog. Everything is serene and bland as suet.

Best love to you both,
Larry

Dear Larry—

Just as well you're snug and safe in dear old England. Stay there till the smoke clears away. Glad to hear two more of your books are coming soon. I got the volume of verse and read a poem a day—as I do with St. John Perse, one of the three living poets I can read, enjoy and marvel over.

Good to hear you have your little girl with you. Val's little thing was written last Christmas when she was just ten. Notice atrocious spelling of American kids—quite common.

Had about 18 books published this year, mostly translations. One in Hebrew with wonderful illustrations by Schatz due out this month. Spain publishing the *Colossus* for South America.

Your book on Cyprus should be exciting. I love the one on Rhodes.

I suppose you're nowhere near Wells, where Joey's wife lives? You'd like the spot, and as for the cathedral, I'm crazy about it, especially the facade. Hard by is Glastonbury—do you know the place?

Here we listen in on world news and arrive nowhere. The good aspect of it all is that the leaky vessel is foundering. Pumps won't work any more. The despised peoples will come into their own, bombs or no bombs. Don't you rather enjoy the paralysis at U.N. and elsewhere? Picasso could solve it alone overnight—or even Chaplin. Don't lose touch—and best to Claude and love to the little girl. Have you a photo of her?

Henry

[Big Sur]

Dear Larry—

Just got your *Justine* and have almost finished it, in one sitting. Fascinating! And what writing! Nobody can wield the English language like you. Hair-raising sometimes. What a picture of Alexandria!

I will write at length in a day or two. Have more to say about it. (Je crois bien.) This is just to felicitate you. Luck to have Book Society recommend it. You should be able now to sell it to an American publisher. If not already contracted for, tell Faber to send copy to Mr. M. Lincoln Schuster of Simon and Schuster, New York. He's fond of me, because of my spiel on Powys. May well take it. It's a good, live house. Also tell Faber to send me 3 copies of book with bill. And can you dig up your *Pope Joan* book for me—lost my copy. Will pay.

Still trying to do something with your *Sappho*. This is a great work, I think. You are certainly not falling behind. Your troubles have done you good.

I've just been elected a member of The Institute of Arts and Letters, which is our apology for a French Academy.

Are you still in the dumps—still broke? Write soon.

Henry

———◆———

T HE correspondence resumes its old tempo when Durrell moves to France, finds a home in a tiny town in
Provence, and settles down as a full-time writer. When
he sends *Bitter Lemons* and the first two volumes of *Justine* (as he calls the *Quartet* at first) , Miller responds with
a number of ringing accolades like those with which he
greeted *The Black Book* 20 years back. Again and again
he writes, full of wonder and admiration and amazement:
"How did you do it with all your troubles?" "*Justine* will
make a hit—it can't help but do so. I repeat—it's magnificent!" Miller helps Durrell to get published in four
or five foreign languages and assures him that the stars
are turning in his favor at last. And sure enough, 1957
marks the turning point. By the end of the year Durrell
has finished three volumes of the *Quartet* and begun to
gain widespread recognition. *Bitter Lemons* becomes a
best seller and is awarded the Duff Cooper Prize. Claude
sends Miller an amusing account of their journey to London for "the Solemn Investiture of Larry at the hands of
the Queen Mother."

*   *

[February 1957]

My dear Henry!

A little hotel off St. Sulpice. Everything a good deal more expensive but the same ambiance. I have been walking round your quarter today with great affection and emotion. So little has changed—Alésia, Rue de la Tombe-Issoire. A quiet drink at the Closerie des Lilas—still out of fashion and quiet enough to write a book in. Chez Henriette is still exactly the same. In fact apart from multiplying your bills by three or four Paris is securely anchored as ever in her rational serenity—mesure and grand style in every local wine and cheese—what a place! Where are you? Write c/o Fabers for the time as I may be going south.

Larry

Villa Louis

[February–March 1957]

My dear Henry—

We have finally fetched up here in the Raimu country. A medieval town asleep on its feet. A castle whose history nobody knows. It just happened. And all built very insecurely on the arm of a river which floods the whole place every other year, carrying away people and houses. Nobody seems to care. Life is a good deal cheaper than in Paris and the people I think much nicer. They do not behave like logical positivists with a high temperature. We want if we can to try and settle in France—Claude is French by nationality. Her first novel has just been accepted in England and the U.S. agents are enthusiastic. Somewhat to my surprise Dutton have bought *Justine* in the U.S.A. and offered quite a handsome advance on it.

310

All this of course doesn't mean much, but it's a ray of light under the door. If I could earn the smallest steady money . . . There are lovely little—no, big, huge— village houses for sale all along this coast for about £400 —1000 dollars isn't it? If we could get one! They are all built round large courtyards, stone, well-tiled. Over a period one could make a lovely house of any of them. Idle dreams! I'm glad *Justine* interested you—première ébauche merely, first stage of an etching I hope will carry three more cuttings—hence the apparent obscurities in the first book. My book on Cyprus comes in September and will rustle a few dovecots, I hope. What are your prospects of visiting France this year? Do keep in touch if you get on the move. It would be so wonderful to meet again after all these years and gros rouge is still only a shilling a bottle in France.

Love,
Larry

Big Sur—Easter

[1957]

Happy Easter, O Master of the Heraldic Line!

Have just read first chapter of Cyprus book and am already enchanted. How you are writing these days! Not that it is a sudden change of style, but now all the work of the past years shows in every line. I don't see how intelligible English prose can be pushed any farther. And now I recall how you looked on the balcony in that little house at Corfu, with a pencil and pad, scribbling, scribbling, polishing your style, rewriting, writing some more, bathing, drinking, singing, laughing, but always coming back to the pad and pencil. One can see how you have struggled to master the medium, and not just the medium, but the language itself, the English, the King's English.

Now I read you enviously. Why didn't I say that? What a marvelous adjective! What an image! That whole duck shoot in *Justine*—something out of this world . . . like Louis Armstrong with his trumpet. Turgenev would have died happily to write this way.

And now tell me, has this book been sold yet to an American publisher? All our old big publishers are doubling up with other firms. The paper backs have won the day. And why not think of Penguin for a pocket edition right now—on Cyprus book, I mean?

Yes, and what are you doing toward getting your other books published here in America? Now is your time. I feel it in my bones. These things come in waves. If I knew your horoscope I could tell you better. Now it is just a hunch. But if you know your hour, date and place of birth, send it to me again. I know a woman who has been most accurate. She's Danish.

Henry

Villa Louis

[June 1957]

Dear Henry:

Just got back from Nimes where we went with Richard Aldington and his lovely daughter. A good lunch and a touch of mistral but the vines doing well, stretching away to the horizon in every corner of the sky. I think I must still be rather a baby because it is such a big thrill to talk to a writer who knew Lawrence for years and was with him when he died; and the span of whose literary life started around 1910. Imagine, as a young man he was corresponding with de Gourmont and Proust. He is now sixty-five and in poor health and has recently fallen into disfavour for attacking some of our more notable buggers; but in good heart otherwise. It is fun to let his memories run on . . . Middleton Murry, Katherine Mansfield, Eliot, Ouspensky, etc. . . .

This week Roy Campbell was killed in a motor crash. I don't know whether you know his work, the finest and most flamboyant poetry of the day. He was a bullfighter here in the arènes of Provence. Aldington is very cast down about it, but Roy, the old devil, with so many unforgivable satires to his credit couldn't have died in bed. I'm sure he has already lampooned St. Peter and been put in irons.

I mustn't forget to tell you of a rare stroke of luck I've had. Someone must have been dozing in the committee. The Book Society have chosen the Cyprus book. Of course this doesn't mean very much as it does in the USA where the book clubs run into hundreds of thousands; it means about ten thousand copies. But as a kick away and publicity for the others it's a good thing to happen. Meanwhile of course I am so glad to feel that I don't have to find another job until at least next year that I have finished *Justine II*. I'll route the MS via you to Dutton; tell me if it stinks. It is only the second of four. The next one is totally different in style, a naturalistic job. Then I hope to add the fourth dimension—Time—in the last volume. Claude is starting to type the old nightmare out this week. Her own novel comes out from Faber in September.

The more I see of France the more convinced I am it is the only place to live despite its expense today. In the country it is not bad and the income tax set-up is so good I am declaring for it, registering from England as an "emigrant"!

I think in a year or so we shall have had a chance to really see Provence. Aldington says there are ravishing, completely overlooked and forgotten medieval towns tucked away north of us, more remote than Spain, where one could find a house like we have and a river or lake to swim in. I am going to investigate all this most carefully before thinking of buying. But even here it's lovely on this gracious river, something like Stratford plus Canterbury, if you know them. When the devil are you coming to Europe again? Couldn't you manage some time over here now you are so famous? A lecture or two perhaps?

Love as always,

Larry

Villa Louis

[June 1957]

My dear Henry,

I'm terribly ashamed at all the time you spend writing about me instead of yourself. Surely for an autobiographer this is a terrible waste of energy. I don't know how to thank you, or what I can do in return to show my gratitude. The foreign rights of *Justine* have gone to French, Swedes and Germans; but best of all is a really interested U.S. publisher—Dutton's. This has encouraged me to grapple with the second book which I finished yesterday, and which I think will amuse you more than the first. The ground plan, if I can do it, is four books of which the first two fit into each other—different but the same book—Giordano Bruno. The next which I shall start after tea today is a big orthodox novella interpenetrating the two previous ones at many points. Anyway, to hell with it all, we shall see. *Justine* has had a tremendous press in England—rather a worried plaintive note from the dovecots where our literary men drowse but enthusiastic withal. I'm curious to see what the second one does.

In France the moral atmosphere, even down here in the provinces, is just right. And they are wise and witty and do not bother you like the Italians and Greeks, who are as sentimental as spaniels: want to sit in your lap all day and feed you sweets. In short living in the southern Mediterranean has its trials. People won't leave you alone. It is like living in an Italian movie—great fun if you have nothing to do, as they never seem to have. But just try to read or work. Now these people have marvellous reserve as well as being really friendly. They read. On the buses you will see the conductor at a stop fish out *Figaro Littéraire!* And the mania for artists is so endearing—they never ask if you make any dough. At Nimes, the Inspector General of Taxes, when he found I was un écrivain, stood up at once and shook my hand with real congratulation which meant "By God, I envy you, I wish I was." Yesterday I had lunch with Richard Aldington in Montpellier. He told me that last week he was sent a summons by the vice squad to appear; a puzzling thing—he has no vices. It turned out that the head of the police vice squad was a writer who admired him and wanted him to check over an essay about his own work which the cop had written for the *Police Quarterly* about Aldington's work. Can you beat it? And well written, too. He showed me a copy. Of course I've always known and loved this about France, but it is good to see that it hasn't perished under the successive waves of Anglo-American dollar-itis. Ordinary life still has the passionate cool authenticity of a line by Molière. And here in the south the heartlessness which you always criticised in the Parisian, but which is only a big town, as opposed to village, phenomenon is missing. They are generous to a fault, Provençal as well as French. Of course there are bastards here too, but the frame which protects the individual life is marvellous—though so venerable and of so slow a growth it is modern, modern as tomorrow. Ach, but you know all this. We've cut the marvellous picture of you out of that French mag—with

315

the caption, "Freedom, is it French?" It looks good on the wall. Of course it's French. You never spoke a truer word, O Master!

Bless you Henry,
Larry

June 21st—Summer!
[Big Sur, 1957]

Dear Larry,

Your letters are piling up and I've had no chance to reply lately. Now my two children are here, and they may possibly stay on indefinitely with Eve and myself. Big job. Tony is near nine, Val near 12. Wonderful kids, but high-strung, active as dynamite, undisciplined, etc. etc. etc. I love them.

Richard Aldington, a neighbor. How strange. A man of sixty, you say. Why, I am now 65, don't you know? However, I'm hardly different than at forty. Get ired quicker, for one thing. I mean hopping mad. And less patience with bores and nit-wits. And fighting like a demon (wrong thing) to achieve more peace and solitude. Impossible here. Simply invaded continually.

Lectures! I get offers every day, from $200 to $1000 per lecture. Never accept. Hate public meetings. Loathe gatherings. Detest readings. Especially poetry readings. Do you have a phonograph that will play long-playing records? If so I'll send you the two recordings I made in New York with Ben Grauer. Just out.

Looking at the photos you sent. How unchanged you look! Amazing. You and Fred. Eternal youth! Hurrah! And Claude, I can't make her out from the photos. Have to meet her in the flesh.

Wonderful about Aldington and the police. Reminds

316

me of my run-in with Fernand Rude, préfet of Vienne—
see *Big Sur* book. There was a scholar! Also, Francis Raoul
of the Paris Préfecture. If I had not had good French
friends like these men I would still be getting my visa
O.K.'d. That Paris Préfecture is a veritable nightmarish
labyrinth. Positively frightening. But there I sat with
M. Raoul, talking literature, cool as a cucumber, and
everything I had done or said (in my papers) was wrong.
And the meeting with the Paris Juge d'Instruction. Marvelous. I felt like Baudelaire after that meeting. A real
honor and privilege to be haled to court there.

I remember standing with my bike and looking at that
Pont du Gard in 1928. I remember the Nimes amphi-
theatre—first bullfight I ever saw. And Arles. But have
you been to Montserrat where the last of the Albigensians
were walled up? Or to Sète, to visit Valéry's grave—very
simple and inconspicuous.

Time's up. All morning answering letters. What a life!
If I don't get a secretary soon I'll die of congestion.

Carry on, and send me pages of *Justine 2* any time.
Then I'll reread *Justine* (1) again. I wish I could read
your horoscope. I'll bet there are great things ahead for
you, right quick. Don't laugh! You've had your years
of martyrdom. I think your path is clearing up. I sense it.
I pray for it. You deserve it.

> Avance Toujours!
> "Ma main amie" (Cendrars)
> Henry

> *Big Sur*
> July 31st, 1957

Dear Larry:

I finished reading the second book of *Justine* yesterday
and am sending it off to Curtis Brown now. It's fabulous.

317

Every bit as good as the first volume and full of the most amazing incidents and events. The carnival scenes are out of this world, hair-raising. I like the Interlinear too. I can't make criticism. I am too spell-bound. Will only say that the two letters at the end seemed a trifle unnecessary and a bit of a let-down possibly. But don't take me too seriously. I read it with great difficulty over a period of ten days, interrupted each day, several times a day, so that sometimes I was able to read only a few paragraphs in a day. But even under that disadvantage I was enthralled. I really don't see how you can improve on this writing. You are at the top of your form. And, strange to say, in some ways you remind me of Paul Valéry. Those aesthetico-religious-metaphysical speculations especially. I'll say this, there is nothing like this *Justine* in all English literature—what I know of it, at any rate.

I've already received the American edition of Book One, and it looks good. I meant to tell you that you received a marvelous tribute over the air by the American writer, Kenneth Rexroth, who wrote the preface to one of my pocket books (*Nights of Love and Laughter*).

Never have I been subjected to more intrusions, more invasions. I am going nuts. I can't even find time to answer my letters regularly. If it continues I am going to quit Big Sur. Cheerio!

Henry

Villa Louis

[August 1957]

THIS LETTER REQUIRES NO ANSWER!
My dear Henry:

Marvellous! Just finished first reading of your *Oranges*. You achieve real Japanese hokku effects in the prologue, and the centre panel had the great pug-marks of genius one always finds when you become airborne. I found you perhaps too indulgent to your neighbours who don't sound a wildly thrilling lot, but then indulgence and affection in you never ceases. Look how indulgent you have been to your juniors, not the least of whom is yours truly. And living together casts a powerful spell over one and roots out egoistic dispathies (Rolfe's wonderful word). I couldn't help being amused by your groans about correspondence. Why, you devil, you adore writing letters. I must have held you up for weeks on *Capricorn* with my letters from Corfu which you answered at such length. Self-indulgence. I had hoped by now you could afford a bodyguard to expel visitors and sift your mail of all trivia because I know that the sight of a Chinese stamp would make you answer a perfectly pointless letter from a student written in pigeon: pidgin. Anyway, I don't write to bother you, just to salute you. Thanks to your efforts, *Justine* goes into four languages and thanks to Rowohlt's contract Faber has come across with a contract which, if I can honour it with two books a year, should enable me to drop everything and *write*. Wonderful. A new avenue opening up, I hope. At any rate I needn't try for a job until next summer now so I hope to get Justine III off my chest pronto. Fabers seem very excited by II so far and are setting it up. Germany has bought *Sappho* too and promise a production next year. With a bit of a shove I shall push the barn doors down, I hope.

Claude just back from London, having sold her second novel to Faber. I think you'd adore her; she is an Alexandrian Becky Sharp, gay, resourceful and good tempered. Luck! How I hope you manage to get to Europe this year, even via Cambodia. For me Europe from now on and the true heart and pulse of it (France) if humanly possible. Always wanted to live here. Now it looks possible—thanks largely to you.

Love to you both,

Larry

Dear Henry :

A quick flash in your direction to thank you, from this children-tormented house, and to hope your boy is safely over the tonsil operation. How worrying these things are I know too well. We have been lucky up to now. The three kids are having a whale of a time, bathing in the river, eating grapes off the vines, sleeping under mosquito nets outdoors among the vines, fishing—and every few days a Provençal bullfight. Not the ritualised murder of the Spanish corrida but the most manly, thrilling and dangerous sport in the world—trying to snatch prize cocardes from the fiery Camargue bulls in full run. Danger and skill and speed. By God, you should see the way these Provençal razateurs fly before the bulls and leap the stockade deftly as swallows. The children are thrilled. And the odd thing is that the bulls are the heroes. They get all the applause for a sharp and dangerous run. What a sport! U.S. cowboys, please copy. It goes back by tradition to ancient Crete! On the vases there are pictures of them doing it.

What else? I'm working like a demon on the Book III —*Mountolive*—again a slightly different angle, a straight naturalistic novel. Then in the fourth I slope back into my roman fleuve style again. I must try and tell you what I'm at formally; but I'm hoping you'll see with the 3rd Vol.

Love ever,

Larry

Dear Larry and Claude:

Haven't written for a good week or more—too many chores. Must tell you how much I enjoyed those last photos. You look good, the two of you, and Claude just delicious, reminds me strongly of some one I know, but can't think whom. Anyway, very feminine.

You seem to want to write something about me. I don't mean to dissuade you, but only to urge you to hold off till you're through with all you wish to write. To finish the Justine quartet is a feat in itself. I can wait and so can the world. The longer I live the less important everything seems. Once through with *Nexus* I don't care if I ever write another line. The hack work which it entails, answering fool letter writers, all sorts of demands, slays me. I spend half my day wading through this crap. I'd rather paint, by God.

It's quite useless, too, to think you'll make any impression on the English. Americans at least get abroad frequently and buy the banned books. Not the English. Not any more. And now that a half million people have read me, what does it mean? About two dozen people are all I really count as understanding admirers. It was worth winning them perhaps. Perhaps.

It gets more and more difficult to do any continuous work here. Living on the land, two children, endless visitors, endless chores, no recreation except pingpong and a half hour's reading a day—no more!—no contact with vital people, no interest in the cultural, or less and less, desirous only of learning how to live easy and relaxed and in the world but not of it, the urge to write recedes. I do want to travel, yes. But it's a great problem. Right now, for example, I am a thousand dollars in debt, and begging my publisher in New York (New Directions) to advance me 500 dollars to tide over. I need quite a few thousands to pick up and travel with a wife and two kids. I want to see Japan, Burma, Java, Jugoslavia and France again. But it all seems far off just now.

However, as I often tell you, my life is one of unexpected breaks. I can't seem to work for anything—it has to happen of its own. And it does, time and again. Right after writing T. S. Eliot, when Fred was here, asking if he would lend me a thousand (and getting a no, polite, to be sure), I received a few thousand from France—back payments due me which I didn't even know about. So it goes. Trust in Providence. Or as George Dibbern put it : "Serve life and life will take care of you." Which I do. Sometimes I think I am nothing but a servant—of any one who comes along. "A votre service, monsieur." Oui. I rarely say no to anything or anybody.

Of course if you saw this place you would understand much better. It is virtually ideal. And I have just sunk about ten thousand dollars into renovations—mostly a studio for myself, and a place for the kids. We moved into a one-room house originally. I drive a Cadillac, 1941 vintage, for which I paid $300. Very cheap. We have an old broken-down station wagon too. I spend a day a week in town, seeing my feeble-minded sister and shopping. I play with the kids. I walk the hills. I play pingpong with any one who happens along, and if not, with the kids, who are very good. Tony's nine now and Val, the girl, 12. She has a horse of her own. Stabled eight miles away. Must go fetch here three times a week. All costs. Food here horrendously high. Costs us $200 a month, *at least*. In fact, right now I am spending almost a thousand dollars a month on everything. Good reason for being broke, what!

All now. The toilet's out of order. Must drive miles to find a plumber. This winter (here) will be a terrible one, it is predicted. We may be marooned by heavy rains for several weeks. Laying in food supplies now. So if you don't hear much after Christmas you'll know it's the weather.

Cheerio, you two!

Henry

Villa Louis

[December 1957]

Dear Henry:

Just got back from London after an exhausting trip to collect the Duff Cooper prize, which enabled me to have a long evening session with little Joe, a marvellous long evening of reminiscence and good talk. Got back to find your good letter and the French *Justine* which I have sent off to you under separate cover—the translation is marvellous and your preface a terrific accolade. I can't thank you enough for it. I am just finishing the third book in the series so that I shall have two fat novels for next year; *Balthazar* comes in April—I should have copies soon. Dutton seems at last to be getting worked up about me, and I may unload some back titles on the U.S. market. Anyway we eat this year for certain.

I brought back the old disc of you and yesterday we had an orgy. Played the lot twice over. It is marvellous to hear you actually reminiscing in the house! Yes, I have been re-reading you from the start, as if I didn't know your work at all, making notes. I found somewhat to my surprise that *Sexus* which I once was so shocked and disgusted by is really as great as *Tropic*—only it is very unpruned. I was very much struck on the disc by what you had to say about phagomania, and Claude who is reading *Plexus* suddenly pointed out how closely the food and fucking references march together; in some places you

323

actually describe the act in terms of food. A great deal of Rabelais in you—the great meal and the great fuck march together and there are even strange connections—as in that wonderfully hypomanic scene after your marriage to June where you get drunk on water and *eat* a painting. I have never really thought about you as a psychology, but there are wonderful things to be discovered here because of the truth of the narrative line.

I learned much about Big Sur and how you live from Joe, and I must say it sounds wonderful; but the lack of people to talk to must be a bore. Incidentally, you can't, simply can't, travel round the world with the children. Not only is travel upsetting itself, but the Orient is a pretty dirty place. Remember I was a child in the tropics and I remember how my parents had to slave to keep me fit. Unless you moved from one great air-conditioned hotel to another you would certainly run into trouble. Do think most carefully about it, won't you? From what Joe says Eve sounds a wonderful ménagère. Let her advise you. As a woman she will know all these things. And besides, on such a trip you must be free to feel, and not full of anxieties. Go alone with Eve!

I was struck in your letter by the great amount of money you are spending. Jesus! For that amount you could live en prince in France even today. But I suppose the scale of everything in USA is larger than life and the cost of living twice anywhere else. Anaïs has just sent me the incomparable Keyserling *Travel Diary*—so I am travelling too while sitting still. What marvellous observation! Do re-read him if he is to hand. It will put you in the groove for travel. Myself, I am so happy in this exquisite Roman walled town with its quiet river and vines, and the whole dramatis personae of *Clochemerle* to talk to that I wouldn't move out of France for anything. By the way, I am going to pay French income tax this year and become a resident—do you know that it is one third of U.S. tax or English tax? Why not try an exploratory year in France? Come over alone, rent a place and have the kids over here?

Languedoc is primitive and dusty, but wonderful wine country. They have never heard of a toilet and we have imported a couple of camp ones from England which they regard with awe. They shit outdoors with the mistral blowing up their assholes. Our rent is only £100 a year for a decent size villa with lovely rooms, part furnished. We eat for about £40 a month when we are extravagant, but can cut down to about thirty without eating badly when the need arises and money pinches.

Yes, I have the order of your books right; and there are no gaps. But I've started again at the beginning and have just got to *Plexus* now. I'm not going to hurry over it. I thought of a book about Art and Obscenity worked around your importance and the meaning of your work. We shall see. Meanwhile now you are getting an English edition out, PLEASE consider rearranging the material. I would be inclined to keep stories together and essays ditto. I think a volume of your short stories in one lump would show your greatness better than a miscellany and your claims as a thinker would be better supported by a complete selection of essays (two volumes if necessary). Because your great books cannot be issued, there is every reason for you to study your line of attack with the books that can, and every reason to rearrange the stuff to achieve maximum impact. What do you think? I may be wrong.

Must go down to town and buy some brandade for lunch. Every good wish to you all—and for Christsake don't feel you have to answer me at length. I just post off to you whatever I think might amuse you and write when

I feel like it. But even when I hear nothing I have the feeling that you are always there, like Blake.

Love,
Larry

Villa Louis
17 Jan.

[1958]

Henry—

Hope all goes well. I have just surfaced after finishing the third of the bloody quartet. As we have to get it in by next week, the gallant and spirited Claude is typing it. (She is a speed typist. 140,000 words in 14 days flat is good even for a professional!) We have just bought a canoe for the children to play on the river with—the upper reaches are very Huckleberry Finn, full of Red Indians. Now we can really explore a bit. I'm writing some silly stories for the States. Your papers pay enormous sums for just a few words. In February I slack off and start shaping up my notes on a fruitful re-reading of your two big volumes. What a huge arc you describe in literature—a cathedral, a forest of statues, Angkor! By the way, be cagey about my address in France, will you? I'm beginning to get letters from the USA promising me a personal call. Provence is crawling with tourists in summer and I'm quite determined not to become a port of call for bores and curious people—as you have done from sheer goodness of heart. Padlocks on the garden gate for me. Why should one be tormented in this way? I feel I'm earning the seclusion I need by hard work and have quite enough old friends without wanting new. "We just came to say that . . ." But of course your Big Sur book won't alleviate the trouble. I'm not writing a word about Provence. I need a few months to tank up before tackling the last volume. My eldest daughter (Berengaria, Penelope, Pinky) is coming out in June to stay 3 weeks. She's a ballet dancer and very beautiful and clever—avant garde. Sapphy (7) is coming in August. Claude has just received a letter from you the length of a novel! Improvident man! You who complain about letters!

Love to you both,

Larry

Villa Louis

[January 1958]

Dear Henry:

Just sent off the huge *Mountolive* MS. They want it set up now so I should have a proof in a while which I'll route via you as a curiosity. I wanted you to read *Balthazar* as it was countersprung and have a clue as to the form. This big novel is as tame and naturalistic in *form* as a Hardy; yet it is the fulcrum of the quartet and the rationale of the thing. With the fourth I can plunge back into the time-stream again as per *Justine*. You may yawn your head off over *Mountolive* and whisper, "Shucks." We'll see. Meanwhile I have a small optional contract for bit writing from the *Sunday Times*, which not only leaves me free as a bird, asking only six articles a year on anything I like, but amounts to a tiny steady income—about half what a plumber would get. But by God, it is steady. It is a basic wage. I always was a timid bugger about that basic wage. Never understand where you got the courage to walk out on it.

I didn't send you *Esprit de Corps;* thought you mightn't find it funny. I had to pay for the baby's shoes somehow and wrote it in a very short time. To my surprise *Harper's, Atlantic,* etc. bought bits, so perhaps it is not too British after all—or perhaps Americans sometimes enjoy sodden

British jokes. Anyway I'm sending it along for you to see. Six thousand copies in a month! And the *Times* is mad about Antrobus and offers to run one a month at forty guineas! They take me twenty minutes to write. Only 1000 words. All this is very perplexing to my fans who don't know whether I am P. G. Wodehouse or James Joyce or what the hell.

I am "resting" this way for a month or two before I start on *Clea*—the last volume of the quartet. The weather has been pretty bad this last month but today at last we get a halcyon spring day, real Provence blue. Almost warm enough to plunge in among the water lilies. Your kids look lovely, both of them. Lucky man to have come to anchor in such a place. I sympathise with you not wishing to voyage around. One's own house is such a step. Alas, I shall never get back to mine—thanks to our fatuity and Turkish imbecility and Greek pottiness. But maybe if I can put some dough aside slowly, I can buy something right here. This would suit me very well indeed, I think.

The Mediterranean for me. You'd have got along swell with the queen mother. She is very attractive and has a mischievous eye—a merry widow look which doesn't appear in her pictures. Certes, une vrai femme.

love to you all,

larry

villa louis

[February 1958]

dearest henry:

We are in the process of being evicted these days, and the feeling that we may find ourselves on the road again without a settled habitat is unsettling. But I'm going to loose off at Joe one day this week. I'll send a carbon along

to you so you can see how the correspondence rides. . . .
My plan was to deal with you only as an illustration of the
naked work of art . . . the outrage on the established
sensibility. And by the way, Duttons *are* going to do *The
Black Book* with Faber sheets; and I suddenly remembered that you (poor you, always prefaces and boosts)
had already written a BOOST for the *BB* in *The Booster*.
I couldn't remember it but wondered whether it wouldn't
reproduce and so give you a moment's peace and quiet,
free from your importunate juniors. But I have no copy.
Perhaps Joe has.

Barker sounds quite a poet from what you say; and I'm
with you about the Jap forms; the trouble is with us lack
of a metaphysical resonance in proper nouns. Their impact in terms of affect is nearly always personal, or traditional. That is why Valéry flew to mathematics and chis-
elled out his stuff as fine as a cobweb, to achieve the
heraldic ideogram. When a Jap writes "cherry," "moon,"
"grass," the ideogram has a mystical-metaphysical ring
quite different from the set of associations we stir by
using them; hence the image-making that we have to put
into it. I work hot to cold like a painter. Hot noun, cold
adjective ("mathematical cherry" rather than "sweet
cherry"). Or on a sour abstract word like "armature" a
warm and sweetish one like "melodious." The Chinese
ideogram carries the "given verb"; our syntax dictates a
subject-verb-object copula in order to create a complex of
affective sounds. Tough on us, isn't it?

No other news; bad weather. Claude is writing a book
about France in the form of letters. *French Letters*. If
Fabers run true to form they will make her change it to
Gallic Missives without moving a muscle.

love,
larry

Dear Larry,

Here it is at last, the Preface. Having rewritten it twice I didn't bother to retype—hope you don't mind the ink corrections. If it isn't what you want, say so. I could try again. The publishers may wince when they read it, but what the hell, am I to worry about *their* feelings?

I have never given any one your address there thus far. (Except one or two of your own dear friends.) You may think you will keep them away, the fans and the reporters, but just wait! For every new success you pay dearly. Some days I truly despair. Last night, at 2:00 A.M. we were awakened by two people opening the door to our room with flashlight in hand. The woman, who was drunk, had come to bawl me out for something I had written. Imagine that! We never use locks or keys here, you know.

So you finished the third volume. What a wizard you are! Reminds me of my more fruitful days—in Clichy and in Villa Seurat. By the way, do you remember the canoe I bought in Corfu from the Countess' son? And that night came the mobilization.

Sometime send me photos of your two daughters, will you? I often wonder about them. Suppose one day they'll be knocking at my door.

I get letters all the time about your *Justine*, from readers. Some recommend it to me! I hope the German edition is out soon; there I feel it will not only sell but get marvelous reviews, and over the air too!

Cheerio!

Henry

———————◆◆◆———————

T HE correspondence now takes on a startling resem-
blance to that of the prewar years. Here they are once
again, after 20 years, exchanging letters at the same rate,
about the same issues and subjects, chiefly writing, chiefly
their own—Miller's for the moment. Durrell now resumes his study of the Master, this time in the form of a
correspondence with Perlès. They send carbons on to the
subject until he can no longer contain himself and jumps
down into the ring with a letter (the sixth in *Art and Outrage*) which Durrell describes to Perlès as "the most com-
prehensive statement of aims and intentions he has ever
written anywhere." Durrell's letter of April 1958, here
printed, shows his reaction. Durrell is also busy rereading
all of Miller for the third or fourth time, preparing the
long-postponed anthology—which task leads to further
exchanges.

There are two specific, striking parallels to the prewar
correspondence. Just as 20 years before he wrote appre-
hensively before sending on *The Black Book*, now Durrell
writes a number of deprecatory letters announcing
Mountolive. Once again Miller responds with a series of
hallelujahs after reading the proofs of *Mountolive*. He is
less enthusiastic about the light feature articles Durrell
is writing for money. Just as earlier he told Durrell to
stop writing as Charles Norden, so now he tells him just

as flatly: "Don't buy any more shoes for the baby! Believe me, they are better off without."

*   *

Henry:

What a stupendous letter! You have stepped in and banged our fat heads together! Makes us look like a couple of punch-drunk hacks cutting paper dolls. But this important statement must be published—either separately or as a postscriptum to our book if it ever shapes up. We are still, as you see, circling warily round each other. I don't know yet what will come of the project, but if we over-write and then cut down we may have what, in effect, could be a brief introduction to H.M. for the British, blast them! The question of intention! Anglo-Saxons tend to view art as didactic. If you want to write merde they at once think you are inciting people to mess the sidewalk. You have been poorly served by lack of detailed criticism and unavailability in UK and several of your younger admirers have a distorted view of you in one sense. They don't realise the central nature of your search, and that the books are a sort of spiritual by-product of the search. In other words they don't get the rationale behind what they call your "deliberate obscenity"—without realising the true meaning of its "deliberateness." Meanwhile of course I don't know which way Joe will see things and how he'll respond. Easy does it. But meanwhile have you kept a copy of your letter? Have you sent a carbon to Joe? You must seriously consider publishing. I will have it copied back to you if you haven't kept it. It is so marvellous. Actually it would make the perfect point de départ for the third volume. For *Nexus*. It is like the play within the play in *Hamlet*.

No, they are not going to bowdlerise *The Black Book* at all; and the few cuts they want in *Mountolive* are so laughable that I let them do it. The French will do it now —in toto—I am at ease. One, by the way, is the Latin word *fellatio*. I don't think anyone in England would understand it except Marie Stopes. It is too absurd.

Baby's shoes! I am in the process of learning to write by a process of progressive unselfimportance and my experience of *forms* is paying off; I can write in several different modes without strain by suddenly realising how unimportant it is to write at all. Learning to relax at last. At least I hope so. And if I can eat for six months at the cost of an 800-word feature I do it before breakfast. I am resting awhile now before beginning the fourth book. "It rests by changing" (Heraclitus) .

love to you both,
larry

Big Sur
5/9/58

Dear Larry,

Here we are again—just a few minutes to spare before mail man arrives. About that letter you found so good— "intentions." I don't mind it being reproduced somewhere, only when time comes, let me know; may be able to improve it. Wrote it right off like that, you know. . . . I'm on *Nexus* again, but it's pick and shovel work right now. Breaking the ice. So difficult.

One thing, when you say "perfect point of departure for *Nexus*" . . . No, I have in mind to one day write *Draco and the Ecliptic*, long promised. Can only do it when *Nexus* is written. This was to be, and still will be, I hope, a brief, cryptic account of what I believe it's all about—the "autobiography," I mean. Now and then I get glimpses. I want to be able to review my work, as I once did my whole life (Villa Seurat) , as from Devachan. See the pattern, the essence, the significance.

Good news that *B.B.* will be unexpurgated. Fabers is

really getting audacious, what! Hold out, I allus say, and you'll make the bloody bastards come round to your way of thinking.

The pictures of the kids came—they look adorable. We too put on a play here once—which they wrote and acted themselves. Good too.

More soon!
Salut!
Henry

Dear Larry:

I'm enclosing a letter from Laughlin, which will clarify things for you, and a copy of my answer, one of them. Will try to track down your "schema" for Reader now. Would think one other category, at least, might be introduced: Portraits (Varda, Reichel, Fred, Delaney, etc.)—no? Not all, but some. And what you classify as "Great thoughts" might be subdivided into categories, no? For example, on Art, on Astrology, on Metaphysics, on this and that. When it comes to the final decision on what or what not to include, I am almost ready to let you take over. I'm not always the best judge. As for that "either-or" you give me, I know damned well I don't want a row with our legal authorities. I know in advance it's hopeless. The only change in attitude, in recent years, has been this, that the pocket book people have gotten away with murder but in the wrong way: what sex material they include is of a perverse, sadistic nature. This is the trend in America, a most unhealthy one. My kind, which is frank and open (and often humorous), seems to shock more. It's pure. That they don't want. Nor England neither, I take it. Note: in the *UNESCO Courier*—a good

monthly!—I saw recently the list of most widely translated authors in the world. The Bible is now fifth or sixth
on the list. Lenin tops them all, by far! But who comes
after the Bible? Mickey Spillane.

More anon . . .

Henry

Big Sur
July 4th, 1958

Dear Larry,

I've just written Girodias (he's no longer Kahane) to
mail you a complete set of the banned books. I will also
send you copies of those New Directions books you lack.
Never use the British editions as nearly all of them were
castrated and in one or two cases whole sections missing.

I feel guilty, I must tell you, presuming on you this
way, when you're still grappling with your tetralogy. It's
a huge job, particularly when it comes to finding those
"gems"—the aphorisms, as you call them. The big blocs
are relatively easy to single out, but this other stuff means
digging. Get what help you can from Cowley, Shapiro,
Fred, anyone you trust. I hate to go into it myself—I
would fall into a trap. And I'm struggling like hell with
Nexus—not to write, it comes easy, but to find continuous
writing time. Some weeks I get only two or three days for
the book, and then only an hour or two at a time. I have
had to train myself to write without thinking. What the
result will be I don't know. I've got 250 pages done, out
of a possible 1200 or more.

I got Joey's "Third Letter" to you and I am going to
write you both about it today or tomorrow. It hit me
again—in a good spot. I have a lot to tell you about my
unworldly life, about reading, and about writing too.
Will probably give you something about Homer too; I'm

almost finished now with the *Iliad*. It's an epic of carnage without parallel that I know of. And there's a powerful lot of what you would call "bad writing" in it. But more of this anon. I hope you won't find me stymying you in this correspondence. My only wish is to incite you. And you must always remember that no matter what I say about myself or my work you have the privilege of ignoring it or proving it false. There is no one truth in such matters; remember the Tibetan business about the soul being a bundle of fasces, a thousand personalities. (I have just ordered a new edition of Milarepa. Don't overlook him when you talk about "influences." He meant more to me than Buddha or Jesus. I could explain why too, if needed.)

I was also delighted to hear about Anais' visit. We had a long letter from her about you and Claude. Her picture of you as being quiet, contained, and all that, seemed a little off. Fred has just written me of *his* visit. That's more like it! If I ever hear that you have quieted down, that you no longer laugh explosively, that you are not doing a hundred things at once, that you are not miserably happy and effervescent, I shall die of a broken heart.

Only the other day, at the hot springs, I was trying to explain to two ex-Yale men whom I knew fourteen years ago and who are now men of almost forty that even though I don't see you or Fred for interminable stretches you are as close and alive to me as ever, that you sustain me, that I still go to bed laughing or wake up laughing, thinking of things you said or did so long ago. That is why I sent you the book about Fargue; it is so beautifully nostalgic, so full of Paris, talk, books, men, streets, dreams.

I would give a lot to be there with you for just ten days. I never, never have a good talk with any one here— unless it's a French visitor. Once *Nexus* is done I want to travel and perhaps never come back. And I don't want to write any more.

Give Claude a good hug. I want to talk to her in Hebrew and Arabic some day. What a woman you've got! Are the kids there now? Send more photos when they do come, eh? We love them.

Cheerio now!

Henry

Villa Louis

[August 1958]

Dear Henry—

Books all arrived and I've started in; it is quite frightening, the magnitude of your achievement—all stacked up here on my desk. One's brain spins wondering how the hell you've done it all and kept sane. I'm in direct touch with Laughlin and won't bother you until we have a complete typescript for you to see and approve. While I want the thing to give a good account of your protean genius I am also keeping a wary eye on reduplication of material which has already been made available in other forms. This should be both representative and as new as possible. Laughlin presses for an introduction—but hell, one does not introduce one's reverend seniors. Even if one heads the clever-but-so-what list of young novelists. We shall see. First the work. I'm trying to use your letter to Joe and me.

Gerald Sykes will be posting you on the proofs of *Mountolive* soon; keep them for a rainy day and don't swear at the pedestrian naturalistic form. It's only the third movement (rondo) of a symphonic poem. When one has all four they will I hope all swim in solution like clockwork fish and the whole job float like a Calder mobile. Espérons!

I have found a desolate little "mazet" on the garrigue. Seventy square miles of heath, moorland, sage, holm-oak. Dry rocky soil, sunburnt. Like an abandoned corner of Attika. We move there around September 15th when the children fly back to school. With any luck I shall be in the clear next year and can finish *Clea* easily without writing rubbish for the *Times*. Whoopee! Things are moving my way now—wind is changing quite perceptibly. *Holiday* magazine want me to go up the Nile! What next? I bet *you'd* love it; but I loathed Egypt! (Not a word.)

I paused several times reading the *Oranges* to wonder (from your hair-raising description of the behavior of the kids) whether you were not doing for children what Jean-Jacques did for the imaginary Noble Savage—a sort of idealised belief in their world. I know what pain and delight they give, of course, but in my case have decided that we use them as objects of self-gratification emotionally. No man can be a mother!

Both my daughters dance wonderfully, particularly the baby. We've been a-swimming for two whole days at the Saintes-Maries—the headquarters of all the gipsies in Christendom. Why the hell don't you take a year off in Europe? Joe is planning to make the jump soon, and so is Anais. Why not a French lycée for your kids?

Love,
Larry

Do you know Eiluned Lewis's marvellous aphorism— "Children are only grown-ups with their eyes open"! Goodnight!

Big Sur
August 29, 1958

Dear Larry:

I've just received a copy of Laughlin's recent letter to you about the H.M. Reader. He urges you to write an introduction. Evidently you were thinking not to. Out of modesty? Or what? You would be the one, no mistake about it. I often think of that gem you wrote for *Horizon* and of the one in *Booster*, "Hamlet, Prince of China," remember? Rather prophetic, what! What I'm thinking is, Larry, that in a preface from your pen, and as coming from a friend, you could say all those things I think you ought and want to say—about my weaknesses, my limitations, my bad writing, my obsessions, my lack of self-criticism, etc. etc. etc. I've had plenty of laudatory comments and lots of picayune criticism from little shits, but you could really blast me—it would be fun. And it would also teach the "critics" how to fire with two guns at once —and remain a friend and a loyal reader. You could also make mention of lots of things the average reader does not know about me or my work, for example—the many prefaces I've written (and the many more I refuse to write), the many texts for foreign reviews, for which I seldom receive any payment, the book reviews I've done, the correspondence I wage with all and sundry (to my utter detriment, to be sure, but one of my "weaknesses" —of character, perhaps). And how this vice has happily made me the kind of writer I am and not a literary figure. And—quite important, as I hinted before somewhere— how in one and the same period I am writing in quite different vein—sexual travesties, metaphysical pish-posh, analyses of books, pen portraits, landscapes, fantasies and so on. Or how (or why) the sexual is so often larded with humor, and, though often verging on (sic) the pornographic, never perverse. At the worst, I'm a "voyeur" and of course a filthy "voyou." And, or, how difficult it is to predict the coming direction or trend in my work, seeing as how I don't know myself. In the oven lies a sort of infantile Céline-like blast against "adults" called *Lime Twigs and Treachery*—from Brahms' Love Waltzes (sic). Or that the only revolution which means anything to me is in the field of education. That I've given up the adults as hopeless, now and forever . . . that all I care about are children. And a few adults who come near being children—"the happy lunatics," as the Zen master might say.

And here's another thought for you . . . did I ever broach it? As time goes on I care less and less (and how!) for literature, especially "good literature," recognized literature, yet . . . now when I do find a good book— good for me—I am more enthusiastic, less critical, more completely taken in, mystified, reverent, than ever before in my life. In short, completely vulnerable. This I must regard as one of God's great gifts to an erring soul. How thankful I am that it took me twenty, thirty, sometimes more, years, to come upon certain books. Because now, only now, am I ready for them . . . ready to enjoy them, I mean. And I must stress it again, though it's boring, that from the so-called bad books I got as much as from the good ones. "One man's meat is another man's poison." To this day I haven't the slightest idea how a book gets written. It remains for me in the realm of the miraculous. I know less now, in other words, than when I began. I do know this, if it means anything, that a book, like a life, is the result of what you are every day, includ- ing the bad days and the lazy days and the infertile days. No estimable critic can evaluate the sublime leaven of idleness for a writer and for a liver of life. As I said to Joey in the "Postface," do less and less! Being is all.

Larry, I feel sorry for you. I'm just adding to your worries. Take what's useful out of all this and throw the rest in the garbage can.

And do take a bit of royalties, won't you? Don't stand on pride or honor. There's more than enough to go round. I wouldn't miss it, even though broke, I can tell you.

341

Every day I continue to live in this frightful country I have less and less respect or understanding of money. It means nothing here . . . absolutely nothing. The harder I work the less I have. If I had nothing I imagine I would be supremely happy. I was checking up in my mind, just the other day, the invitations I have had in the last few years from fans and friends all over the world. If I gathered the family together and took off, I could keep traveling from place to place for the next ten years—rent free, good food, good talk, no worries, seeing the world. Why in hell don't I do it? I belong out there. I could also not budge. Drôle de con, quoi!

Well, enough! Love to Claude and all the little ones!
"Other rooms, other voices!"

Henry

Mazet Michel

[October 1958]

Dear Henry—

Just a swift line to answer yours. We are still in a hideous mess here with masons, etc. I got a windfall of a thousand dollars from the States and decided to build a small lavatory. Tired of having to bury the stuff. The soil here too rocky. Hence all the mess. It is odd, isn't it, temperamental likes and dislikes in writing? Stendhal bewitches me with his curious shyness and tenderness and the sudden flashes of mordant humour and irony. Quite unFrench in temperament and yet at the same time he couldn't be anything but a Frenchman. I tried *The Glastonbury Romance* years ago while we were all in Paris. But it seemed to me to have varicose veins. Perhaps I'd think differently now. I don't know. At the moment I am reading to learn about novels and how they are made. Don't bother with *Mountolive;* it's a genre which I know

342

you hate as much as I do, the naturalistic novel. But some of the big cinerama bits are quite fair, I think. Now for *Clea!* The piece of yours, "Children of the Earth," is absolutely marvellous. Shapiro just sent it. It should go into the anthology as soon as Laughlin has studied the question of length. He says he is in favour of a big book. I think he is right. Wish he would get a real book designer to make it up. Your English *Big Sur* was beautiful, I thought. And the cover of the American *Balthazar* was the best bit of commercial display art I have ever seen. Economy and total impact.

love to you all,
larry

Mazet Michel

[October 1958]

Dear Henry—

"Mock-up" is printer's English for a "maquette"—a dummy. Probably common usage either side of the pond. I don't know. As for "influences," I was asked who my "guides and mentors" were and replied : "Among writers Miller for or rather by example and Eliot for advice." This is exactly it. Old TSE was a masterly critic and a very helpful publisher. Any poetic reputation I have is due to his persuasion—to cut out dud poems, verbose ones, poems bulging with connective tissue. I often thought him wrong and attacked; but patiently, wisely, he really did convince me. As for that rogue Miller . . . the debt isn't yet repaid nor ever will be. Another ten days of Bedlam here with carpenters and plumbers, and then I can get out some paper and do your preface. Fear and trembling! Imagine introducing the author of, say, *Moby Dick* to his own countrymen while he was still very much alive

and in full production. What would you say? We shall
see.

Pray for me Saturday, October 11th—*Mountolive*
comes out in England: it is the fulcrum, the *clou* of the
quartet, and if it has the same reception as the other two
I shall be sitting pretty next year.

All of everything to you both,

Larry

By the way, I don't believe you could read Eliot's *Four
Quartets* without that interior music which good stuff
starts up.

Mazet Michel

[October 1958]

Dear Henry

I dotted you off a preface to the anthology yesterday
which you must look at, and tell me if you like or not.

We are still in a hellova mess, tidying up. Soon I must
get down to this blasted fourth volume. A complimentary
of *Mountolive* is on its way to you. You'll probably find it
stinks if you like Kerouac; I have only seen one sent me
by Anais. Found it unreadable; no, I admire it in a way,
as I admire *Catcher in the Rye*. It is social realism as the
Russians understand it. But ouf, the emptiness really of
this generation of self-pitying cry-babies. We have our
own group in England. And how can you not see that
God or Zen is simply a catchword, as Freud was in our
time? It doesn't really mean anything.

It is only here that I think America is really harming
you, making you critically soft. Beware of cowboy evan-
gelism and Loving Everything and Everybody Everywhere! Or you'll be doing a Carl Sandburg with a portable harp! Sharpen up the Miller harpoon! Batten down on
the soft, the lax, the self-pitying, the self-indulgent. Have

you seen the excellent article on the "beat" boys in the new mag *Horizon?* It is really good. Pinpoints them. But I guess I am perhaps too vieux jeu to mistake lumberjack's manners for art. And it don't really touch me at any place. They are turning the novel into a skating rink; I am trying to make it a spiral staircase.

Here's a quote from de Rougemont to ponder and perhaps pin up somewhere: "When under the pretence of destroying whatever is artificial—idealising rhetoric, the mystical ethics of 'perfection'—people seek to swamp themselves in the primitive flood of instinct, in whatever is primeval, formless and foul, they may imagine they are recapturing real life but actually they are being swept away by a torrent of waste-matter pouring from the disintegration of the ancient culture and its myths."

Ouch! Watch that large-hearted self; keep the handloom turning at full pressure!

Bless you,
Larry

Big Sur
10/30/58

Dear Larry,

Just got the Preface to the *H.M. Reader* and I do like it! And why not, since you flatter the shit out of me, as Joey would say. One thing surprised me—the reference to message from Keyserling. Did I really get that message or did you make it up? Since then, of course, I've had hundreds of extraordinary messages from extraordinary people, not the least of them coming from an Indian guru via a physician in Ismailia who had cured him of some illness. That and the one from Tagore via our mutual firebrand Hindu-Communist friend (in London—forget his name now) are outstanding in my memory.

There's just one sentence I want to comment on, for your benefit. It needn't be altered, however. It's where you say that I am reconciled—"to judge by his latest book"—to my native land. That's dead wrong. I am not even reconciled to Big Sur, though I have accepted it and made the most of it. But America . . . I loathe everything about it more and more. It's the land of doom. I will yet escape, I feel. How, I don't see yet.

And this leads me to Kerouac, that book I sent you. No matter what you may have read or tried to read of his before, don't pass this up. I say it's good, very good, surpassingly good. The writing especially. He's a poet. His prose is poetry. Or, shall I say, the kind of poetry I can recognize. How representative he is of the Beat generation I can't say. I know little of these boys, I avoid them, I don't read them. As for growing soft in criticism, never fear. Whom have I praised among American writers—contemporaries? None of the celebrities do I read or can I read. The publishers send me their dreck and I chuck the books over the cliff. I don't even bother to pass them on to some poor bastard who can't afford to buy a book. I wouldn't waste his time.

Aside from yourself, Céline, Cendrars, Giono and good Friar John—what a book, I repeat, is *A Glastonbury Romance*—I see none. Wasteland. No Moses trekking across it and no Sinai to reach. Rubbish. Drivel. "Social realism," you say? Worse.

All this for the record . . .

A good note. Just got Rowohlt's handsome German edition of the *Big Sur* book. A honey of a book. Beautiful jacket, good paper, good print, good format. Why, oh why, can't the English and Americans bring out such productions? And did you see Ernst Rowohlt's touching encomium to you (*Justine*) in a recent issue of *Das Schönste?* You're a success already, in Germany. With this review came a copy of *Du* from Zurich—issue devoted entirely to Hermann Hesse. How tender! And what wonderful photos of him at all ages. Especially one with a beard and black-rimmed glasses: there he is the poet, painter, musician and magician all in one. I'm going to frame it. To put beside that strange-looking guy Gurdjieff! Does *he* look like a master, wow! Well, enough. Hope the mistral blowing through the garrigue doesn't destroy the mazet. Mock it up!

Henry

le mazet michel

[November 1958]

Dear Henry:

Keyserling! I saw you get the telegram and exclaim. Afterwards we were lunching with Joe at L'Escargot and he told me what was in it, and you had the grace to blush as you admitted the soft impeachment. You were quite shy, and deeply delighted—as who would not be? It stuck in my mind, and an accolade from a philosopher somehow seemed to give point to your reputation not as a mere novelist etc. but as a thinker, visionary etc. . . .

About Kerouac, whose new book has arrived, what am I to say? Question de goût, I suppose. I can't go along with you. I found it really corny, and deeply embarrassing (read pages 30–33 aloud in a strong American voice) and worst of all pretentious. All these nincompoops crawling up hills with their food in polyethylene bags and attitudinising about religion like Oxford Groupers. You have done the most devastating satires on this kind of savin' and keepin' line in *Black Spring*. And I remember once dragging you to a movie where Bing Crosby, in a dog collar, sang a little jazz about Jesus from a pulpit in a penitentiary; and you were so god damned mad you

347

wanted to throw rocks at the screen. No, this really seems campus stuff. All those cute little fucks stolen in the name of Zen (just substitute the word Jesus and see what you make of the content). It is hick stuff. Remember the nursery odyssey?

> Ma's out, pa's out,
> LET'S TALK DIRT!
> Pee, po, bum, bottom, drawers!

Sorry if you think I'm unjust but it seems to be about Errol Flynn level. And gee, when they open their little peepers to drink in the universe, gee how alloverish they come. No, No! As for the writing, yes, it's fluent with good key changes but it has that breathless wondering lisp, the prattling tone which seems to have been handed down to American writers by Anita Loos. "So I went down to the hotel, grabbed me a corplaster, docked my luggage, and I says to myself, if God don't know (with the mountains so lovely), why I don't know either, and if I don't know, who the hell does? So I went and had a slug of rye and God . . ."

Saroyan has killed himself as a writer in this genre, the breathless lisp of a sweet little boy who is granted all the wonderful, wonderful treasures of God's own landscape. It is fundamentally pretentious-sentimental, and goes along with being tough as hell and hep and yet "so quiet, saintly and Christ-like, just another bum like Krishna was, and maybe even Jesus out there on Galilee . . ."

I'm trying to isolate a tone of voice which irks me. God knows, Kerouac may yet turn into a writer. He's young and hard-working. But what a devastating picture of what young intellectuals are saying and doing over there. They need a week at a French lycée to be taught to think and construct.

Anyway, what the hell! Don't be angry with me for

not going along on this book. Maybe it has fine things in it which are not on my wavelength. No, old fogey that I am, I thank goodness that our Henry Miller ain't this kind of writer, even in his worst bouts of sentimental fantasy! Love to you both. *Mountolive* is a Book-of-the-Month choice. No idea as yet what this means in dough.

Love,
Larry

Le Mazet Michel

[November 1958]

Dear Henry:

Just a swift line. I'm glad that the preface seemed okay, and hope that the book goes forward now if and when you approve.

Yes, I don't think a prolonged siege in USA could do anything but dehydrate one; I think it is wonderful you've stuck it out the way you have. I mean without very frequent visits abroad. Mind you, I don't think it is the people; I really believe that places have their own rhythm and compulsion and some are hostile to artists. But I think the American scene is enriching in another way; a big spiritual potential which isn't being capitalised due to our beastly puritan culture. In England the landscape is good, nourishing; one can work there. There isn't any hostility to the artist. What is killing is the spineless and revolting life they have built up around themselves, the habits, the boredom, the lack of la bonne chère. No belly worship!

Up here on the wild garrigue it is . . . curiously like Greece. The typics of the place are all out of Rabelais, huge mutton-headed, pink-cheeked, potato-nosed belly-worshippers with laughter like a force three gale. There is only one topic of conversation—food, past and to come.

Never money. Often lavatories. Seldom sex. But always food. Just suit you down to the ground!

Anais wants me to preface her first novel to appear in England. Lord. I must be getting quite important with all these prefaces to the work of my elders and betters; well, it's a toe-hold in immortality, I suppose.

every good thing to you all,

larry

Big Sur
11/19/58

Dear Larry:

Don't feel you have to reply to all my letters. Let me write you—I can afford to waste time, what! Writing again today because whole day has gone answering queries from this one and that, and other chores of similar nature. So, I'm wound up. No use tackling *Nexus* with only half hour to go. (I need at least an hour clear.) Just got your last about receipt of American dollars, lavatory, Enfants de la Terre and—this is why I write—your deprecatory remarks about *Mountolive*. My dear man, don't say such things, ever, not to any one. That book is a perfect gem. I am thirty-five pages from the end now; I have read it like a Yeshiva Bocher would read his Psalms.

Some day we're going to have a long talk, tête à tête, about Egypt, Rhodes, Jerusalem, Greece, Jugoslavia, Armenia, Turkestan, Argentina, and so on—where haven't you been? And Cos! My God, when I see how you call up these places, how deeply you have absorbed them, how magnificently you have given us their spirit and essence—even down to the flies—I am dismayed. Who is this man I have been corresponding with over the years? What do I know about him? He was almost a cherub when we parted—in Arcady. Yes, I knew he had genius, but not

350

such genius! And now he is in his forties, and I know him only through his books and letters. What a great pity! I long to know all, the whole man, the whole life—especially all the setbacks, disasters, frustrations, bedevilments, detours, ennuis, alimonies, etc. without which no one could have written such magnificent books. And what a darlint of a writer you are to have kept all this nasty personal dreck out of your books. Hourrah for the Durrells of this world! Hourrah!

No, *Mountolive* is not to me a naturalistic novel, nor indeed any classifiable novel. It fits into the tetralogy like the key in the lock; gives one a thrill to get behind previous scenes, in and under certain characters encountered before. Also to see again these words—"gras, delgat et gen." No, it's masterful, the scaffolding, the armature, the plan or whatever. And the writing never lags, never palls. Same Durrellian level—gem-like, incandescent. What you call the "cinerama" parts—good expression—sure, we look for them, all of us. But do we deserve them? And whence come they—out of what depths, what experience (actualités)? But I find as much thrill, almost, in the way you handle ordinary things, descriptions, characters, conversations, reveries, literary and historical allusions—what a savant you are! You seem to have forgotten nothing you ever saw or heard. No, I read you with a powerful magnifying glass. Nothing escapes me. Even that questionable "boustrophedon" passage—aren't you wrong there? No matter! It's vast, vast, this work, the whole tetralogy. A vast pool from which one can gather what he likes. There's no one alive writing like this. I said before —you're king now. I mean it. You say you got a windfall from America. A thousand only? Man, they'll be paying you in diamonds yet.

Larry Powell (librarian—your greatest admirer in U.S. aside from me) was here the other day. He spoke with reverence of you, as always. "He's come into his own," he said. Yes, I said, it's like watching some great tropical flower open up. Like that moon flower I once saw in Los Angeles, which opens at five minutes before sundown, on the dot, every day.

Tell Claude to serve you an extra good meal this evening.

Kerouac, you see, is just up my street, as far as American writing goes. He swings. Doesn't worry. Good, bad, indifferent—cancer-schmanser. What difference, so long as you're healthy? Something comes through, writing this way. Something that never happens with the usual "good" writers, I mean. We all can learn from this effortless effort. We need to learn to enjoy what we do while doing it. I'm doggoned if I believe one must squirm in labor doing it. Especially not after the fifth book, what! Theory is, if *you* enjoyed doing it, chances are the other fellow will too. I talk enjoyment. Forgive me. That's all I have learned from the books I've pored over.

Do you laugh sometimes while writing? It makes fun, as Reichel would say.

I'm going down now for my apéritif. Here's a new one I'm trying: equal parts of gin, Dubonnet and Cinzano. It clicks. Two and I'm swacked. Just got a case, through friend, wholesale, of an excellent year of Châteauneuf-du-Pape. If I could, here's how I'd do it each night, every night: Nuits St. Georges, Gevrey Chambertin, Château Rothschild, Clos-Vougeot, Vosne-Romanée, Aloxe-Corton, Pommard, Médoc, Beaujolais. Then in reverse. Do you ever taste Verveine (liqueur) there? Almost as good, I think, as Chartreuse Verte. Shit! Wish I were there to talk to your neighbors. Food! What better topic for conversation?

Signing off now. Just had crazy letter from hotel clerk in Monterey, saying he heard a long-distance telephone

352

conversation to *New York Times* from a nut claiming he had proof that I (!) am the real author of *Lolita*. I haven't been able to read that book yet—opened it, didn't like style. May be prejudiced. Usually am. As Reichel says of paintings, "A book should smile back at you when you open it, nicht wahr?"

Henry

mazet michel

[November 25, 1958]

my dear Henry:

The accolade on *Mountolive* was terrific and held me speechless with pleasure for the whole day. I thought the form would tire you too much. But I'm delighted you think it fits in. Phew! But of course I'd give both arms to have written this piece of *Nexus* with its fountain-like effortless rhythms—perfect momentum from start to finish. It is of course poetry; and you are dammit a poet, a psalmist. And now you've reached the stage of "effortless play-automatism" you can pull off these giant trapeze acts; whereas us poor devils still have to build patient ladders up the side of the cliff. But I console myself by the tremendous amount of practice you've had, inner and outer, to achieve this fine rare harmony and balance of forces, and hope one day to start playing. You are right about the not-trying thing, the sich lassen and wu wei; but I think it comes after a long spell of practice and trying out all the disciplines in order to surmount them. In this sense I may have been unjust to Kerouac; it wasn't the loose free and easy thing I wanted to criticise. I was against the Burt Lancaster tone of voice! So rugged without, so tough and crude; yet so tender within, the wondering babe in the wood! Incidentally this tough tone and arid colourless grim-lipped style is being imitated by the young French—Jean Cassou. It is horrible; but they have no sentimental Gary Cooper underneath ready to turn into Davy Crockett. It is pure brutality—which is what the French are (being women in temperament) the minute they try and ape foreign moeurs!

If this American killing brings me some dough I shall buy this place and fix it up good. I think you'd like it here. It is very like Attika, and the Midi types you can see at a glance were Greek in origin. They are quite mad and continue the traditions of Panurge, Tartarin, Raimu, etc. It's a thousand pities that when you got your windfall you didn't buy a little place here—you could have got a château and twenty acres of ground for nothing after the war. Anyway, I hope you'll take a trip over some day to discuss food with the plumber. He rolls a huge tongue about in his mouth as he talks.

love,
larry

JANUARY 1959—

(Durrell in Provence—Miller in Big Sur, Paris, and
Big Sur)

———◆———

THE entire correspondence describes a perfect arc, beginning with Durrell's fan letters and ending with
Miller's. Now it is Miller's turn to acclaim Durrell as
the Master. Now too, in the fullness of time, they finally
meet again—after all these years of war, travels and
troubles. The closest we come to overhearing their talk is
the letter Miller writes when he returns to Big Sur, the
last and by far the longest of the correspondence. After
25 years he is just warming up and writing a letter that
goes on for days.

*   *

[January 1959]

Dear Henry:

Delighted to get Eve's second letter which confirms you are on the way. HURRAH for you! The first letter was so exalté that I couldn't really believe the idea at first. Claude wrote a long letter of advice and so on, asking for more dope, without which it is impossible to act. If it was just you two it would be easy, mais avec le régiment . . .

I am buried deep in *Clea*, this last bloody volume. I gather that Jean Fanchette is worrying you for tributes and things. Listen, don't bother with it; I've sent him a copy of your long letter about *Mountolive* and suggested that he ask permish to print it and save you trouble. Aldington has come up with a little essay on the books. By the way, important afterthought: in interviews for press or radio or television, say you are going to Antibes or some other Wimbledon. The "arty" tide is now at Aix, and beginning to slop over; only the mistral and mosquitoes prevents Languedoc being overrun. God, how I've been so glad to feel that within forty miles there are no celebrities! And once they come of course UP GO PRICES. I want you to explore this end for a whole summer at leisure, and then pick on a spot to stay; remember the kids could go to the diplomatic school (American) in Paris. Enquire when you are there about it. Make a bivouac this summer and explore the area; tremendous variety of landscape and weather within a mean circuit of 100 miles, forest, lake, mountain, desert . . . every damn thing you can imagine. Alors, Balbus, quarter the tenth legion and spy out the land!

every good thing,
Larry

Dear Henry:

Claude is writing Eve direct about the tiny flat. **My** own hope is that this three months will finally decide you to stick and settle here; my only terror is that having done so you will write a *Big Sur* about the Languedoc and start a landslide! I've just turned down two handsome offers to do a travel book about this part; having fouled my own nest in the same way in Greece, I'm not taking any chances, no sir! I sign my books "Ascona"! But . . . I believe that IF you take the flat and IF it works as it may well, you will experience an entirely new reunion with France—a different France; that is why I am so anxious that you should be the ONLY foreigners in the little town, which is quite unencumbered. You would wake up every morning in the Middle Ages; and every Saturday morning your balcony would hang above a sea of coloured tents —Market Day; the forains pour into the little square, spread out their huge coloured marquees and set up their stalls; and the Provençals from the surrounding villages come in to buy boots and aprons and pitchforks and tractor spare parts; and the cafés fill up with hundreds of Raimus in berets. All day you hear the click of boules. Such a variety of character, too; placed in such an intimate contact with the town the characters of people come up clear, and within ten days you will be simply delighted by your talks with Lopez the mason, and Serafim the hairdresser (he paints horribly), and the butcher, baker, etc. When I think of the terrible poverty of the human material you describe in the *Big Sur* (despite your marvellous writing *about* them, their lack of shape and interestingness came through, reminding me of Joe's grim description of you sitting surrounded by genial morons), when I think of them thar and the people you will meet in the

357

Languedoc, I can see you simply hop with joy! As for the children, they are Anglo-Saxons, and like ours will hate the smells, the sanitation, and the fact that movies and comics are in French; but love the river (fishing for your boy), the old fort, the market, the Glacier ice cream, the cake shop, etc. etc. Moreover this particular situation is the best of getting a real bird's eye view with a view to settling; a forty mile radius gives you a bewildering variety of landscapes and altitudes. You will own the only flush lavatory in the place; the two hotels have Turkish loos, one per landing; and nobody has ever heard of a bath. In short you can revisit medieval France, quite unchanged, quite untouched; notaries out of Balzac. But I told Claude to tell Eve to read *Clochemerle!*

Phew! signing off now. As soon as we have a peep from the Stes. Maries we'll signal you. Mum's the word and I duck under.

Larry

3/8/59

[Big Sur]

Dear Larry, dear Claude—

Yes, all's set—passports, visas, tickets. All I need do is relax. Working feverishly to finish rewrite of *Nexus* before leaving. (Just had letter from Fanchette. He's using the text I wrote expressly.) Think we have a place in Paris —at a hundred dollars a month. The flat is cheap— these days. Hope it's livable. If not, I'll forfeit the rent and find a good hotel somewhere. Can't abide medieval conditions any more. America spoils one. And my ideal now is Japan. Why live like dogs in the age of the atom? Isn't it ridiculous! But don't worry—we want to be near you. For me it will be a tonic! Incidentally, don't be frightened either that we will eat into your working day.

I am most sensitive about that, living as we do at the mercy of any Tom, Dick or Harry who takes a notion to visit us. Before we go south—while in Paris—I may go to Copenhagen, Brussels, Amsterdam, Stockholm, Hamburg. Maybe I'll take the kids with me. Eve wants to stay in Paris. For me it means nothing any more. Ghostly.

I got the German edition of *Justine* and Dutton's of *Mountolive*. Both look good. With that Book-of-Month biz here in U.S. you should soon be sitting pretty. And in Germany Ledig says you are doing well. I don't think you'll ever be poor again.

About keeping my whereabouts secret, I'll certainly try. I'm curious to see how successful you will be in warding off visitors. They find out, you know, eventually. Are you coming to Paris for the launching of your book chez Corrêa? I told Buchet I wanted none of it for my book.

Well, those 12 little cafés au bord de la Vidourle sound wonderful. Maybe I'll find a pingpong table there! It's great fun, pingpong. Today I'm walking like a cripple after strenuous rounds of p.p. with Tony who is awfully good at it. The kids love to swim. Val rides (an old nag). I just hope to Christ the mosquitoes are not there! I'm also trying to estimate (from map) distances to seashore, to Die (Drôme) and that beautiful stretch of great wine country from a little south of Beaune up to Dijon. (Et puis, le Puy—ever been there? Et l'Aveyron?)

We made plane reservations to return from Paris about 20th August, I think. However, if the kids liked it, if we put Val in that "Ecole d'Humanité" in Switzerland (it sounds great—Tagore wrote about it!) and Tony somewhere else—who knows? But I am not quitting Big Sur for good—not yet. It's a real haven. Besides, I do want to see Japan, China, Java, Burma—*etc.* And stop writing!

I hope Fred joins us somewhere. He hints at it. It's a must. And to see your dear Claude. I'm sure we're going

to like her! And all those kids of yours and hers! Ho ho!
You know, I'm at that senile stage now where I enjoy
better talking and playing with kids than with adults.
I'm really death on adults. Unless they've grown child-
like.

I'm laughing already.

Cheerio!
Henry

Paris
4/21/59

Dear Larry, dear Claude—

Here at last! Looks same as ever—except that the traf-
fic is terrifying. I wait like an invalid before crossing a
street. Prices almost American. So far nothing but visits,
interviews, dinners, telephones. How I hate the phone! It
rings incessantly. Weather was lousy but now clearing—
"fair and warmer." The best thing is the *cuisine.* That's
still tops.

Fred may run over for a weekend—next or week after.
Then to Copenhagen, Stockholm, Oslo, Amsterdam, Brussels. Avec les enfants.

Happy to see the kids like it here and get on with their
French friends. But I'm longing to get to the country.
Don't like city life any more.

I wouldn't come up especially, if you're still on *Clea.*
Waste of time and money. Discovered Hoffman hadn't
paid you for the rent you disbursed. Let us know what we
owe and I'll send postal money order or American Express
check.

A part cela, comme on dit, tout va bien. I wish I could
start having a real vacation soon.

More à bientôt!
Henry

Dear Larry—

Finished *Clea* yesterday with a feeling that it was a
huge tome. Came away as one does sometimes after at-
tending a bullfight—battered and dazed. Particularly
devastating is that underwater scene—Clea's hand nailed
to the boat. And then the dervish dance. And then—the
Hand!! An ending à la da Vinci. A note of sublime and
delicate horror. But from the beginning there is the incessant flood of poetic imagery. One drowns in it—will-
ingly, voluptuously.

What I missed, by obtusity no doubt, was what you
told me to look for. Unless it was in those notes of Pursewarden. This part—like an interpolation—seemed weak-
est to me, though containing much profound observation
on art and life. But, for me, it had a sort of surgical quality, a sort of desperate last-minute opening up and sewing
back again. The humor didn't always come off, for me.
To be frank, of all the characters in the quartet Pursewarden is the least interesting to me. Darley and he seem
to be the two halves of a coin—like Lawrence in *Aaron's
Rod*. I never get the conviction that he was the great
writer you wish him to seem. I think he'd come off better
—forgive me!—if you sliced down his remarks or observations. They get sententious and tedious and feeble sometimes. Too much persiflage. (By the way, doesn't something of the sort occur in *The Black Book* too?) What I
mean, more precisely, is that one is not sure at times
whether the author is taking his double-faced protagonist
seriously or ironically.

Keats you handled wonderfully, I thought, and in the
few pages devoted to him, in *Clea*, you gave a picture of
war with its multiple aspects that was tonic. Keats we feel

will become a writer. As for Darley, one feels sometimes that the self-deprecation he employs is unwarranted, exaggerated—false modesty. The man who recounts and observes, whether the author in disguise or not, can not be this crippled writer!

Forget all this trivial criticism. I don't know why I pass it on to you, except that I feel I owe you such frankness. What *is* important for you to know is that all four books have the same specific gravity. Throughout the quartet there is a repetition of technique which reminds me of the divisions in a bullfight. Always, à la fin, the mise à mort. The cape work always remarkable, thrilling, *dangerous*. I like too the way you handle the lesser figures—they remain unforgettable. But Scobie again seems to have received undue weight and importance. (From the reader's standpoint. I can understand an author's infatuation for a minor character.)

Oh, by the way, the bit about the homunculi—so marvelous! But, I wonder if you knew that in one of his books Cendrars has a very similar situation? (Forget which one now.) One ought to do a whole fantastic hair-raising book on this theme. It gets under one's skin, what! And I liked your preparatory explanations—Da Capo's. You have a *book* there!

To come back to Pursewarden. Maybe I should reread all four books and see afresh. No doubt I've missed the boat somewhere. Another lesser point . . . Because of the condensed aspect, lack of new paragraphs, conversations set apart—know what I mean?—*Clea* takes on a heaviness not just. Too packed. It's a book of 500 pages really, not 200. (I do like the way you will end a long paragraph with a single line in quotes—a remark. It does something.)

And, oh yes! no doubt whatever that the city itself, Alexandria, is the real hero. You've made it immortal. It communicates always by and through the senses. It also gives the impression of being inexhaustible—like a god. Bravo! (How different, in essence and in your handling of it, from my Brooklyn and New York.)

One curious question to put you. This propensity of yours for making characters speak through exchange of letters. Has it some special value, in your eyes? Each time it happens I have a feeling you are about to lose your grip. You don't, of course. But it gives the effect of heavy breathing (whilst sitting on a rock) after violent exertion. Your last letter to Clea, for example—isn't it a bit like slackening a taut rope? And, at the end, to give that much space to Darley's new job, new residence, future plans, France, and all that—it weakens the book, all four books, it seems to me. Clea's response, of course, is a shocker. One will never forget that steel Hand, never! or the wonderful "lesson" imparted by implication—to wit (as you have stated explicitly or implicitly through one person or another throughout), that the hand, or whatever the implement, resides in the psyche. Yes, you have said many, many wonderful things (even through Pursewarden) about the nature and purpose and aim of art. Bravo! I repeat. And I see you re-introduced "the heraldic universe." Let us clap our hands. It all needs rereading, careful, scrupulous rereading. Not the intoxicated draughts such as I indulged in.

You know with whom, in some ways, you have a kinship? Malaparte! Because of the "horrors" employed. I think of so many episodes—the chopping up of the live camel, Leila's disfigurement, Narouz himself—a magnificent horror, Liza's blindness—cruel and disturbing always—only to mention a few—and the *lovely* horror of the drowned Greeks standing underwater in their canvas jackets—and that most excellent touch of growing familiar, even playful, with them whilst swimming below! And (but this is no horror!) the perfectly marvelous touch of swimming in a phosphorescent sea, after the storm! Je te salue! All this wonderful sun-and-sea period with Clea (I always transpose Claude for Clea) is better, far better, in my poor opinion, than the vaunted beauty of Homer. Yours is the distilled essence of the Greek world. Homer reminds me so often of the clotted, catalogued passages in the Old Testament, everything dragged in by the hair and at the wrong moment. (Was *that* Greek, I ask you?)

And then over all and above all, I must say that you seem to have harpooned once and for all—*morality*. The moralities, better said. Alexandria—your Alexandria— is the whole pantheon of Homer's bloody, senseless gods —doing what they will, but conscious of what is done. The Homeric gods are more like blind forces, components of the now exposed psyche—atomic, in other words. Whereas Alexandria—through and by her inhabitants, climate, odors, temperament, diversity, freaks, crimes, monstrous dreams and hallucinations (but why imitate *you?*) —gives the impression of living herself (her pantheonic self) out, of washing herself clean through complete enactment. Alexandria *enacts* for us—that's it. The act and the actor, the dream, or vision, and the drama— all in one. Do I make myself clear?

And your Nessim, to switch a moment. Do you know that he has the qualities of a great and gentle monarch? A royal personage, truly. I feel towards him as towards a great brother—not spiritual so much as an enlarged human. He moves with the dignity and felicity of a panther. His recovered happiness makes one's heart swell. He, Narouz, the mother—what a world you created—to say nothing of the decor in which they swim!

No, by God, if I let myself go, try to review it all in

memory, even patchily, it's overwhelming. And to know that it was done so swiftly! No, it's incredible.

What matter, then, if the ground plan escapes me. I become just another reader, avid for more, unquestioning, glutted yet insatiable, crying as he reads—"Hosanna! Hosanna in the Highest!"

We'll probably see you chez vous demain, or whenever Eve said by postcard. Prepare the fatted calf. Must drink to your health, your arrival like a nova on the firmament of creation.

Apologies for handing you these reflections in such shoddy fashion. When I travel I'm dispersed. I ingest only —but like a bivalve.

More à viva voce!

Henry

P.S.   Yes, Claude, I know you are there. How are you? It will be good to see you again.

Big Sur

9/2/59

Dear Larry,

If I remember right today is the day you sail for England. We are back home about ten days now, after a spectacular jet flight from New York to Frisco—$5\frac{3}{4}$ hours at a height of 30,000 feet and all smooth as oil. I had a real vision of the future during that flight. Of our immediate future, I might say. One thought kept hammering itself home all the time—that we are now, already, definitely in the era of the Mind. It won't be long, I think, before the whole mechanical age will crumble, and with it the fuel and power business. When they build rockets which will take you from Los Angeles to Paris in forty minutes—and they plan just such by 1975—won't they see the absurdity of power-speed and find out what motion (or real power) is and just harness it? You can't bust atoms still farther. The next step is mind, or imagination. Anyway, in the plane, I could see it all clearly—what would come to pass. Inevitable. We are like men of the Old Stone Age with one foot in the Atomic Age. But the Atomic Age will be even more short-lived than any of the preceding ages. The clock speeds up with each change. No, all that we now see is doomed. We're having a last look. There *will* be space travel, but it will be a space such as we have only dimly imagined. And the planets will be quite other too, believe me. We are being compelled to realize that imagination is all. We won't be able to live with anything less.

I'm going through some sort of crisis. Never felt more desolate. Yet underneath very hopeful. Two nights ago I got up in the middle of the night with the firm intent of destroying everything—but it was too big a job. So I'll hang on and finish *Nexus* (Vol. 2), then see. Writing seems so foolish, so unnecessary now. Not yours, of course, but mine. As for you, I feel such a glorious future for you. You've just opened the vein. And with what a salvo! Go on, you bring joy everywhere. As for me, I seem to feel that all I have done is to create a booby-hatch. Now I can throw the letters away without replying. It's easy. The next step is to throw myself away. That's harder. One thing seems certain—that I've built on sand. Nothing I've done has any value or meaning for me any longer. I'm not an utter failure, but close to it. Time to take a new tack. Years of struggle, labor, patience, perseverance have yielded nothing solid. I'm just where I was at the beginning—which is nowhere. And perhaps that's good, real good. Perhaps I'm getting to that stage of utter doubt which will dissolve all doubt.

I think of our talks in Engances, Sommières, Stes. Maries, Nimes, Paris. They meant much to me. I would love so much to be near you, talk to you when I felt like it. I like the underneath gravity which you have acquired over the years, without loss of effervescence, enthusiasm, spontaneity, joy. I must have been a sorry sight most of the time. A dud. Too bad. But I shan't forget those evenings under the tent, over a vieux marc, stepping out under the stars, the road to Uzès hard by, the ride through Nimes and the villages between, all so unlike anything here. And dear Claude. Such wonderful dishes she cooked up, such wonderful talks, such good, honest friendship, such regal hospitality. Now it's all like a dream.

Our kids will be going to live with their mother in a few days—perhaps for the whole school term. And Eve will be staying with her mother in Berkeley till she dies. I will be alone as I was when I first came here, but a different aloneness now, harder to bear, considering all that has happened here since I first came. Maybe it will be good for the "work"—ha ha! If only the "work" seemed more important, more urgent.

Stop! When I think of all you have endured these past fifteen years or more and of how discreetly, tactfully silent you have been, I grow ashamed of myself.

I do hope you'll have some good innings with Joey there in London. Haven't heard much from him since Sommières. Give him a good hug for me. Be good to yourselves, as he always says.

Cheerio!
Henry

Big Sur
9/10/59

Dear Larry,

Our friend Larry Powell, head of the library at Los Angeles, was here and we had a good talk. Among other things he brought up the subject of our correspondence over the years, saying he thought it the time now to get it published. (I mentioned Rowohlt's interest in this subject and then we both wondered if that meant doing them in translation—not so good, what?)

Anyway, he suggests that if your friend Alan Thomas is holding my letters to you that he get them all microfilmed and Powell would do the same with yours; then, when reproduced he would assort and put them together in chronological order, so that they could be presented in good fashion to prospective publishers. He says Thomas has facilities in London and is sure he would do it; I don't know who would foot the bill, but I imagine Powell would.

You know that he and Thomas are working on a bibliography of yours—difficult task too, it seems. He is still trying to track down a very early book of yours, by a title I don't recognize, published under your right name, not Norden. Says it's virtually impossible to find, though he did see a copy at the British Museum library. Otherwise he has just about everything of yours, including magazine pieces, privately printed items, etc.

Anyway, I too have a hunch that the time may be ripe for such a publication. And we wouldn't have to do any work—ain't that grand?

Cheerio now. Weather fair and warmer. Cool breezes off the ocean. Occasional fog. Have a good time!

Henry

The mazet
(Rainy weather but by the fire)

[October 1959]

Dear Henry:

I told you we got back pretty tired and found a bloody mess here; the mason had run the well dry, drunk all our wine, fired off all my shells, disamorced the fucking electric pump . . . everything; so it's taken us about a fortnight to bring order out of chaos. Luckily *Sappho* has been postponed by a few weeks; I was really dreading more travel. In fact I've come to hate travel entirely, and would gladly sit here on my arse and not move. Old age? All countries seem the same, less interesting than France. Though in justice I must say that England was *marvellous* this time; you really would have been startled to see what three months of solid sun (first time in 200 years) can do to my compatriots; such humour, kindness, serviability, exquisite manners, rugged laughter. It was uncanny! It was like a real move forward. People were sparkly, alive, forthcoming, devil may care; and all as brown as berries. Food's improved too—or else my fame is rating me higher class meals. But the day we left the rain closed in again, that heartbreaking steady drizzle! We dragged a whole load of books and papers back here and I'm sorting out stuff I haven't seen for years and years, and mostly your letters; they are going to be a job to microfilm as the earlier ones were written north south, and then south north, and then sideways, and many not dated at all; but I think I have almost every scrap. Unlike Joe who tears everything up. I felt they'd come in useful sometime, maybe pay Tony's gambling debts! Anyway they'll make a fine book even on their own; but I won't bother with scraps like postcards etc. etc. I'll keep those to give away as presents to your fans when they call. Among other things I've found the little Jupiter diary which you wrote for me in '39; do you know there are about 30 Zen quotations in the book? You had the impression you only heard of Zen postwar, but it ain't so. I also have some amusing scribbles—your first Greek lesson (transliterated), and a few pages of impressions of Athens. All this I will hoard for my daughters on condition that if ever Val or Tony are in need they will turn them over. We are waiting for a telegram from Hamburg about the play, and another about a film team coming to photograph the master in his natural surroundings. What absurdity! But the three little rooms Giraud is building are going on apace and will be done by Christmas. Big fire. Pot au feu. Claude is correcting the French and Italian translations of *Mountolive* by it. I really want to sit by this fire indefinitely, that's all.

Clea is to bed in UK and USA. Don't know how things will turn out. We must wait upon the event. So much depends on luck; so far the French and German critics who've seen it in proof are thrilled. But I fear that it is too explicit, too simple to please our domestic highbrows. They suspect the easy; if it don't bore a little they feel cheated. However we'll see. *Mountolive* really does sound magistral in French, better than English and much more exotic. The Saxon shock-points don't shock here, and many Saxon commonplaces seem wildly rare and exotic to French people.

Anyway, what the hell; don't drive over that bloody cliff until you've done another dozen at least. You'll be the home-grown doyen of Yankee litcheratewer yet, mark my word.

Love,
Larry

Mazet Michel

[October 1959]

Dear Henry:

I've brought back all your letters and am sorting them before sending to Alan for microfilms, as Powell wants. There is some marvellous stuff here about your work and ideas and should make a good book. I hope however that

Powell doesn't want to print mine. I have tender feelings about my private affairs and private life and don't want to exhibit my sore spots to a wondering world. Your position is different and these letters make a fine pendent to your work.

Hamburg has put the play back a fortnight until November, and it looks doubtful now that I shall be able to get away as there is a television team coming down here to picture the animal in his natural surroundings; unfortunately as originally planned I was to be back here by the first of November. However what will be will be.

I got a very good reception in England; I think the French and German press treatment of me rather stung them, so they extended quite a hand to the wandering boy, and most people seem to think that *Clea* will get through the hoop all right and wind up the bloody quartet. Now . . . I have a dozen plans and don't know which to start on first. On the other hand I may just lie about and be bad tempered for a few months. I've overfulfilled my norm and there's such a block of books to come out that it seems silly to produce more for the time being. I might tidy up my play *Acte* for the Germans instead. I rang Joe in London but couldn't make contact in that madhouse he works in. He's editing *The Booster* all over again in book form; I don't know why. I have stumbled among my papers on a haul of interesting letters which I thought I'd lost from people like Dylan, Shaw, and so on; they make amusing reading.

The well is dry; and the mason has made a bloody mess in starting the children's cabin. Well. But the garrigue is so nice, smells good. First frost and rains coming. More soon.

love,
LARRY

371

Dear Larry,

How good to get your letter at last! You say the garrigue is lovely now; so it is here. Divine days, and threatening to continue on into the New Year. Somehow I'm full of expectancy. Sometimes I'm up before dawn, filling the bird bath or watching Venus fade out. She's at full candle power now and becoming more and more beneficent.

Before I go on a word about the letters. Larry, you simply can't withhold your end of the correspondence. You know, there's hardly ever anything very personal in your letters. I'm the one who blurts things out; you're discreet, reserved, veiled. The reader will hardly know whether you're talking about a wife, a mistress or one of the characters in your books. Your personal life is bound up with places, fauna and flora, archaeology, the planets, mythology. You're always "heraldic." No, I won't let them publish mine alone. Besides, yours are far more interesting. You take us places. Think it over. Don't be squeamish! After all, you're not British, you're Irish, a Mediterranean Irishman at that.

This morning, after three hours of cleaning up around here, I took a seat on the bench under the oak tree (it's a pew my sister got for me from a Baptist Church), and I began reading the page proofs of Delteil's *St. Francis*. I read only the Preface (20 pages) and I was delirious. You know, I've written you from time to time about Delteil, that you ought to get to know him better. He *is* a saint, a modern one, who knows how to wield the pen. (Writes in bed, with a quill, I believe, before having breakfast.)

But do you know what Joseph is talking about in his

Preface? He wants us to start all over again, from the beginning. Back to Paradise, no less. I thought I was the only fool who talked this way. One can never go back? Nonsense, he cries. Why change the world? *Change worlds!* (St. Francis) He talks of poverty, of Francis electing for it. Liberty in poverty. Not the miserable suffering kind of poverty, but the privilege of being poor, the privilege, in short, of rejecting all that we do not need, did not ask for, do not want, cannot use, etc. In short, the kit and boodle. For Francis, he says, it was a matter of throwing overboard, of rejecting completely 30,000 years of civilization. What he railed against, in praising holy ignorance, was our bookish culture, our crazy, deadly sciences.

Familiar? All too, perhaps. I recall your disdainful laughter when you handed me back Maillet's book. The true Christ! How naif! you said. Did Jesus really live? Which Jesus? Etc. As if it mattered whether a man named Jesus lived or not. He lives. And we live in him, or live not. Socrates, Gautama, Milarepa, le Comte de St. Germain—did they live? Astound me, if you can! I believe. I know. Don't talk about God—be it! Find the place, the formula (Rimbaud). Ecrasez l'infame! Or, as Lord Buckley renders it—"Stamp out the terror!"

Ah, Larry, it isn't that life is so short, it's that it's everlasting. Often, talking with you under the tent—especially over a vieux marc—I wanted to say, "Stop talking . . . let's *talk!*" For twenty years I waited to see you again. For twenty years your voice rang in my ears. And your laughter. And there, at the Mazet, time running out (never the vieux marc), I had an almost frantic desire to pin you down, to have it out, to get to the bottom. (*What is the stars?* Remember?) And there we were on the poop deck, so to speak, the stars drenching us with light, and what are we saying? Truth is, you said so many marvelous things I never did know what we were talking about. I listened to the Master's Voice, just like that puppy on the old Victor gramophone. Whether you were expounding, describing, depicting, deflowering or delineating, it was all one to me. I heard you writing aloud. I said to myself—"He's arrived. He made it. He knows how to say it. Say it! Continue!" Oui, c'est toi, le cher maître. You have the vocabulary, the armature, the Vulcanic fire in your bowels. You've even found "the place and the formula." Give us a new world! Give us grace and fortitude!

All I was trying to say, bedazzled as I was, and it was like trying to put a knife into a crevice, was: "What's it all about?" After the last line, *what?* After the television appearances, after the Académie, *what?* Remember my visit to Valéry's tomb with Rowohlt? What a day! Such a view from the cemetery! And later, along the river bank, the curving line of facades like a Guardi, the puffing launches, the masts bobbing up and down, the nets spread out to dry, oysters, prawns, crabs, eels glittering on the ice, and Rowohlt thirsty, his eyes moist with friendship, thinking back, the two of us, along the ancestral stream—Walther von der Vogelweide, the Hohenstaufens, Friedrich Barbarossa, Parsifal, the Minnesinger—oh yes, I would come to Hamburg, to Bremerhaven, to Hannoversch-Münden, we would go here, there, everywhere—but it was so good just to sit, just to watch the river flowing, the boats passing, the facades changing color. Just to look into Rowohlt's eyes was something. Such an honest man, such a tender, loving soul. A brother. A blood brother. (Did you ever remark how different he looked when he removed his spectacles? "Two Brown Eyes." I used to play it on the piano for my dear Tante Melia before she went mad. A special from Hamburg, it was.)

It was always a sort of thick talk we had, Rowohlt and I. Guttural, soupy, sentimentalisch, quoi. Sometimes we merely grunted. The waiter always filling the glasses. And Jane, that pale odalisque with the most beautiful feet I've ever seen, sitting serenely drinking it in, interrupting only to add more flavor, more celery salt, more brotherly-sisterly love . . . what a woman, what lazy delicatesse! A sort of Germanic geisha whose pleasure it was to please because she was too lazy to do anything else. A divine slothfulness. He really loves her, I believe. And she loves being loved.

Where was I? The knife in the crevice. Or the chink in the armor. More and more I'm intrigued by simplicity—simplicity of act, word, thought. Reading plays, for example, I'm fascinated by all that's left out. The bare bones—how wonderful! Looking back over my more tumultuous writings I begin to wonder if perhaps I was not trying to hide something? Or perhaps I was hiding from myself. You know, for example, that when you are "emotional" you're not really feeling. You're pumping it up. You put something outside that should be inside. Right? Now I would like to be able to make the reader laugh and weep by a few well-placed words, a phrase, a short sentence—or an exclamation. Fuck the hammer-klavier and the well-tempered clavichord.

Having done battle for so many centuries, I feel now more expert in the use of the rapier, the stiletto—or the axe. I love the Japanese sword play with the grunts, the heavy breathing, the slow, steady footwork, the shift of stance, and then presto—cloven through the middle—one swift, clean stroke. Just one. (The opposite is Alexandre Dumas via Douglas Fairbanks, get me?)

But I can't change horses in mid-stream. For *Nexus*, Vol. 2, I've got to stick to the last. I wonder, though, if you, you especially, ever realized that from the very beginning of the trilogy I was trying to be more simple, more straightforward. I didn't succeed, of course. But the intent was there. What I feel like saying sometimes—when the whole bloody *Crucifixion* comes to an end—is "Ladies and Gentlemen, don't believe a word of it, it was all a hoax. Let me tell you in a few words the story of my tragedy; I can do it in twenty pages."

And what would be the story? That, wanting desperately to become a writer, I became a writer. In the process I sinned. I became so involved with the Holy Ghost that I betrayed my wife, my child, my friends, my country. I fell in love with the medium. I thought—if one makes a stroke on the blackboard that is the thing in itself, the reality. I almost fell in love with myself, horrible thought. I recorded what I saw and felt, not what was. To explain . . . it's a bit like what happened to the Jews. In the beginning there were men who talked with God. As the power or faculty dried up men began talking *about* God. A world of difference. I would like to talk to men or with men in a different way now. Like Parsifal, not Pagliacci. My heart was never broken. I'm intact, comme dit Rimbaud. I held on by a thread, no doubt.

Two or three days later . . . Just had a letter from Fanchette telling me of his visit with you recently. Says he saw that dummy which I wrote for you—where? Corfu, was it, or Paris? How does it sound now? Only a few months ago I got a photostatic copy of the one I wrote for Reichel. I fell in love with it. Never will I be able to say things as I did then. It was hallucinating, especially the bit about Madame Ginsbourg, our landlady at the Villa Seurat. Do you remember her, the old harridan? I had pasted a photo in the dummy, at this section, showing a freak from a sideshow with an extra pair of legs, useless ones, to be sure. That was Madame Ginsbourg. I'll never forget the day that Fred, overcome with remorse for smashing the window panes, went downstairs and sat on her lap and billed and cooed, called her his darling mother, etc. etc., while fondling her big cabbagey breasts, and she loved it—and we never had to pay for the repairs.

Excuse me for running on. This is a warming up exercise. Sooner or later I've got to get down to work. I left off, at page 3, vol. 2., where Mona and I have registered at the Grand Hôtel de la France, rue Bonaparte. I'm standing on the balcony listening to the bells of St. Germain. It's May and spring has come to Paris. But here's the point. I don't fall for Paris immediately. I had thought it would be more exotic. Soon I will buy bicycles and Mona will take lessons in that narrow little street, the rue Visconti, where Balzac had his publishing house and failed heavily. Not far away, a parallel street, Oscar Wilde had lived—in a modest hotel, I see it clearly still. We will be leaving for Fontainebleau by train, there to start our cycle tour. I don't know then that the great Milosz lives there, with his birds, his poems, his Lithuanian memories —and "the key to the Apocalypse." Maybe I didn't even know that Gurdjieff had his sana there, or whatever he called it. And that Katherine Mansfield would be one of his patient-disciples. Or that, much later, I would be weeping in the Noctambules whilst listening to Francis Carco (born same place as Mansfield—New Hebrides, New Caledonia?) recite his poems. In the lobby outside his books are on sale. Piles and piles of them. He must have already written 50. Think of it. I wept for all the poètes maudits that night, myself included. It was glorious. In the morning the birds sang as usual, and as usual I took my constitutional before breakfast along the exterior boulevards, arriving always breathlessly at the Place des Peupliers, where there was a sort of scaffold, it seemed to me, though I never heard of anyone being executed there. Blissful days, those. Time for everything then. Once a week I'd visit Moricand in his attic and study horoscopes. Thus I acquired a cane belonging to Kissling

——or perhaps it was Modigliani. I lost it in Rocamadour, in a fit of ecstasy one night. Just before visiting the Gouffres du Padirac.

Listen, if you and Claude ever travel up the Rhone again, take the left bank and stop at La Voulte. It's absolutely insane—people and architecture. Also a good hotel there with excellent food—near the bridge. *But*, it was somewhere near there, between Vienne, I imagine, and La Voulte, that on that bicycle trip with Mona—Paris to Marseilles—we stopped at a café one hot day and while in a trance, a blissful one, the spot so fixed itself in my memory that it was more real than reality. Like a spot you recognize—the déjà vu business—from another incarnation. Maybe I sat there, at that very spot, in Roman times, my chariot parked nearby, and I knew the Vandals were coming, knew that all was changing forever, and I was having a last look. I do wish I could find that place again!

You see what my task is. I have to write about a Paris I haven't yet become acquainted with. I must walk certain streets I later regard as brothers or sisters of mercy as if I hardly noticed them. The rue St. Dominique, the rue Mouffetard are not yet discovered. The Rotonde is a café where every afternoon a German girl, Magda I think it was, used to meet us by accident. That is, meet Mona, whom she was in love with and hoped to mulct for a few hundred francs. She loved her hats, her gowns, her cape. They would always excuse themselves to run off and do a few errands. Errands! What kind of errands!? And I'm too much in love (with my wife) to give heed to the vultures who surround me. Besides, I had no French. About all I could muster was a "Oui ou Non, Monsieur" and "L'addition, s'il vous plaît!" Oh yes, I could also ask how to get to the lavabo.

Oh yes . . . Then one day, when I'm by my lonesome, sitting again at the Rotonde, a woman gets up from the terrasse of the Dôme and starts crossing the street. What a creature! Only twice have I met the like. (Once with Fred, on the grands boulevards, when a magnificent cocotte with violet eyes—but *violet*, I tell you!—passed us, and like automatons we wheeled around and passed her again—just to see those eyes.) But this one at the Dôme was a bit like your Nancy, tall, willowy, with auburn hair which fell down her back like a waterfall. She had the walk of a queen—something out of the Arthurian legends. Definitely English. Irish-English, I'd say. So stunning that I trembled from head to foot. Then I was up and following her. No thought of accosting her. Ah no! Just to follow and gaze and feast my eyes. A long walk, up and down side streets. Finally she ducked into a dress shop. I walked over to the opposite side of the street, went as far as the corner and turned back. Imagine my astonishment when, just as I pass the shop, I find her lifting her skirt over her magnificent fall of auburn hair. She stands there in her slip, more willowy now than ever, more ravishing. And she is totally oblivious of anything outside. Innocent as a dove . . . That's all. I never saw her again. I was happy. I had seen her. Maybe she was an actress from the Gate Theatre. Maybe it was Lady Gregory. Maybe she was a pawnbroker's mistress. For me, it was as if I had seen Guinevere. And I knew later why the good, the glorious Arthur had to be betrayed by his friend Launcelot. He had taken Beauty (Rimbaud) but had forgotten to sit her on his knee. It was too noble a betrothal. Guinevere's infidelity always moves me deeply. It makes her a woman. She had to step down or be lost in legend. And as she sinks Arthur rises. How wonderful is Arthur with Launcelot. Stop! I may grow maudlin.

And now I must tell you a strange thing. Just before

leaving for Europe I received two or three rather weird letters from a man in New York, telling me that he knew who the real Dr. Kerkhoven was, that in fact, he had been his patient only recently. Further, that Kerkhoven knew of me and would welcome hearing from me. I thought he must be a crackpot. I went off. When I got back here I looked up the correspondence on an impulse and I wrote to Dr. Kerkhoven. Lo and behold, I got an answer. A beautiful letter, full of modesty, simple, warm, utterly human. He said Wassermann had used three men to build his Kerkhoven, that Jung was one, and he another. I forget the third, a name unknown to me. He had just been through a grave crisis, he said, and instead of wrestling with the spirit had submitted to an operation. Now I am rereading this book. It is one of those books which, as a reader, one feels is addressed to oneself personally. Every page is marked and scored. Kerkhoven is as close to me as my skin. The reading shakes me to the very foundations —and this is the third or fourth reading, mind you. The wonderful thing—this ties up with what I mentioned earlier—is the sloughing off of the built-in man (the man of society, tradition, education, background, etc.) and the emergence of the new man relying upon his intuition, knowing that whatever it is he is practising is "magic." The certitude that grows and grows, until, like a Christ, one can say: "Get up and walk!" And the man walks. So, many times, when I am sorely baffled, I will say to myself—"Write it, put it down! What difference whether it makes sense or not." And then it's as if some panel inside one slid open, the musicians are there, the note is sounded, the walls give way, the images beckon—and you find yourself saying it without knowing it. Fatal to pause and reflect. On! On! Until the strength gives out. Then, in quiet, after a prayer of thanks, you read—and you see the traces of another's hand, God's maybe, or maybe your own, your concealed, your suppressed self. All one. God needs us as much as we need Him. Dixit.

And so I say to you, or ask you rather—imagine us still under the tent—when we arrive at this stage, even if only once, must we not question this power, must we not feel chastened, must we not blush when signing our own names? If, whenever we sat down to write we could summon the spirit, would we want to go on writing? How often have I told you that the books I wrote in my head were the best, that nothing manifested in print ever approaches them? What we put down on paper is but a pale imitation, a faint and faded remembrance of these sessions with the silent spirit. What we are doing, I sometimes think, is to trace the outline of our irrepressible ego. Instead of the act we give a performance. The author is in the wings, the writer is dazzled by the footlights. Rimbaud leans out of the wings. His shadow, at least, is visible to all.

Interruption again . . . A fan, all the way from New York, sans sou and famished. And I had had such a marvelous dream, during my brief nap. I was going to insert it for you—gratis. Then this lad whom Eve should have shooed off but didn't because—guess why!—because he resembled our beau-frère de Jérusalem when he was 19. I was riled. And sometimes when I'm riled I recommend Maxim Gorki or Meister Eckhart. I told him it was good to be a slave, to crawl like a worm, to bark now and then, to stand on one's hind legs, etc. He was slightly bewildered. (What he really wanted was food, but he didn't have the courage to ask for a crust of bread.)

Anyhow, that was yestereve. Now it's 7:30 A.M. next day and I've already bathed, shaved, eaten, walked the dog and cleared the crumbs off the table.

Whenever I rise at dawn I put the gramophone on real loud—usually Monteverdi's madrigals. Or else Gaspard de la Nuit. Or the Fifth piano sonata of Scriabin. So doing I fill the bird bath and place a few bread crumbs around the edge of it. Dante, whose plaster head is cemented to the bowl, is always gazing at his reflection in the water. Thinking of Beatrice, no doubt. If the fog has rolled in I wait for the nimbus, i.e. the magnification of my image with halo and all, cast on the iridescent soap suds below by the sun which has just come over the mountain in the rear. Then I think of the Lord Buddha—"I obtained not the least thing from unexcelled, complete awakening, and for this very reason it is called unexcelled, complete awakening." Could anything be clearer?

When I rise before dawn I feel horsey. Think of Nijinsky trying to climb out of the orchestra pit like a horse. Think of Gogol—what horses! "Russia, where are you leading us?" Etc. The day begins with the sign of the pit, the chasm, the gouffre. Means I will tumble into my own pitfalls. *Attention!* Méfiez-vous des femmes! On one side of the chasm the dodo, on the other the totohotsu or whatever the bugger is called. (He appears only in phantasmal landscapes.) I may start for the hot baths and end up in the forest. I will have written ninety letters, three plays and a half and started a romance. Night will find me at Nepenthe ordering a gin and tonic. There, while shaking hands and saying "Happy to meet you," "Yes, thank you, I'll have another," I plan the next water color move. Something allegretto, something very subtle and delicate. In the midst of it I suddenly remember : "Darling, where are you?" That's a tentative title for a play rolling around in my noodle. You can't imagine what I can put into that *darling!* And so with Eric Barker on one side of me and Ephraim Doner on the other, both talking rubbish by now, and the owner staring me in the face like a majolica hand-painted pisspot, I weave into the opening. The scene is always two in the morning, time same as always.

Always begins in the middle of a sentence. For decor a table, a coffee pot and a half-finished bottle of some ratgut or other. The talk began hours ago. Just getting to the boil as the curtain rises. Comes the familiar phrase, like a gong—"You want the truth, do you?" Here I get fuzzy, because the truth is like a tapeworm—you never get rid of it.

In this house, or rather in this play, truth is served up at all hours. Always on tap, so to speak. You can have it cold or hot, scrambled or fried, varnished and unvarnished. Usually it's predigested. Sometimes given in powder form. Always soothing and conducive to nightmares. The house is divided into sixteen marriages, forty peccadillos and a few amourettes. The slats between the walls thrum like loose banjo strings. The alarm never goes off. Flanking the bedrooms are the slave quarters where the Master plies his varying vocations. . . .

But enough of this. To come back to Scriabin, a first love and a lasting one. I started a long extravaganza about him in *Nexus*, Vol. 1, but cut it down to a cadenza because I had already run off the trolley too many times. I felt I had to stick to the leitmotif announced in *Capricorn:* "On the Ovarian Trolley." But anyway, since I'm doing a marathon, let me give you a quote or two about him from a Communist Russian's book:

"Bitter fate mocked the composer. He, the messiah in his own imagination, who had dreamed of leading mankind towards 'the last festival' (must have read Rimbaud, the bugger!), who had imagined himself God, and everything, including himself, his own creation, who had dreamed by the force of his tones to overthrow the universe, died of a trifling pimple. . . .

"Scriabin's insanity did not lie in his ideas, but in the central role which he wished to play himself, in his self-opinionation and self-love. His insanity consisted in not knowing his own powers. (sic!) Taken apart from this 'evil,' Scriabin is neither insane nor monstrous, but a man who was painfully absorbed in thinking and who wished to arrive at a joyous solution of the problems of the world. And in his music was reflected this joyous and impotent urge toward something 'absolute.' "

I was twenty-five when I first heard Scriabin. It began about nine o'clock one evening, in a Russian café on Second Avenue, and lasted till dawn. It was like an inoculation—I never got over it. They talk of jam sessions. But what's a jam session to a night of nothing but Scriabin—played by a mad Russian who will hang himself a few days later? Before the year is out two other friends have hanged themselves. (One of them made a living writing jokes for the newspapers.) I never liked the feel of the rope, else I might have tried it myself.

Now, some ninety-five years later, it's pleasant, as Virgil would say, to remember these things. Then I had to wake people up in the middle of the night to tell them of this new discovery or that. Now I send it out over the waves—to the birds and fishes, to the snails and the sowbugs. If nobody gets it, tant pis. Nothing's lost, not even yesterday's garbage. "Good morning, Mr. President. How do you like your new home?" (meaning the White House).

Reminds me of Fred after a night's debauch. Saying: "We sacrificed to the elementals last night, didn't we, Joey? How do you feel?" And I would answer: "I feel fine. And you?" And then he would put me in stitches, saying how his gal had the curse or a short leg or something unromantic but he did his best. Followed by "When do we eat, Joey?" And then a grand cockalorum about the 20-page letter he was writing to his inamorata in Dalmatia. Maybe I could add a few lines, he was running dry. The evening after a night like that would be a poetic one for me. A long walk alone, preferably in a drizzle, and always in an unfamiliar neighborhood. Thoughts would ooze out like pus. Perhaps I'd recall incidents or characters I meant to elaborate on, things I had forgotten, things I had skipped in the rush of spilling it out. Or I'd think of rhythms, think of the book as a symphony. (There was a whole period when I knew a man from Hong Kong who lent me his Chinese records. Got to love stone music and the faint sound of gongs dropping their aspirates.) Coming home I'd be ready to write. Sometimes it was too good, I couldn't write it down. I would just flop on the bed, clothes and all, and enjoy the writing that went on in my head. Next morning I'd be up bright and early; again the constitutional, the Place des Peupliers, maybe a chat with the children on the bench near the scaffold. Swinging into the Villa Seurat I'd be singing to myself. And like that, one morning, just as I've struck the right rhythm, who walks in on me but Tihanyi, the deaf painter, remember? He tells me in his cluck-cluck language (which he always supposed we understood, but no one did, not even his Hungarian friends) that I should go right on writing, he would talk to me as I wrote. And by God, I did! And it was amazing that I wrote as well as I did—nothing lost, as I said before. He talked for twenty minutes while I polished off two or three pages—of "The Wild Park," I believe it was now. All he had come for was to tell me he had fixed a goulash for me. When I got there that evening he was lying beside the telephone, dead.

To be continued.

Henry

Lawrence Durrell Chronology

Born February 27, 1912, India.

Attended College of St. Joseph, Darjeeling, and St. Edmund's School, Canterbury.

Worked at various jobs in London, e.g., Blue Peter Night Club.

Married Nancy, spring 1935. Daughter Penelope Berengaria born June 3, 1940, Athens.

Corfu, 1935–39; visits to Paris and London, 1937, 1938–39.

Met Henry Miller in Paris, September 1937.

The Black Book published in Paris, 1938.

Greece, 1939–40, teaching at Institute of English Studies in Athens and Kalamata; in Crete until April 1941.

Cairo, 1941–44, Foreign Press Service Officer.

Alexandria, 1944–45, Press Attaché.

Rhodes, June 1945–March 1947, Director of Public Relations, Dodecanese Islands.

Married Eve (Gipsy), February 26, 1947. Daughter Sappho-Jane born May 30, 1951, Oxford.

Argentina, November 1947–November 1948, Director, British Council Institute, Cordoba.

Yugoslavia, July 1949–December 1952, Press Attaché, Belgrade.

Cyprus, 1953–August 1956, Director of Public Relations, Government of Cyprus.

Provence, since February 1957.

Awarded Duff Cooper Prize for *Bitter Lemons*, December 1957.

Justine, 1957; *Balthazar*, 1958; *Mountolive*, 1959; *Clea*, 1960; published as *The Alexandria Quartet*, 1962. *The Black Book* published in U.S., 1960.

Married Claude, March 27, 1961.

Born New York City, December 26, 1891.

Grew up in Brooklyn. Attended City College of New York for two months, 1909.

Worked at a great variety of jobs, ranging from father's tailor shop to employment manager of messenger department, Western Union Telegraph Company, 1909–24.

Married Beatrice, 1917.

Wrote first book ("Clipped Wings"—never published) during three weeks' vacation from Western Union, 1922.

Left Western Union to become a writer, 1924.

Married June, 1924.

Toured Europe for one year, 1928.

Moved to Paris, 1930.

Tropic of Cancer published in Paris, 1934; *Black Spring* Paris, 1936; *Tropic of Capricorn* Paris, 1939.

Visited Lawrence Durrell in Greece, 1939.

Returned to America, 1940; made "air-conditioned nightmare" tour, 1941–42.

The Colossus of Maroussi published in U.S., 1941.

Settled at Big Sur on the California coast, 1944.

Married Lepska, December 18, 1944. Daughter Valentine born November 19, 1945. Son Tony born August 28, 1948. Lepska departed, leaving children at Big Sur, 1951.

Tour of Europe, 1953.

Married Eve, December 29, 1953.

Returned to Europe with Eve and children for reunion with Lawrence Durrell, 1959.

Tropic of Cancer published in U.S., 1961; *Tropic of Capricorn* published in U.S., 1962.

INDEX

(With Explanatory Notes)

Acte (Durrell's second play), 371

Advocate (Harvard), 10

Air-Conditioned Nightmare, The (Miller, 1945), 169, 172, 180, 183–85, 194, 213, 251, 389

"Alcoholic Veteran with the Washboard Cranium, The" (Miller), 229, 240, 254

Aldington, Richard (English poet, novelist, and biographer), 76, 80, 312–13, 315–16

"Alexandria" (poem, first published in *Middle East Anthology*, 1946), 255

Alexandria Quartet, The (Durrell, tetralogy, 1957–60; published in one volume, 1962), 179, 307, 311, 313–14, 320, 326–38, 363–65; see *Balthazar, Clea, Justine, Mountolive;* also "Book of the Dead"

Aller Retour New York (Miller, 1935), 3, 10, 12, 198

Anand, Mulk Raj (Indian novelist), 117, 197

Anne of Dumfries (wife of Alfred Perlès), 189, 307

"Aquarians, The" (experimental prose piece by Durrell, 1938; never completed), 130

Aram (Armenian soothsayer in Athens), 162; see *The Colossus of Maroussi*

Armstrong, Louis, 312

Art and Outrage ("a correspondence between Alfred Perlès and Lawrence Durrell [with an inter-

mission by Henry Miller]," 1959), 325, 328–29, 331, 333, 336

"Asylum in the Snow" (Durrell's "Christmas Carol," 1936), 43–45, 58, 137, 242, 244

Atlantic Monthly, 327

Baltazian (Alexandrian banker and occultist), 202

Balthazar (Durrell, second volume of *The Alexandria Quartet*, 1958), 306, 309, 313, 317–19, 323

Balzac, Honoré de, 37, 140–41, 143–44, 152–53, 158, 358, 377; see *The Wisdom of the Heart*

Barker, Eric (poet living at Big Sur), 329, 382

Barr, Cecil; see Kahane, Jack

Baudelaire, Charles, 128, 231, 317

Beach, Sylvia (owner of Paris bookstore, Shakespeare & Co., first publisher of Joyce's *Ulysses*), 17, 35

Beat Generation, 344–48

Benn, Gottfried, 111

Bergson, Henri, 254, 261

Big Sur and the Oranges of Hieronymus Bosch (Miller, 1957), 293, 318–19, 326, 339, 343, 357

Bitter Lemons (Durrell, about Cyprus, 1957), 293, 305, 307, 309, 311, 313

Black Book, The (Durrell, 1938), xiv, 33, 35, 38, 49, 60, 63–65, 75, 77–85, 120–21, 123, 126, 135, 137–40, 144, 151, 171, 198, 201,

389

204, 207, 222, 230, 249, 263, 298, 300, 329, 331, 333–34, 361, 388; sends to Miller, 68–69; Miller's response, 71–74; Miller's second thoughts, 91–95, 98–108; expurgation? 101–109; published in Paris, 131–32

Black Spring (Miller, 1936), 3, 8–9, 12, 22, 30, 36, 53, 66, 69, 75, 84, 90, 92, 152, 199, 231–32, 243, 265, 374, 389

Blake, William, 326

Blakeston, Oswell (English critic and writer), 118, 120

"Book of the Dead" (title of a planned book, mentioned first 1937; later applied to project culminating in *The Alexandria Quartet*), 105, 157, 192, 201–202, 224–25, 229, 246, 283

Books in My Life, The (Miller, 1952), 169, 280–81, 284, 290–91

Booster, The (erstwhile house organ of the American Country Club of Paris; 4 issues edited by Perlès, Miller, Durrell, & Co., September 1937–January 1938; succeeded by *Delta*), xii, 109–10, 113, 115–22, 189, 211, 228, 246, 291, 340, 371

Brahms, Johannes, 340

Brandes, Georg, 55

Breton, André (leader of the French surrealist movement), 19, 44, 247

Bromage, Bernard, 150–51

Brown, Curtis (Durrell's literary agent), 32, 76, 107, 115, 242, 317

Bruno, Giordano, 314

Buchet, Edmond (publisher of Corrêa), 359

Bucke, Richard Maurice, 172

Burford, Roger, 119

Cahiers du Sud, 46

Cairns, Huntington (American "censor" with whom Miller and Durrell correspond 1937–38), 89, 91–92, 95, 131, 152

Campbell, Roy (South African poet and bullfighter), 76, 80, 313

Carco, Francis, 377

Carroll, Lewis, 16, 19

Cassou, Jean, 354

Cavafy, Constantine (Greek poet of Alexandria), 193; see *The Alexandria Quartet*

Céline, Louis-Ferdinand (French novelist, author of *Journey to the End of Night*), 90, 176–77, 234–35, 340, 346

Cendrars, Blaise (French writer, wrote first review of *Tropic of Cancer*), 8, 90, 158, 269, 317, 346, 362; see *The Books in My Life*

Cézanne, Paul, 17, 53

Chaplin, Charlie, 307

Chaucer, 27

"Children of the Earth" (Miller, in *The Prairie Schooner*, Fall 1958), 343

Chirico, Giorgio di (father of surrealist painting), 30, 256

Churchill, Winston, 176, 279

Circle (Berkeley, Calif.), 207, 230

Cities, Plains, and People (Durrell, poems, 1946), 201, 207, 221, 230

Claude (Durrell's third wife), 304–305, 307, 309–10, 316, 319, 321, 323, 329, 337–38, 342, 352, 356–60, 364–65, 367, 378, 388

Clea (Durrell, fourth volume of *The Alexandria Quartet*, 1960), 313, 328, 339, 343, 356, 360–65, 371

"Clipped Wings" (Miller's unpublished first novel), 233, 388

Cocteau, Jean (French poet, critic, dramatist, and novelist), 30, 90

Colossus of Maroussi, The (Miller, narrative of trip to visit Durrell in Greece, 1941), 142, 159, 171, 175, 180, 192, 196, 198, 212, 224, 240, 307

Comfort, Alex, 199

Communism, 58, 264, 277, 279–81, 283–84

Connolly, Cyril (British critic, editor of *Horizon*, 1940–50), 8, 95, 235, 260, 263, 271, 275

Cornaz, Roger, 275

Corrêa (French publisher of Durrell and Miller), 359
Cosmological Eye, The (Miller, first book published in U.S., 1939), 75
Cowley, Malcolm, 336
Creative Writing, 160
Criterion (edited by T. S. Eliot, London, 1922–39), 30, 46, 48, 144
Crosby, Caresse, 185

Dark Labyrinth, The (Durrell, first published as *Cefalù*, 1947), 201, 207, 214, 216
Dekker, Thomas, 39
Delaney, Beauford (New York Negro artist), 335; see *Remember to Remember*
Delta (successor to *The Booster*, 3 issues, Paris-London, 1938–39), 43, 113, 141, 147, 150, 189
Delteil, Joseph (French surrealist writer, friend of Miller and Durrell), 372
Devil in Paradise, A (Miller, Part 3 of *Big Sur and the Oranges of Hieronymus Bosch*, 1957), 237, 305
Dibbern, George, 285, 322
Doner, Ephraim, 382
Donne, John, 27
Dos Passos, John, 81
Dostoievski, Fëdor, 17, 58, 108, 145, 191
"Draco and the Ecliptic" (Miller's long-projected book), 148, 263, 334
Dreiser, Theodore, 81
Du (Zurich), 347
Dudley, John, 183
Durrell, Gerald (brother), 114, 218, 241, 244, 300, 305–306
Durrell, Leslie (brother), 199
Durrell, Louisa (mother), 243
Durrell, Margaret (sister), 218, 241, 244
Durrell, Penelope Berengaria (daughter), 164, 172–73, 176, 178, 180, 260, 263, 327, 339, 388

Durrell, Sappho-Jane (daughter), 257, 286, 289–90, 294, 296, 298, 300, 302, 305, 307, 327, 339, 388
Dutton, E. P., and Co. (Durrell's American publisher), 310, 315, 323, 329, 359
Dyn, 195

Eastman, Max, 81
Eckhart, Meister, 381
Economos, Homer, 175
Edgar, David (American friend of Miller in Paris), 77–79, 83–84, 115, 182, 185, 188–89, 211, 247
Editions du Chêne, 198
"Elegy on the Closing of the French Brothels" (Durrell, poem, 1947), 222, 232
Eliot, T. S. (as editor of *Criterion* and director of Faber and Faber, corresponded with Miller, published and encouraged Durrell), 4, 30, 32, 37, 46, 69, 90, 102, 113, 116–17, 128, 135, 137, 182, 185, 188, 192, 241, 313, 322, 343–44; Durrell meets, 115–18
Elizabeth, Queen Mother, 309, 328
Ellis, Havelock (English sexologist), 113, 117–18
Emerson, Ralph Waldo, 261
"Eos" (projected literary quarterly in Corfu), 34–35
Epstein, Teresa, 211
Esprit de Corps (Durrell, sketches of diplomatic life, 1957), 257, 327–28
Etiemble, René, 200
Evans, Sir Arthur, 38, 59
Evans, Patrick (poet, friend of Durrell in Corfu), 40, 67, 74, 118
Eve (Gipsy, Durrell's second wife), 192–93, 201, 205, 214–16, 223, 226–28, 231, 235, 239, 250, 253, 289–90; meets in Alexandria, 189–90; to Rhodes, 210; Sappho born, 286; illness, 293–94, 301–302, 304, 388
Eve (Miller's fourth wife), 289,

296–97, 324, 356, 358–59, 365, 367, 381, 389
Existentialism, 223–24, 235

Faber and Faber Ltd. (Durrell's English publisher since 1937), 32–33, 39, 64, 68, 72, 74, 101, 113, 124, 180, 185, 204, 207, 239, 305, 308, 310, 313, 319, 329, 334; and *Black Book*, 102–106
Fanchette, Jean (co-editor of *Two Cities*), 356, 376
Fargue, Léon-Paul (French writer, subject of André Beucler's *The Last of the Bohemians*), 44, 337
Faulkner, William, 158, 174
Faure, Elie (French art historian), 261
Fechner, Gustav, 195
Fielding, Alexander ("Xan," British secret agent and writer), 191, 212, 232–33
Figaro Littéraire, 315
Ford, John, 38
Fowlie, Wallace, 195
Fraenkel, Michael (friend of Miller in Paris, his antagonist in the *Hamlet* correspondence), 3, 10, 25, 29, 33–34, 36–37, 43, 50–53, 55, 73, 85, 87
Freud, Sigmund, 209, 215, 261, 278, 344

Gascoyne, David (English poet, briefly poetry editor of *The Booster*), 119
Gauguin, Paul, 17–18, 53, 76
Gawsworth, John (English writer, friend of Durrell), 76, 118
Ghika (Greek painter), 244
Gide, André, 88
Gilbert, Stuart (British author of *James Joyce's Ulysses*, lives in Paris), 37, 47
Gillet, Louis, 46
Giono, Jean, 346
Gipsy; see Eve (Durrell)
Girodias, Maurice (son and successor of Jack Kahane, publisher of Obelisk Press), 198, 204, 213,

222, 230–31, 259, 266, 280, 284, 298, 336
Goethe, 193, 268
Gogol, Nikolai, 382
Gorki, Maxim, 381
Gotham Book Mart (New York), 171
Gourmont, Remy de, 312
Grauer, Ben, 316
Greville, Fulke, 39
Groddeck, Georg (German psychologist, subject of one of Durrell's "Studies in Genius," in *Horizon*), 204, 209, 222, 229
Guardi, Francesco, 374
Gurdjieff, Georges Ivanovitch (occult philosopher, author of *All and Everything*), 347, 377
Gutkind, Erich, 262

Haggard, Henry Rider, 281
Hall, Joseph, 27
Hamlet ("A Philosophic Correspondence," an exchange between Miller and Fraenkel, ostensibly about *Hamlet*, 2 vols., 1939–41), 3, 10, 12, 20–21, 23, 25–33, 37, 39, 43, 46, 49–55, 69, 132, 240
"Hamlet, Prince of China" (letter by Durrell, 1937), 43, 49–52, 53, 340
"Happy Rock, The" (Durrell, 1945; title essay in a book of Miller appreciations, considered for expansion into book-length study of Miller, but dropped in favor of *Horizon* article, July 1949), 179, 190, 199, 213, 215, 233–34, 240–41, 287
Harper's Magazine, 327
Harriss, Wayne, 171
Hemingway, Ernest, 128, 225
Henry Miller Reader, The (edited by Durrell, 1959), 237, 251, 254–55, 258, 323–25, 331, 335–36, 338–42, 345
Heraclitus, 334
"Heraldic Universe," 15, 19–24,

44, 65–66, 105, 203–204, 363, 372

Herald Tribune, 272

Hesse, Hermann, 347

Hiler, Hilaire (American artist), 36; see *The Air-Conditioned Nightmare*

Hitler, 133–34, 156

Hoffman, Michael (Miller's agent in Paris), 360

Holiday, 339

Holve-Barrows (Miller's friends, Holve and Barrows, publishers of *The Angel Is My Watermark*, Fullerton, Calif., 1944), 183

Homer, 108, 336–37, 364

Hopkinson, Tom (English magazine editor), 227

Horizon (edited by Cyril Connolly, London, 1940–50), 199, 204, 258–60, 263, 271–72, 340

Horizon (New York, 1958—), 345

Houghton, Claude (English novelist, author of *Julian Grant Loses His Way*), 175

Houseman, John, 247

Hudson, Barclay (American writer, mutual friend of Miller and Durrell), 5–8, 19–20, 22–23, 40–41, 66

Hugo, Victor, 37

Huxley, Aldous, 64, 76, 88, 90, 174

International Post, 154

"Ionian Profile" (prose piece contemplated by Durrell, 1936), 33

Jannings, Emil, 166

Jonson, Ben, 22, 51

Joyce, James, 4, 20, 22, 28, 46, 76, 328

Jung, Carl, 53, 261, 380

Justine (Durrell, early title for *The Alexandria Quartet;* later limited to the first volume, 1957), 293–94, 298–300, 302–304, 306, 308–12, 314, 317, 319, 321, 323, 327, 330, 346, 359

Kahane, Jack (English expatriate, founder of Obelisk Press, Paris; publisher of Miller's and Durrell's banned books; author of *Daffodil* and other erotica by "Cecil Barr"), 12, 16–17, 31, 46, 73–74, 80, 86, 93, 96, 98, 102, 105–107, 114, 120–21, 124, 132–35, 137, 139–40, 152, 157, 198, 201, 241, 244

Katsimbalis, George (Greek raconteur, the "colossus" of Miller's *Colossus of Maroussi*), 159–63, 165–68, 180, 188–89, 197, 205, 212, 231, 244–45, 248, 277, 293, 295; in postwar Athens, 218, 221, 223–24, 226

Kerkhoven, Dr. (protagonist of *The Maurizius Case*, trilogy by Jakob Wassermann; cf. Miller, *Maurizius Forever*), 176, 380

Kerouac, Jack (beatnik novelist, author of *The Dharma Bums*), 344–49, 352–54

Keyserling, Hermann Alexander (German philosopher, mystic, author of *Travel Diary of a Philosopher*), 97, 324, 345, 347

Key to Modern Poetry, A (Durrell, lectures in Argentina, 1952), 237

Kisling, Moise (painter), 377

Koster (friend of Durrell in Corfu), 67

Kretschmer, Ernst (German psychologist), 54, 66

Krishnamurti, J., 214; see *The Books in My Life*

Ladas, Diana, 305

Laforgue, Jules, 256

Lao-tse, 17, 21, 65, 168, 192

Laughlin, James (founder of New Directions, Miller's American publisher), 33, 36, 45, 58, 83, 99, 134, 198; *Aller Retour*, 10–11; *Black Spring*, 30–31; *Air-Conditioned Nightmare*, 194; *Henry Miller Reader*, 254–55, 335, 338–39

Lavrin, Janko, 284

Lawrence, D. H., 3, 6, 8, 9, 12, 17–

18, 22, 27, 34, 46, 52, 56, 64, 72, 108, 217, 228, 312, 361; see "The World of Lawrence"

Lawrence, Frieda, 217

Léger, Fernand, 243

Leigh Fermor, Patrick (British secret agent and writer), 212, 232–33

Leite, George (editor of *Circle*), 207, 222, 230, 242, 244

Leite, Nancy, 249

Lenin, 336

Lepska (Miller's third wife), 199, 228, 250, 252–53, 284, 288, 389

Levesque, Jacques (editor of *Orbes*, where first review of *Tropic of Cancer* appeared), 31, 37

Lewis, Eiluned, 339

Lewis, Wyndham (English writer, painter, and polemicist), 28, 30, 76, 80, 251

Life and Letters Today, 47

"Lime Twigs and Treachery" (Miller), 340

Litvinova, Ivy Low, 175

Loos, Anita, 348

Loti, Pierre, 38

Lowenfels, Walter (American poet in Paris, friend of Fraenkel), 36, 81, 87

Lundkvist, Artur (Swedish poet, translator of Miller), 37, 58

MacCarthy, Desmond, 90, 118

Maillet, Albert, 373

Mairet, Philip (editor of *New English Weekly*), 29, 46, 56

Malaparte, Curzio, 363

Mansfield, Katherine, 313, 377

Marlowe, Christopher, 27, 39

Marston, John, 27

Marx, Karl, 18

Maugham, Somerset, 31, 250

Max (friend of Durrell in Corfu), 67, 160; see *The Colossus of Maroussi*

Max and the White Phagocytes (Miller, includes "Max" and "Eye of Paris," 1938), 36, 55, 59, 96, 114, 140, 151

Melville, Herman, 191, 194, 225, 343

Mercure de France, 46

Middleton, Thomas, 39

Milarepa (of *Tibet's Great Yogi Milarepa*), 261, 337, 373

Miller, Henry (father), 170

Miller, Tony (son), 253, 288–89, 316, 320, 322, 359, 367, 370, 389

Miller, Valentin Lepska (daughter), 213, 216, 227, 233, 235, 288–89, 303, 307, 316, 322, 359, 367, 370, 389

Milosz, Oscar Vladislas, 377

Miró, Joan, 182

Modigliani, Amedeo, 378

Molière, 315

"Mona," 377–78

"Money and How It Gets That Way" (Miller, pamphlet in parody of economic theory, 1936), 29, 117

Monteverdi, Claudio, 381

Moore, Reginald, 194

Morgan, Charles, 76

Moricand, Conrad (astrologer friend of Miller in Paris, villain of *A Devil in Paradise*), 133, 139, 211, 230, 237, 244, 247, 250, 252, 305, 377

Morley, Frank (publisher and author), 102, 116–17

Mountolive (Durrell, third volume of *The Alexandria Quartet*, 1959), 313, 319–20, 326–27, 330–31, 333, 338, 342–44, 349–53, 356, 359, 370

"Murder the Murderer" (Miller, pamphlet, 1944; reprinted in *Remember to Remember*), 186, 200–201, 225, 254

Murry, John Middleton, 313

Musset, Alfred de, 128

Mussolini, 107–108, 134

Nancy (Durrell's first wife), 38, 41, 49, 53, 60, 65–66, 71, 74–75, 81, 94, 99, 106, 114–15, 122, 125–26, 135–36, 138, 145, 172–73, 176, 178, 180, 388

Nashe, Thomas, 39
Neiman, Gilbert, 173
New Directions (Miller's American publisher) ; see James Laughlin
New English Weekly, 10, 30–31, 46, 135
Nexus (Miller, Book 3 of *The Rosy Crucifixion*, 1959), 280, 284, 321, 333–34, 336–37, 350, 353, 358, 366, 375, 383
Nietzsche, 55, 105, 261
Night and Day, 106
Nights of Love and Laughter (Miller, 1955), 318
Nijinsky, Vaslav, 189, 211, 382
Nin, Anaïs (novelist, friend of Miller and Durrell in Paris), 36, 41, 71, 74, 83, 114, 182, 198, 211, 232, 291, 337, 339, 350
Norden, Charles (pseudonym of Durrell in writing *Panic Spring*), 101, 104–108, 114, 332
Nouvelle Revue Française, 7, 31, 152

Obelisk Press (Paris publishers of the banned books), 8, 16, 48, 114, 133, 198; see Maurice Girodias; Jack Kahane
On Seeming to Presume (Durrell, poems, 1948), 231
Orbes, 16, 31, 37
Orwell, George, 117; reviews *Tropic of Cancer*, 10
Ouspensky, P. D., 313

Panic Spring (Durrell, 1937), 32, 64, 101, 107
"Parthenon, The" (Christmas card by Durrell, 1945), 221
Perlès, Alfred (alias Alf, Fred, Joey, and Joe, "Viennese French writer," Miller's crony in Paris, author of *Sentiments Limitrophes*, later *My Friend Henry Miller*, 1955, and *My Friend Lawrence Durrell*, 1961), 3, 8, 15, 36, 67, 101, 113, 116, 119, 133, 139, 145, 147, 173, 176, 178, 185, 205, 211, 214, 227, 237, 239–40, 244–47, 249–50, 253, 257, 259–60, 271–73, 275–77, 285–87, 293–96, 305, 307, 322–24, 335–39, 341, 345, 347, 357, 359–60, 367, 369, 371, 379, 384; *Hamlet* correspondence, 10; inherits *The Booster*, 109–10; emigrates to England, 141; *My Friend Henry Miller*, 303; *Art and Outrage*, 331, 333

Personal Landscape (published in Alexandria, 1942–45, by Durrell and other English writers in Egypt; selections published as *Personal Landscape, An Anthology of Exile*, London, 1945), 179, 186, 190, 207, 209
Petronius, 57, 275, 288
Picasso, Pablo, 146, 149, 262, 282, 307
Pied Piper of Lovers (Durrell's first novel, 1935), 3
Plexus (Miller, Book 2 of *The Rosy Crucifixion*, 2 vols., 1953), 268–69, 271, 275, 285, 290, 298, 323, 325
"Plight of the Creative Artist in the United States of America" (Miller), 169, 182
Pope Joan (translated by Durrell, from the Greek of Emmanuel Royidis, 1954), 252, 308
Porphirios, Father, 215–16
Porter, Bern (publisher of *The Happy Rock* and other Milleriana, Berkeley, Calif.), 199, 213
Porteus, Hugh Gordon, 119–20
Potocki of Montalk, Count (poet and Royalist Polish exile, editor and printer of the *Right Review*), 117–18
Pound, Ezra, 18, 28, 76, 81
Powell, Lawrence Clark (head librarian, University of California at Los Angeles, friend and collector of Miller and Durrell), xiv–xv, 169, 237, 255, 280, 286, 351–52, 367–68, 370–71
Powys, John Cowper (British novelist, author of *The Glaston-*

bury Romance), 284, 286, 297, 346

Pringle, Alan, 102, 116–17, 118

Private Country, A (Durrell, poems, 1943), 179–80, 185

Prospero's Cell (Durrell, 1945), 63, 179, 180–81, 188–89, 192, 198–99, 201, 207, 210, 239

Proust, Marcel, 181, 191, 240, 312

Rabelais, 16, 57–58, 63, 324, 349

Raimu (French film actor), 310, 357

Ramuz, Charles Ferdinand, 222

Rank, Otto, 261

Raoul, Francis, 317

Ravagli, Angelino, 217

Ray, Man (American photographer-artist in Paris), 235

Read, Herbert (English poet, critic, surrealist, and anarchist), 15, 29–30, 128, 211

Reavey, George (English poet and translator), 118, 120

Reflections on a Marine Venus (Durrell, 1953), 207, 307

Reichel, Hans (German painter, friend of Miller in Paris), 75, 96–97, 121–22, 126, 211, 230, 247, 335, 352–53

Remember to Remember (Miller, 1947), 234, 252, 254

"Reunion in Barcelona" (Miller, a letter to Alfred Perlès, 1959), 293

"Reunion in Brooklyn" (Miller, from *Sunday After the War*), 240, 254

Revue des Deux Mondes, 46

Rexroth, Kenneth, 318

Rimbaud, Arthur, 61, 94, 203, 256, 301, 373, 376, 379, 381, 383; see *The Time of the Assassins*

Rolfe, Frederick ("Baron Corvo"), 319

Ros, Amanda (British novelist), 119

Ross, Patience (literary agent), 199

Rosy Crucifixion, The (Miller, trilogy, 1949–59), 175, 183–85, 194, 198, 225, 227, 240, 243, 250, 259, 262–63, 270, 376; see *Nexus, Plexus, Sexus*

Rouault, Georges, 146

Rougemont, Denis de, 345

Rowohlt, Heinz Ledig (son of Ernst Rowohlt, German publisher of Miller and Durrell), 359, 374–75

Rowohlt, Jane (wife of Heinz Ledig Rowohlt), 375

Rowohlt Verlag (Durrell's and Miller's German publisher), 319, 346, 368

Rude, Fernand, 317

Russell and Volkening (New York literary agency), 171, 173, 183–84

Ryan, Betty (American painter, resident of Villa Seurat), 115, 189, 211, 291; see *The Colossus of Maroussi*

St. Augustine, 228

St. Francis, 373

St.-John Perse, 307

Sand, George, 143

Sandburg, Carl, 344

Santayana, George, 90

Sappho (Durrell, a play in verse, 1950), 229, 282, 285–86, 303, 308, 319, 369, 371

Saroyan, William (American writer, contributed to *The Booster*), 30–31, 34, 36, 116, 225, 230, 348

Satyr Book Shop, 173

Schatz, Bezalel (Israeli artist, Eve Miller's brother-in-law), 222, 307

Schliemann, Herman, 59

Schnellock, Emil (American painter, lifelong friend of Miller), 133

Schönste, Das, 346

Scriabin, Alexander, 382–84

Seferis, George (alias Seferiades, Greek poet and diplomat), 159, 163, 165, 168, 171, 180, 189, 193, 197, 205, 212, 217, 244–45, 287, 289, 293, 300; in postwar Athens, 219, 221, 223; to Durrell on Cyprus, 298; see *The Colossus of Maroussi*

Sekilianos, Anghelos (Greek poet), 220

Selected Poems (Durrell, 1956), 305

Seneca, 51

Seven, 137

Sexus (Miller, Book 1 of *The Rosy Crucifixion*, 2 vols., 1949), 280, 285, 288, 302, 323; Durrell criticizes, 264–77

Shakespeare, 16, 20–21, 27–28, 50, 56, 64–66, 154–56, 285

Shapiro, Karl (American poet, editor of *The Prairie Schooner*), 336, 343

Shaw, George Bernard, 76, 80, 89, 118, 371

Sitwell, Sir Osbert, 185

Skelton, John, 27

Smile at the Foot of the Ladder, The (Miller, 1948), 243

Southern Review, 37

Southwell, Robert, 27

Spencer, Herbert, 261

Spengler, Oswald, 213, 261

Spiro "Americanos" (Greek taxi driver in Corfu), 210, 230, 242; see *Prospero's Cell*

Stein, Gertrude, 21–22, 28, 76, 81, 128

Stendhal, 278, 342

Stephanides, Dr. Theodore (naturalist, author of *Climax in Crete*), 118, 189, 210, 232; see *Prospero's Cell*

Stern, James, 36

Strauss, Harold, 107

Summers, Romilly, 212

Sunday After the War (Miller, 1944), 215, 220, 225

Sunday Times, 327–28, 339

Surrealism, 15–16, 18–24, 29, 34, 235

Suzuki, D. T., 153, 301

Swedenborg, Emanuel, 144

Swift, Jonathan, 16, 19, 23

Synge, John Millington, 227

Tagore, Rabindranath, 345, 359

Tambimuttu (Sinhalese editor and publisher), 190, 200–201, 209

Thomas, Alan (antiquarian bookseller, lifelong friend of Durrell), xiv–xv, 84–85, 89, 93–94, 98, 237, 368, 370

Thomas, Dylan, 44, 119, 199, 241, 284, 371

Thoreau, Henry David, 261

T'ien Hsia Monthly (Shanghai), 47, 95–96

Tihanyi, 385

Time of the Assassins, The (Miller, 1956; published in French as *Rimbaud*, 1952), 218, 222, 240, 243, 254, 275, 286, 301

Titian, 17

Tito, 277

Tonio (Antoniou, Greek poet, captain of a small ship), 160, 163, 168, 220

Tourneur, Cyril, 27, 33, 47, 69

Town and Country, 234

transition (Paris, 1927–38), 111

Tropic of Cancer (Miller, published novel, 1934), xiv, 3, 8–13, 27, 35–36, 41, 53, 56, 61, 75–76, 84, 90–91, 95, 129, 175, 179, 189, 192, 194–95, 198, 201, 211, 231–33, 240, 243, 262, 265, 273, 288, 291, 388; Durrell praises, 4, 6; first draft of, 225, 233

Tropic of Capricorn (Miller, 1939), 36, 57, 96, 123, 127–29, 142, 149, 151, 179, 190, 194, 198–99, 201, 222, 231–32, 240, 243, 262, 291, 388; finished, 131–32; published, 157–58

Turgenev, Ivan, 312

UNESCO Courier, 335

"Universe of Death, The" (Miller, fragment of projected "World of Lawrence," printed in *Max and the White Phagocytes*), 22, 36

Valéry, Paul, 317–18, 329, 374

Valeurs, 200

Van Gogh, Vincent, 17, 214

Van Norden (Durrell's twenty-foot

Bermuda-rigged sailboat), 24, 40, 67, 71, 85, 99, 106, 114, 124; see Charles Norden

Varda, Jean (artist who introduced Miller to Big Sur), 335; see *Remember to Remember*

View, 195

Villa Seurat (Miller's headquarters in Paris, 1935–39), 3, 5, 12, 32, 37, 77, 101, 114 ff., 119, 128, 135, 139, 211–12, 225, 237, 240, 259, 291, 330, 334, 385

Villon, François, 7, 19

Warner, Rex (English poet and novelist), 244

Wassermann, Jakob (famous German-Jewish novelist), 176, 380; see Dr. Kerkhoven

"Waters Reglitterized, The" (Miller, pamphlet, 1950), 217

Watts, Alan, 153

Webster, John, 27, 38, 69

Welles, Orson, 247

Wells, H. G., 22–23, 80

West, Rebecca, 117

White Eagles Over Serbia (Durrell, 1957), 257

Whitman, Walt, 37, 153, 225, 261

Wilde, Oscar, 377

Williams, William Carlos (American poet), 76, 81

Wisdom of the Heart, The (Miller, 1941), 140–41, 143–44, 152–53, 254

Wodehouse, P. G., 328

"World of Lawrence, The" (projected book by Miller), 9, 46–47, 57, 78–79, 237; see "The Universe of Death"

World of Sex, The (Miller, 1940; second edition, completely revised, 1957), 290

Yeats, William Butler, 90, 149–50

Zarian, Ivan (Armenian writer in Corfu), 33–34, 36, 42, 71, 81, 118, 210, 282, 300–301; see *Prospero's Cell*

Zen, 151–53, 262, 301–302, 341, 344, 348, 369

"Zero" (Durrell, 1936), 43, 71, 137, 242–44

Zola, Emile, 231